Changing the Subject: Women in Higher Education

edited by

Sue Davies, Cathy Lubelska

and

Jocey Quinn

Taylor & Francis
Publishers since 1798

UK   Taylor & Francis Ltd, 4 John St., London WC1N 2ET
USA   Taylor & Francis Inc., 1900 Frost Road, Suite 101, Bristol, PA 19007

© Taylor & Francis

First published 1994

A Catalogue Record for this book is available from the British Library

ISBN 0 7484 0281 0 (cloth)
ISBN 0 7484 0282 9 (paper)

Library of Congress Cataloging-in-Publication Data are available on request

Typeset in 10/13pt Times Roman
by RGM Associates, Lord Street, Southport

Printed in Great Britain by Biddles Ltd, Guildford and Kings Lynn.

Changing the Subject

This book is fondly dedicated to Shauna Murray (1941–1993): feminist, teacher, colleague and above all, friend; who enriched all who worked with her.

Contents

Contents

WHEN
(Women in Higher Education Network)

WHEN brings together women working and studying in higher education at all levels. It aims to foster networking and debate which will raise the profile of women in higher education, address issues of importance to them and challenge the male dominated ethos of higher education.

Founded in Cambridge University, co-ordination of the network then moved to Nottingham University, and is currently held by the Univesity of Central Lancashire. To initiate their period of responsibility for WHEN, the co-ordinators organized a conference on Women and the Higher Education Curriculum in November 1993, at the University of Central Lancashire, Preston.

The success of the conference resulted in this collection of selected papers, which incorporate discussions and ideas from conference participants. Most papers were presented in a workshop format to encourage debate, and then written up taking into account feedback from other women. They reflect the collaborative process which the conference sought to engender, and issues regarding the empowerment of women at different stages in higher education, including students.

The aim of the conference was to stimulate discussion, provide support, share information and highlight examples of good practice. This collection reflects these goals and seeks to share the experience and ideas of women involved with a wider audience.

For further information regarding WHEN please contact:

Sue Davies/Jocey Quinn
Equal Opportunities Development Officer
University of Central Lancashire
Preston PR1 2HE

1

Introduction

Sue Davies, Cathy Lubelska and Jocey Quinn

Why should women in higher education want to change the subject? The subject–object relationship raises issues of power familiar to feminists: the subject is active and acts upon the object. Within this analysis, who are the subjects in higher education? Who are the initiators of action within the institution, the controllers of the space and the agenda? As this collection reveals, they are largely men or male-identified. Like other institutions, the University perpetuates a sexual division of labour, men hold the majority of senior positions, whilst women predominate in lower-paid, insecure, part-time jobs (AUT, 1992). Usually men decide whether those women will even have a job next year. Of course, power and control go much deeper into the structures of the University, its committees, its working parties, its informal lobbying groups. Even where women have gained some representation, the very style and discourse of meetings tends to be male-defined.

The agenda of the University is determined by both external and internal forces. New and old universities must jostle and compete for financial survival, determined by assessments from a central government which remains unregenerately patriarchal. All decisions made are value laden and gender determined, for example, the growing emphasis on research and the downgrading of teaching skills are clearly not neutral in their effects. Traditionally men have had more access to research and publishing networks, more domestic support to facilitate research and better promotion prospects, whilst women have been encouraged into caring pastoral roles within the University, which can give little time or opportunity for self advancement. These factors still persist. The deep and surface structures of higher education, its values and its processes, all declare that men remain the subjects; their actions, agendas, knowledge and power are still predominant.

As these papers show, however, it would be naïve to assume that all women are outsiders in the academy, and that all play equally subordinate roles. Some women do gain access to power, but, whilst gendered notions of success predominate, it is often at the cost of their sense of identity as women, or their solidarity with others. As long as women are still classed as 'the other' they must either lose or deny their difference to join the elite, or face endless conflict and self doubt (Davies, 1994). A dominant theme in this collection is the rejection of this bad bargain. For writers such as Pauline Leonard and Danusia Malina, their 'subjectivity' and self worth as women/mothers will not be bartered away. We want to be our own subjects within the University, and not honorary men.

If the university 'subject' is male, it is also predominantly white, able bodied, heterosexual and middle class; and attaining access to privilege and status is, therefore, much easier for some women than for others. Levels of silence and exclusion amongst and between women are acknowledged and addressed by contributors such as Khalwant Bhopal and Julie Matthews, revealing a wide range of differing needs and disadvantages for women in higher education. Many papers clearly reveal the limitations of most approaches to equal opportunities which lump all women together as a homogeneous group (Quinn, 1994). On a positive and proactive level, they present ideas and strategies for the articulation of the differing voices and needs of women.

For 'subject' one can also read 'discipline' or 'discourse'. Authors in this volume recognize the centrality of curriculum issues in any debate on change in higher education. What is taught and how are key considerations. This is not to say that the 'subject' is protected from change. Market forces and ideologies shape content, form, structures and methods, to produce a climate of flux in today's University. Material conditions, such as increased teaching loads and cuts in student grants, impact upon the curriculum. However, underlying judgements about what constitutes valid and valuable knowledge continue to be made largely by minorities of white men, whether on instrumental or ideological grounds, or both. As Marilyn Schuster argues 'In questioning the paradigms we use to perceive, analyse and organize experience, we are pointedly asking not only what we know but how we came to know it.'

Although the traditional image of the higher education institution is of the 'ivory tower', so well dissected by Millsom Henry here, authors in this volume also set higher education firmly within its social and political context. As feminists with experience and understanding of grass roots issues, they deconstruct the interplay between women's lives in and out of the institution, recognizing the importance and interdependence of both.

'I used to keep my books on top of the ironing board to look at them when I was ironing and when he came into the kitchen I used to quickly hide them under the ironing' (mature student interviewed by Madeleine Leonard). This image is a resonant one. A woman's freedom to change and become an autonomous 'subject' in higher education is constrained by many external forces. Like this student, we may be forced into strategy and subterfuge to get what we want. Recognizing the barriers to change, whilst being determined to achieve it, is a central theme within this volume.

Making our Voices Heard: Women in Higher Education

The papers in this section reveal the complexity of women's lives and the contradictory nature of women's experience in higher education. They question the dominant interests of those within the academy and the ways in which these are presented as neutral and objective.

The authors explore ideas about what it is to be a woman, about our different and diverse identities and whether, given the patriarchal nature of academia, it is possible to be both a woman and an academic and to retain a sense of identity. The contradictions that have to be managed, the frustrations, joys and pleasures of our often fragmented lives, give a rich pattern to the text that is repeated and echoed in the other sections of the book. Breda Gray acknowledges the difficulties of being an 'Ambivalent Academic', someone who has achieved under the *status quo* and has an investment in defending existing 'academic requirements' yet at the same time wants to challenge them. Barbara Bagilhole described how success in academia 'requires knowing colleagues who can provide guidance, support and advocacy to the apprentice'. In exploring how far we do and might fit into academia, the papers raise many questions, not least about the construction of the knowledge, procedures and structures on which traditional notions of academic success are predicated. In considering these issues it becomes clear that there needs to be a marrying of the formal and informal arenas in which we live, if we are not to feel as if we merely have a toe hold on both sides of a precipice.

Women are outsiders in academia. We are disadvantaged by a system where our differing values and interests are seen to be of little or no importance. Disadvantage, difference and their inter-relationship are recurrent themes in this section. Millsom Henry, Chris Corrin, Pauline Leonard and Danusia Malina all explore aspects of difference and its personal and political consequences. In order for us to challenge patriarchy successfully in higher education we first need to develop a more coherent understanding of the nature and consequences of our different and often multiple identities. Higher education is dominated by masculine values, masculine power and masculine discourse, but while power can be a weapon of oppression it is not always wielded equally and women are not equally oppressed. Barbara Bagilhole has argued elsewhere that while women working in higher education are in privileged positions relative to many other women, they are in weak positions relative to most men within the academy (Bagilhole, 1992). However, as Millsom Henry argues 'The racist, sexist and elitist ideologies in society continue to be reflected and reinforced in the Higher Education system which tends to ignore Black Women's experiences.' While many women enjoy the support and confidence of other women, the papers also explore areas of tension and conflict. Women, as well as men can manipulate and wield power in ways that oppress others and women, as well as men, can become the instruments or perpetrators of oppression. Are many of the problems being addressed by white women in higher education merely the problems of the already privileged? Pauline Leonard and Danusia Malina position themselves as white middle class women but find their experiences as mothers mean they stand outside the norm and that this can be both a burden and a blessing. The pregnant woman brings home into work, she is clearly a maternal and sexual being with a life outside the institution in which she works, she can be marginalized because of this but can also draw strength and vigour from it too. Chris Corrin explores how the 'unquestioning and unambiguous presumption of heterosexuality' oppresses lesbian women and can 'silence discussion before it has begun'. Again, she draws attention to the significance of the informal social interactions that take place and how these can make lesbian women feel particularly vulnerable or excluded. If women have to conceal from colleagues aspects of their personal identity and deny the existence of friends and lovers how can they feel anything but 'other' in the institutions in which they work?

These papers, however, look forward. One of the questions that Chris returns to in her paper is, why do we, as lesbian women, heterosexual women, feminists, need each other? The answer that she proposes is that we need each other to develop our understanding of ourselves, particularly if we want to empower ourselves to resist prejudice and challenge oppression. Millsom, in 'Ivory Towers and Ebony Women' argues that change has to start somewhere, and that black women, 'cannot afford to wait for the right social, political and economic constraints to disappear before they feel empowered to make their own valuable contributions to society'.

These women are not passively accepting their own oppression. All the authors here emphasize the need to challenge privilege and discrimination, and to find ways of making their voices heard.

The Empowerment of Women in Higher Education

The authors here discuss ways in which women can attempt to empower themselves in higher education. In considering the development of appropriately enabling strategies for women, recurrent themes emerge: the importance of establishing what we mean by Empowerment; why it is necessary for women to empower themselves; and whose empowerment is desired and affected.

An acknowledgement of the patriarchal structures of power and knowledge in the academy, and the ways in which these can disadvantage women can help to foster a sense of collective identity between us. The importance of mutual support is emphasised in the alternative, woman-centred approaches explored here. This is reflected in the way in which all these papers are centrally concerned with women's experiences and are, to a greater or lesser extent, autobiographical. As Mairead Owen points out in her paper, a feminist, experiential focus serves to illuminate not only the commonalities between women, but also the extent to which these can obscure differences and inequalities amongst us too. In considering how we might empower ourselves as women the importance of recognizing and validating the diversity of women's experiences is stressed. To do this we need to acknowledge our different resources and needs as women, as well as the existence of privileges and inequalities amongst us. These papers point up the inadequacies of simple equal opportunities approaches to women's empowerment, which assume the existence of the illusory 'level playing field', where women continue to be disadvantaged in relation both to men and to each other. Yet as Mairead implies, an appreciation of our diversities and multiple identities as women can be a critical resource in the empowerment of all women.

The following two papers in this section make explicit the ways in which women in the academy can exclude and marginalize each other. Kalwant Bhopal's discussion of the whiteness of the academy and of the successful women within it illuminates the ways in which black women have been silenced, under-represented and mis-represented within the curriculum and the academy as a whole. Drawing upon both her own experiences as a black woman in higher education and the insights of black feminist theory, Kalwant explores the interplay of race and gender in shaping structures of power and knowledge in higher education. Julie Matthews, also writing from an autobiographical perspective, raises similar issues in relation to disability. Her focus upon the prevalence of prejudices and assumptions about those who are seen to be 'different' and 'other', complements Kalwant's concern with the perceived 'deviancy' of black women, and serves to highlight the ways in which women can actually disempower each other. Yet both papers indicate agendas and strategies through which we can begin to address and resolve the issues raised here.

The importance of recognizing the diversity of women's experiences and resources as a pre-requisite of their empowerment is also foregrounded in the last two papers in this section. Here two very different case studies of approaches to empowerment focus upon women's differing needs and how these can best be met. Trev Broughton's reflexive account of how she attempted to tackle the problems of getting down to writing with a group of Women's Studies students highlights the importance of the gendered and diverse experiences, attitudes and needs of women in shaping both the problems which they encounter and successful strategies for dealing with these. It is seen as important to confront how we, as tutors and students, are disempowered in order to identify how our needs can be effectively fulfilled.

The joint paper of Rebecca D'Monté, Sally Kilmister, Deryn Rees-Jones and Joanne Winning is a collective, largely autobiographical account and appraisal of the development of a woman-only post-graduate support group. Each voice offers different, though complementary focus on the principles and processes which were involved. Although the benefits are tangible and diverse, the aim of self-empowerment through the creation of a safe space for women proves to be problematic. The fact that some women clearly felt more empowered than others here is discussed within a context of concern with education politics, institutional structures and issues of privilege for women.

Crucially, the processes of empowerment detailed in these papers exist in tension with the character and values of the academy and its curricula. The expressed need for radical change rather than assimilation presents us with both a challenge and an opportunity to transform the curriculum and priorities of higher education in a positively inclusive way.

Women Challenging the Mainstream Curriculum in Higher Education

Feminists in higher education are often faced with the dilemma of either retaining a radical, but marginalized position, or demanding a place within the 'malestream' which ultimately leaves them feeling compromised or incorporated into the *status quo*. Authors in this section address how far women can initiate positive change within traditional disciplines at the heart of the academy, and the role of feminist perspectives and values here. Both 'curriculum' and 'feminism' are presented as complex and problematic. Curriculum encompasses areas such as the nature of the disciplines — their methodologies, subject matters and perspectives; teaching approaches, relationships and experiences within the institution, as well as the wider educational and social context. Whilst feminism cannot be easily categorized, all the authors share a consciousness that women are oppressed; an oppression interwoven with issues of race, class, disability and sexuality to produce a variety of differences and disadvantages which are rarely reflected in the curriculum as it stands. All strive in different ways for a feminist praxis uniting theory and practice, which will develop non-patriarchal knowledge and new methodologies to benefit women and others practically, in and out of the academy.[1]

Penny Welch's paper establishes a broad perspective, examining feminist pedagogy across disciplines. She focuses on the teaching process as a possible agent of feminist change which can transform power relations and widen opportunities for women students. Her paper sets teaching in higher education within the context of the development of women's movements in the UK and explores the possibilities and limitations of teaching as feminist activism.

Madeleine Leonard's work also indicates clearly how the experiences of women in higher education cannot be divorced from the wider social context, and how affecting change within a limited sphere can sometimes be problematic for students. Here, attempts to encourage access and change the curriculum to meet the needs of mature women students are hampered by patriarchal attitudes and practices in the home. Grounded in the lived daily experience of the students, this paper throws into sharp relief the importance of theory to understanding and positively changing women's role and status within the domestic sphere.

The case-study paper in this section also straddles the world outside and inside of higher education focusing on an area which has a profound effect on women's daily lives: health. In the health professions, women may have dominated numerically, but debate has tended to marginalize their concerns. Theory has prioritized male notions of value, whilst powerful positions in administration and practice have mainly been occupied by men. Doreen MacWhannell presents a practical example of how feminist educators have attempted to change health education using modularization to 'infiltrate' the mainstream. Her paper is not posited as a definitive solution but as an example of work in transition and process.

This sense of feminist curriculum change as a gradual process, which builds on the successes and failures of our own experience as women in higher education, is summed up in the final paper by Marilyn Schuster. Her analysis is based upon work undertaken in the United States, but is clearly pertinent to the current position in Britain. Here Marilyn presents an overview of the stages of curriculum transformation over time, a map where we can place ourselves and our institutions. She argues that the growing sophistication in our under-standing of the processes involved can be informed by an increased awareness of the complexities of feminist politics. She also shows how the empowerment of women through the new curriculum, can be met by fear and resistance both inside and outside the academy.

Clearly there is still far to go, and scope for a great deal of future work, and feminist permeation, particularly in the field of Science and Technology. The papers in this section indicate issues, questions, possible directions, rather than clear cut answers, their approach is open-ended, reflective and feminist:

What we see, we see
and seeing is changing
(Rich, 1968)

Beginning to Change

All the papers in this collection share a women-centred and experiential focus, bringing the concerns of women in higher education in from the margins, to make them the subjects, at the core of this volume. This approach reveals the reality behind the veneer and shows that despite (and, possibly because of) the flaunting of equal opportunities policies and of 'successful' women who have 'made it' by politically correct institutions, most women continue to feel disadvantage and oppression in relation to their prospects, representation and needs within higher education. The wider contexts and multiple identities of women's lives revealed here, and the inter-disciplinarity of much of this work is at odds with the rigid demarcations of knowledge and identity within the academy, with its archetype of the successful, autonomous (male) academic specialist, which continue to exclude and de-value women and their resources.

The principle response to the perceived 'otherness' and outsider status of many women in academic life is radical and assertive in resisting the conformity and compromises expected of them, which merely serve to maintain the status quo. It is not we, as women, who need to change so that one or two of us can occasionally burst through the 'glass-ceiling', leaving the rest of the building intact; rather it is the academy.

All the contributions here are in some way informed by feminist theory and practice. The focus is upon the transformation of higher education in a variety of different ways and in these studies, from the bottom up. Empowerment for women in higher education is seen to be about us, as women, doing it for ourselves, as activists and subjects, aware of the political as well as educational implications of our actions. Yet many of the papers here also stress the need to recognize the challenges posed not only to the male-defined institution, but also to ourselves, as women working in higher education, by the feminist processes and strategies detailed here. Those approaches which seek to make visible and to isolate the experiences and needs of all women serve to delineate our differences and the ways in which inequalities amongst us can be perpetuated and legitimated within the academy. In engaging with such issues, which lie at the heart of contemporary feminist concerns (Lorder, 1984; Adams, 1989, Ramazanoglu, 1989) a consistent theme which emerges is the necessity of combining the assertion and consciousness of our different identities and needs with a unity of purpose amongst those who share the goal of empowering women in higher education.

The emphasis given here to working together in a variety of ways — such as networking, alliances, mentoring, collaboration and coalition — is important as a way to connect and activate not only women, but all those who might share our aims. There are men too, who experience disadvantages within higher education, usually due to some difference — of race, class, sexuality, with whom we might ally over matters of shared concern. Some of our male colleagues and senior managers are supportive, and may have the power which we ourselves lack to advance our cause. We need to give particular thought to working with sympathetic women who have advanced up the career ladder, but can become distanced from the rest of us. They are themselves though, often isolated and vulnerable, needing our support to empower them to help us in ways and contexts which are not available to most women (Flander, 1993). Of course, some of the alliances we make over particular issues may be risky, but they can also provide the opportunity to raise consciousness and the possibility of both broadening the basis of our support and, hopefully, of increasing our power to bring about change in higher education.

The strategies and discussions recounted here provide some promising beginnings and agendas upon which all women can build, they also give grounds for cautious optimism about the possibility, ultimately of transforming higher education into a women-friendly sector.

Notes

1 Debate on these issues has been led by work in the field of Women's Studies, see, for example, Cathy Lubelska 'Teaching Methods in Women's Studies' and M. Humm 'Thinking of things in themselves: Theory Experience and Women's Studies', both in J. Aaron and S. Walby (Eds) (1991), *Out of the Margins, Women's Studies in the 1990s*, London: Falmer. M. Maynard and J. Purvis (Eds) (1993) *Research Methods in Women's Studies*, London: Taylor & Francis.

References

ADAMS, M. L. (1989) 'There's No Place Like Home: On the Place of Identity in Feminist Politics' *Feminist Review* **31**, Spring.

ASSOCIATION OF UNIVERSITY TEACHERS (1992) 'Sex Discrimination in Universities'.

BAGILHOLE, B. (1992) 'On the Inside: A Research report on the position of women, black and disabled people in academic life'. Department of Social Sciences, Loughborough University.

DAVIES, S. (1994) 'One foot in the door. Women's Experiences of seeking promotion at the University of Central Lancashire.' Research report, University of Central Lancashire.

FLANDERS, M. L. (1993) *Breakthrough. The Career Woman's Guide to Shattering the Glass Ceiling*, London: Paul Chapman.

LORDE, A. (1984) *Sister Outsider*, Trumansburg: Crossing Press.

QUINN, J. (1994) 'Equal Opportunities in Academic Affairs? The Differing Experiences of Women Students'. A paper presented at an International Conference on Women in Higher Education, University of Florida, USA.

RAMAZANOGLU, C. (1989) *Feminism and the contradictions of oppression*, London: Routledge.

RICH, A. (1975) *Poems Selected & New, New York* WW Norton and Company.

Part I

The Experiences of Women in Higher Education

Chapter 1

Being Different is a Very Difficult Row to Hoe: Survival Strategies of Women Academics

Barbara Bagilhole

Size and Depth of the Problem

The traditional Japanese saying in the title above (New Internationalist, 1992) describes women in academic jobs. They are 'double deviants', not only working in a male dominated world, but also expecting to receive equitable rewards and recognition (Laws, 1975). They are privileged in comparison with most women, but not in comparison with men. In both the 'new' and 'old' universities women academics remain in a very small minority, representing only about 20 per cent of full-time staff (DES, 1992; USR, 1993). Even this figure is misleadingly optimistic as it includes staff on research-only contracts. The proportion of women in full-time posts which carry both teaching and research duties is more like 14 per cent of the total (Halsey, 1992).

The problem is demonstrated even more starkly when the proportions across academic grades are considered. According to the figures available for 'new' universities, while 30 per cent of lecturers are women, this falls to 10 per cent or less for grades above senior lecturer (DES, 1992). In the 'old' universities, only 3 per cent of professors and 6 per cent of senior lecturers are women (Hart and Wilson, 1992). The Association of University Teacher's comprehensive audit of the salaries of academic staff in 1991 shows that women are systematically paid less than men of equivalent academic achievement, age and length of service. On average, women earn only 83.9 per cent of men's salaries. The main reason for the large difference in pay is the concentration of women in the lower grades (AUT, 1992).

Nearly 20 years ago, Blackstone and Fulton presented evidence of discrimination against women in British and American universities; 'We have shown that women, including those whom, to judge by their research output, it would be insulting to dismiss as lacking motivation or commitment to their work, are not rewarded for their achievements to the same degree as comparable men' (1975: 269). More recently the Hansard Report (1990) has been heavily critical of universities as 'bastions of male power and privilege'. Also, the Committee of Vice Chancellors and Principals have expressed their concern at the proportion of women in universities and of how few are in senior positions, recognizing that discriminatory practices exist within universities (CVCP, 1991).

Halsey, in his third large-scale survey of British academics, acknowledges that the academic profession remains predominantly male and that there is strong selection taking place, but he locates the problem within women themelves. His explanation hinges on the supposition that their domestic responsibilities impinge upon their professional performance. 'The outcome is that women in this privileged profession put themselves, or are put, at a disadvantage in the competition to produce research' (1992: 234). On the other hand, Hawkins and Schultz (1990) in their studies of West Germany and the Netherlands argue that, 'The case for the existence of sex discrimination in academe has been amply documented although there is little empirical knowledge about its nature and the mechanisms that serve to maintain it' (1990: 47). The study (Bagilhole, 1992) reported here investigates the ways that the male-dominated profession and universities contribute to the problem. It explores the perceptions and experiences of women academics themselves, giving a sense of what being a member of this profession feels like to them. It examines the reality of being a small minority working in a male-dominated environment, and explores the solutions and survival strategies that women employ.

The Study

A total of 43 women were interviewed from a university where women make up only 11 per cent of the full-time academic staff; 58 women out of 510 staff. Out of these 43 women, only two were black and ethnic minority women and none were disabled. This reflects the added disadvantage that minority race and disability gives within the academic profession. The sample was made up of all the women who were available and willing to be interviewed during the period of the research project. They came from across all the departments in the university where women are present, and across the range of academic posts. The university's departments are divided into four schools; engineering (4 per cent women), pure and applied science (4 per cent women), human and environmental studies (18 per cent women), and education and humanities (29 per cent women). The majority of the women interviewed were on the lecturer grade (77 per cent), 16 per cent were senior lecturers and 7 per cent professors.

Although this research has been carried out in a single institution, many of the findings do conform to data uncovered by another more extensive international study. Sutherland (1985) reviewed the situation of women who teach in universities in five countries and found that, although prejudice against women was not cited as often as she expected it to be in explanation of women's minority position, 'there does remain the possibility of unconscious prejudice manifesting itself . . . in failure to perceive women as appropriate for initial appointments or for a kind of gradual initiation into the profession' (p. 183). As she acknowledges, prejudice is very difficult to prove, but some of the women she interviewed were of the strong opinion that they had not received appointments because they were women. Also, it is very important to bear in mind that, as Sutherland tells us, we are not collecting the 'most telling evidence of prejudice'. This must come from the absentees, the women who have left the profession or who have been persuaded not to start in it.

The Findings

Women Academics in a Minority

Out of the 21 departments within the university, four have no women academics at all, a further eight have only one, and most have very small numbers. The majority of the women across disciplines and departments viewed this as a major disadvantage for them.

> When I first came here I was the only woman and it had an enormously detrimental effect. It was the beginning of my professional life and I was up against a male environment.
>
> (Lecturer)

> They don't know how to react and respond to me. They are boys together and I don't fit in with that. As a woman, it's hard to penetrate that. They asked me to go for a drink but on a night when I can't go. I feel marginalized.
>
> (Probationary Lecturer)

Kanter (1977) provides a framework for discussing the difficulties of women who are single 'tokens' or in small 'minorities'. They suffer from the duality of being both invisible and extra-visible. Women who are in a small minority experience all the problems of discrimination and isolation characteristic of groups in similar positions. They are less confident of their abilities, less willing to take risks, less able to negotiate for their needs, they experience performance pressures and marginality. One lecturer in a scientific discipline reported her experiences.

> Quite a lot of comments go on. I work hard and they complain that the conversation always gets serious when I'm around but I find that's the best way to handle it. Jokes can get out of hand, where do you stop them? I'm treated as less important and invisible. I'm very aware of being a woman in male environment.
>
> (Lecturer)

Women academics report greater social isolation than men (Yoder, 1985), and they are less integrated into university departments (O'Leary and Mitchell, 1990). This was a problem for nearly half of the women in this study.

> I find it difficult to get to know the place. I don't go to the senior common room because I feel isolated. No-one has set out to exclude me but I don't feel part of it. I'm peripheral. All academics are isolated, but women have an extra dimension.
>
> (Probationary Lecturer)

Interestingly, about two-thirds of the women report that they treat male and female students differently, and they in turn are treated differently by the students. They spend more time with female students and give them more support. In contrast, they sometimes get problems with male students who do not accept their status or authority as academics.

> Male students are more difficult to deal with, they have the power of their maleness. Although it may not be in my mind it's in theirs and it makes it difficult to be assertive. Boys are skilled at manipulating women, they've done it all their lives.
>
> (Senior Lecturer)

> Some male students find it hard to do what a woman tells them and they don't like it. They have difficulties with my authority.
>
> (Senior Lecturer)

Some female lecturers report problems of sexism and sexual harassment from male students. This was particularly so in the male-dominated disciplines in engineering and science.

> I stopped wearing mini-skirts following comments about my legs. I
> have to give as good as I get, sexual innuendo. I can handle it but some
> female staff find it more difficult. I treat the female students differently
> because they treat me differently.
>
> (Probationary Lecturer)

Relationships with Male Colleagues

Women report more difficulties with relationships with colleagues, and more
leave their positions because of negative relationships (Johnsrud and Atwater,
1991). They feel like outsiders, and that they don't belong (Ainsberg and
Harrington, 1988). Women are more likely to have their scholarship trivialized
and discredited (Kritek, 1984). This is very important because women in the
academic profession are often dependent on good recommendations from men.
It is highly probable that interviewing committees will consist of men only, and
this imbalance will continue throughout a woman's career. 'The structure of the
academic hierarchy puts women in the situation of being judged only by those of
the opposite sex on a great many occasions' (Sutherland, 1985: 15).

Over half of the women in this study felt they had a neutral relationship
with their male colleagues, only one reported a positive, supportive relationship.
However, over one-third felt that their collegues had adverse views of them
because they were women.

> I was told by a male colleague that I only got the job because they
> wanted a woman. Their wives have looked after their children while
> they've concentrated on their careers, and they're very macho about it. I
> spend most of my time with the secretaries. It's a common idea that you
> get through the door first, but if you do you get a knife in the back.
>
> (Senior Lecturer)

> It's more like non-communication rather than different treatment. The
> department is male-dominated. They are quite stand-offish. They don't
> tell me things I need to know. They are pleasant but underneath the
> knife is going in. I'm asked to do things at the last minute, literally an
> hour before. Am I being set up to fail in front of the students? You can't
> do the job properly if you're not given information.
>
> (Lecturer)

Role Models and Networks

Being in a large majority men are inducted into the profession under the tutelage of male models and mentors. They have more natural access to these support systems than women as men hold the senior positions. This sponsorship enhances their self-esteem, self-confidence and their careers. 'Generally, the university is a "man's world" and the old boy network is influential' (Sutherland, 1985: 25). Universities are prime examples of Lipman-Blumen's (1976) 'homosocial' institutions, where men are dominant in sex-segregated institutions and act to exclude women from participation. Universities claim to be meritocracies. However, they value reputational status above all, which is heavily dependent upon one's integration into formal and informal networks in the academic community (Thomas, 1990).

Women on the whole have little access to female role models or mentors. Less than a quarter of the women in this study had a role model or professional mentor though the vast majority did feel a need for them and their benefits were appreciated. This was felt most strongly by the women on probation. Success in the academic market place requires a high level of educational attainment, but moving through the system of rewards and status requires knowing colleagues who can provide guidance, support and advocacy to the apprentice. Delamont (1989) argues that, 'It is the indeterminate aspects of occupational performance in elite jobs which prove elusive to women.' These aspects are the 'distinctive modes of perception, of thinking, of appreciation and of action', the 'taste of a group, its characteristic taken-for-granted view of the world', 'tacit, undescribable competencies'. Without these qualities women's success will be limited. They need the same socialization into the profession that men get from male networks and sponsors. As it stands, 'parts of the occupational identity and performance are obscured from women'.

The women in this study perceived their male colleagues' greater access to the benefits of role models and mentors as giving them a large advantage in terms of support and encouragement, and in terms of being better placed for promotion opportunities and to gain research experience. As one women so graphically described it, 'They come off the walls at them, don't they.'

Women are frequently not admitted into the all-male informal networks in departments which are well-established.

> Particularly in research, you see it going on. Men giving advice to other men in private. Sporting activities brings them into contact with staff from other departments, which gives them opportunities that I don't have. Then they make more of the right decisions about research and so

on. I've no access to the grapevine. They intertwine well and it helps their work.

(Senior Lecturer)

Networking is a crucial ingredient in professinal career success and is looked for in promotion decisions (Halsey, 1992). Women have particular difficulty in securing access to this 'colleague system' that brings mutual benefits through collaboration, information exchange, contacts for research resources, career planning, professional support and encouragement and opportunities to publish and facilitates informal interactions and connections to people of influence in the academic environment (Kaufman, 1978; O'Leary and Mitchell, 1990).

I'm trying, but it's difficult to break into the cliques within the department. I have the same research interests as colleagues, but they keep them close to their chest.

(Probationary Lecturer)

Going over to a group of men at a conference and joining in their conversation is difficult. When I start talking to a man it never occurs to me that he might think I'm making a pass at him, but it has happened and it is excruciatingly embarrassing. I try to be professional with them and not be aware of this but it's a problem.

(Lecturer)

Sutherland's (1985) sample of Finnish women academics felt that male cliques could form with women being excluded from informal decision-making that takes place in social gatherings. This was particularly prevalent there in the single-sex saunas. Many women in the present study commented on the difficulty of getting to know male colleagues.

There's a heavy male drinking social life. You're barred from meeting them outside the university because they're involved in sport and bars. Thing I can't participate in.

(Lecturer)

The Effects on Women Academics

These experiences of being in a minority with the accompanying lack of support systems and the difficulties of integrating into a male working environment influence women academics' perception of themselves and affects their careers.

It affects their confidence and impairs their ability to perform professionally. Women express more uncertainty regarding their ability to meet tenure and promotion requirements (Lovano-Kerr and Fuchs, 1983). Many feel that they do not belong and are not true academics. Men's ideas are the 'ruling ideas' in this environment producing a valid hegemony, which has a detrimental effect on women's careers (Acker, 1983; 1992).

Nearly two-thirds of the women interviewed in this study felt that there was a problem with the concept of a woman academic. Some women academics take on the characteristics of their environment, they become 'honorary men' because men make the rules. This was seen as a bad thing for the profession and to deny female qualities and potential.

> Because of the male perception of what an academic is, a male role model. Women are put into a different role model, and men find it difficult when the two come together. If you're a woman academic you are seen as masculine. You just don't fit, it's against all the rules.
>
> (Professor)

> A certain way that academics behave is defined by men because they were there first. You have to divorce oneself from one's femininity in order to be taken seriously as an academic. You have to be harder, more professional because of all the preconceptions about your ability which you have to overcome before people actually see you.
>
> (Senior Lecturer)

> I've been told by many people that I'm not a normal woman. An academic is either male or neutral. I don't know what a woman academic is. Women are only seen as playing at being academic, not a real academic.
>
> (Lecturer)

Solutions and Strategies

Working Harder

One strategy that women academics employ leads them to strive to be incredibly conscientious and dedicated, putting excess pressure on themselves. This is reflected in the fact that over three-quarters of the women in this study felt that they had to be better than their male colleagues to succeed.

You are in the minority. To succeed you have to be one of the better people, better than most men around.

(Professor)

We have to say over and over again that we have a right to be where we are. It's a constant defence of ourselves.

(Senior Lecturer)

You can't show any signs of weakness. If you do these are fastened upon and used to show that you're no good at your job. When female staff go out it's assumed they are going to look after their family, not to work at home or go to the library as with men. You have to be very, very careful.

(Lecturer)

The 'Queen Bee' Syndrome?

Another solution to the problem of being in such a small minority with marginal status is to avoid, as far as possible, being identified with the minority. Hawkins and Schultz (1990) found that most women academics hesitate to support each other. There has been a considerable amount written about token successful women who succeed by using male criteria, and their failure to support other women; the Queen Bees (Staines *et al.*, 1974). They are strongly individualistic and tend to deny the existence of discrimination against women. Sutherland found that; 'For those in senior or isolated positions the role of "honorary man" is easily accessible and has a certain piquancy' (1985: 28).

Kanter (1977) saw these women as fearing the success of other women which would challenge their power. However, Bardwick (1977) questioned this explanation suggesting that the behaviour of Queen Bees had been misinterpreted and that a more likely explanation for not supporting other women was that powerful women rarely saw themselves as powerful. Delamont's (1989) adaptation of the theory of *dominant and muted groups* may help here. A possible explanation for the observed conservative behaviour of women academics is that as a muted group, having expended much energy conforming to the dominant model, they cling to this accommodation and fear a fresh start. The following comments from this study highlight this dilemma:

To become an academic I've had to take on a man's model. I've avoided women's groups and not wanted to be identified as a women's studies person or feminist.

(Professor)

> This is a disadvantage of being a woman. You are categorized. Women with families are put in the worst category. We're expected to be somehow less intelligent and less able to achieve. So you've got to get over that hurdle of male perception. It's very difficult because you can't be too feminist, women's lib, aggressive. You can't display typically male characteristics. You have to be more intelligent, special without being threatening. There isn't a clear path, an acceptable way of behaving and performing.
>
> (Lecturer)

These women have a strong commitment to the male mode of the profession. They do not want to be suspected of exaggerated women identification. In contrast to male colleagues, they do not appear to favour members of the same sex. They behave in accordance with their minority status. They are determined to succeed on the basis of their own merits, with no hint of patronage and expect the same of other women.

> I'm anti pushing women for women's sake. You should get in on your own merit.
>
> (Lecturer)

> I've always held out for academic achievement and professional competence, these mean more to me than being a woman.
>
> (Senior Lecturer)

> I went to a conference the other day with ten women and one hundred men. Every speaker referred to disadvantaged groups needing help, and referred to women among these groups. I resented this because we're equal and have equal opportunities. I'm a woman on the inside not a woman on the outside trying to get in.
>
> (Senior Lecturer)

Alternative 'Women Friendly' Strategies

There was a small minority in the study who had turned to 'women friendly' solutions and called for positive action for women academics. These women are beginning to develop a new support system of their own turning to one another, rather than to men, for help in exchange relationships. Lipman-Blumen recognized that communication networks that passed information about jobs were developing as 'indications of an emerging "new girl network" analogous to the powerful "old boy network" of the male world' (1976: 18).

I'm trying to establish these networks, but it takes time and it's more difficult as a woman.

(Probationary Lecturer)

I network with women who work in the areas I'm interested in. I get information, collaborative work, and get tipped off when things are going to happen. It's a tremendous source of support and encouragement. Without it I would have gone mad.

(Senior Lecturer)

Some women in the study felt that there was a need for a formal mentoring system for women, where the mentors could be chosen to match interests, experience and personal circumstances. This was felt to be important to compensate for the lack of general availability of networks accessible to women. For the most part academic women have not achieved either professional or organizational authority to the same extent as men. However, women with professional information can help others to network by introducing them to colleagues and peers within the discipline. Women with organizational influence can provide guidance, consultation, advice and advocacy for navigating the institution. Nichols *et al.* (1985) argue that given women's limited access to formal authority 'the effective use of organizational and professional influence may be the best hope for accomplishing the inclusion of women in academia.'

The idea of mentoring is not new and is used in other professions. It is obvious that a good deal of informal helping among academics does occur. However, to make a systematic impact it must be formalized as an integral part of an institutional plan for equal opportunities. To be effective in the long term, mentoring cannot be viewed as a peripheral or compensatory programme for women only, but as a strategy for structural and climate changes in the institution. One formal means of socialization is the pairing of those who have successfully negotiated their academic careers with those entering the profession: to facilitate the success of the less experienced academic by providing ready access to an experienced resource person. Ideally, these relationships are based upon mutual regard. The purpose is information sharing, personal and professional support, and career assistance. The intent is to foster self-reliance. On the basis of their experience, senior academic women can anticipate and assist with the problems and issues faced by those with less experience. They can be a sounding board, offer introductions, advice and counsel. Relationships can be mutually enhancing, they can collaborate, build a peer relationship.

Pairing can be based on criteria such as discipline, professional interests and lifestyle issues. Senior women by virtue of being senior are the 'survivors' of role overload, lack of sponsorship, and exclusion from the culture of the institution encountered in their early career years (Clark and Corcoran, 1986). It is critical that women who have weathered the differences and survived help other women. However, it is also important to acknowledge the possible downside of mentoring. Women must not be typecast as mentors in a 'caring role' while men press forward with research and publications. Women who take on the role of mentor must not be disadvantaged with even more work overload, which leaves little time for activities essential for success. One way around this would be to formally reward their contribution of mentoring in other ways, for example, through time allowance in their other duties, recognizing mentoring in promotion criteria, and giving financial rewards. Wunsch and Johnsrud (1993) describe the success of a pilot mentoring programme of new junior women academics that has been running for two years at the University of Hawaii. The programme emphasizes individual professional development and retention issues and includes colleague pairing, mentor training, the use of a mentoring agreement and a multi-levelled series of development workshops, seminars, and networking activities. The goals of the programme are to develop the academic careers of junior women academics, and to ensure institutional change through the retention of these women.

Conclusion

Within the academic profession, women suffer from a lack of role models and informal support systems, which play a major role in enhancing reputations and status, and inducting academics into the reward system. Formal effective procedures are, therefore, crucial for women's establishment in the profession. They are found at the moment to be sadly inadequate for women. Where they do exist they are dominated by men and their ideas. 'The result is a self-sufficient, male homosocial world which need not deliberately conspire to keep women segregated. Merely by ignoring the existence of women outside the domestic, sexual, and service realms the male homosocial world relegates women to the sidelines of life' (Lipman-Blumen, 1976: 31). It is these processes of exclusion that the women in their small minority endure within their professional life. One of the reasons women lack positions of responsibility and power in the university is due to their lack of numbers and seniority.

After exposure to this masculine environment, the majority become convinced that the concept of a woman academic is a paradox, and that they do not really belong. This can lead them to employ survival strategies which puts pressure on themselves to perform better than male colleagues, and to avoid being identified with other women. This means that the women who do succeed as 'honorary men' are in no position to support other women, and the process continues.

The disparity in the experiences and recruitment and promotion rates for men and women in the academic profession requires compensatory approaches to create a supportive culture and an equitable working environment which would enable the full personal and professional development of women academics. Attention to women's socialization and professional growth within an institution encourages retention and advancement. One solution proposed here as an alternative to more negative strategies is a formal mentoring system. It must be visible, fully supported and given due importance by university establishments and have enough structure to facilitate worthwhile activities and motivate individuals.

As Delamont argues, the route to success for women must be strategically planned; 'If it is possible to do so, the route is probably not through publishing more, or even through doing "better" research, but through personal contacts: friendships, correspondence, visits, conferences, seminars, and co-operative work with key actors' (1989: 260). Weston entreats us all to 'remember and remind our successful women colleagues not to pull the ladder up after them' (1993: 7). Since institutional structures are slow to change and women at the moment do not appear to be encouraged to full participation in the academic profession, one strategy is to 'bore from within and to work on informal levels of the organisation' (Nichols *et al.*, 1985). This is not to ignore institutional responsibility for the support and retention of women. The success of junior women should not be the sole responsibility of senior women. Yet for now women helping women within the academy may make the critical difference.

References

ACKER, S. (1983) 'Women, the other academics', in DUDOWITZ, R. L. (Ed.) *Women in Academe*, Oxford: Pergamon Press.

ACKER, S. (1992) 'New perspectives on an old problem: The position of women academics in British higher education', *Higher Education*, **24**, pp. 57–75.

AINSBERG, N. and HARRINGTON, M. (1988) *Women of Academe: Outsiders in the Sacred Grove*, University of Massachusetts Press, Amherst: MA.

AUT (1992) *Sex Discrimination in Universities: Report of an Academic Pay Audit Carried out by the AUT Research Department*, Association of University Teachers.

BAGILHOLE, B. (1992) *On the Inside: A Research Report on the Position of Women, Black and Disabled People in Academic Life*, Department of Social Sciences, Loughborough University.

BARDWICK, J. M. (1977) 'Some notes about power relationships among women', in SARGENT, A. G. (Ed.) *Beyond Sex Roles*, St. Paul, MN: West.

BLACKSTONE, T. and FULTON, O. (1975) 'Sex discrimination among university teachers: A British-American comparison', *British Journal of Sociology*, **26**(30), pp. 261–75.

CLARK, S. M. and CORCORAN, M. (1986) 'Perspectives on the professional socialisation of women faculty: A case of accumulative disadvantage', *Journal of Higher Education*, **57**, pp. 20–43.

CVCP (1991) *Equal Opportunities in Employment in Universities*, Committee of Vice-Chancellors and Principals of the Universities of the United Kingdom, CVCP Guidance.

DELAMONT, S. (1989) *Knowledgeable Women: Structuralism and the Reproduction of Elites*, London: Routledge.

DEPARTMENT OF EDUCATION AND SCIENCE (1992) *Statistics of Education: Teachers in Service, England and Wales 1990*, London: HMSO.

HALSEY, A. H. (1992) *Decline of Donnish Dominion: The British Professions in the Twentieth Cenytury*, Oxford: Clarendon Press.

HANSARD SOCIETY (1990) *The Report of the Hansard Society Commission on Women at the Top*, London: Hansard Society.

HART, A. and WILSON, T. (1992) 'The politics of part-time staff', *AUT Bulletin*, January, pp. 8–9.

HAWKINS, A. C and SCHULTZ, D. (1990) 'Women: The academic proletariat in West Germany and the Netherlands', in LIE, S. S. and O'LEARY, V. E. (Eds) *Storming the Tower; Women in the Academic World*, London: Kogan Page.

JOHNSRUD, L. K. and ATWATER, C. D. (1991) *Barriers to Retention and Tenure at UH-Manoa: Faculty Cohorts 1982–88*, Technical Report, Honolulu, HA: University of Hawaii.

KANTER, R. M. (1977) *Men and Women of the Corporations*, New York: Basic Books.

KAUFMAN, D. R. (1978) 'Associational ties in academe: Some male and female differences', *Sex Roles*, **4**, pp. 9–21.

KRITEK, P. (1984) 'Women's work and academic sexism', *Educational Record*, **65**, pp. 56–7.

LAWS, J. L. (1975) 'The psychology of tokenism: an analysis', *Sex Roles*, pp. 51–67.

LIPMAN-BLUMEN, J. (1976) 'Towards a homosocial theory of sex roles. An explanation of the sex-segregation of social institutions', *Signs*, **3**, pp. 15–22.

LOVANO-KERR, J. and FUCHS, R. G. (1983) 'Retention revisited: A study of female and male nontenured faculty', *Journal of Educational Equity and Leadership*, **3**, pp. 219–30.

New Internationalist (1992) May, p. 231.

NICHOLS, I. A., CARTER, H. M. and GOLDEN, M. P. (1985) 'The patron system in academia: Alternative strategies for empowering academic women', *Women's Studies International Forum*, **3**, pp. 383–90.

O'LEARY, V. E. and MITCHELL, J. M. (1990) 'Women connecting with women: Networks and mentors, in LIE, S. S. and O'LEARY, V. E. E. (Eds) *Storming the Tower; Women in the Academic World*, London: Kogan Page.

STAINES, G., TRAVIS, C. and JATRENTE, T. (1974) 'The Queen Bee Syndrome', *Psychology Today*, **7**(8), pp. 55–60.

SUTHERLAND, M. (1985) *Women Who Teach in Universities*, Stoke-on-Trent: Trentham Books.

THOMAS, K. (1990) *Gender and Subject in Higher Education*, Open University Press, Milton Keynes.

USR (1993) *Universities Statistical Record*, July.

WESTON, C. (1993) 'Women, discrimination and work', *AUT Bulletin*, October.

WUNSCH, M. A. and JOHNSRUD, L. K. (1993) *Breaking Barriers: Mentoring Junior Faculty Women for Professional Development and Retention*, Honolulu, HA: University of Hawaii.

YODER, J. D. (1985) 'An academic woman as a token: A case study', *Journal of Staff, Program and Organisational Development*.

Chapter 2

Caught Between Two Worlds: Mothers as Academics

Pauline Leonard and *Danusia Malina*

Introduction

The task of combining motherhood with the demands of academic life is a difficult one — a fact which is reflected in the relative rarity of mothers occupying full-time academic posts. Although recent statistics are hard to find, Blackstone and Fulton's early study on academic women noted that while men find it easy and socially acceptable to combine family and career, many academic women in the past have 'chosen' to remain unmarried, or married without children (Blackstone and Fulton, 1974; 1975; 1976). Simeone (1987) notes that the vast weight of research shows that there is a basic incompatibility between married life and academic life for women. Compared to men, academic women are significantly more likely to be never-married or divorced, to report less stable marriages, to have fewer children, and to see their families as detriments to their careers. For those academic women who are married,[1] they are more likely to be working or studying part-time, to hold lower rank, to be unemployed or in a job unrelated to their training. Interestingly however, Blackstone and Fulton noted that those few British academic women in their thirties and forties who were married with children wrote and published more than any other group of women (Blackstone and Fulton, 1974; 1975; 1976).

As two thirty-something, white, middle-class women each with a male partner, mothering eight children between us, we daily confront the complex agendas of children, career, partners and personal life satisfaction (Malina and Leonard, forthcoming). Our individual struggles of juggling pregnancies, babies and children, at the same time as building up our academic careers, drew us, the writers of this paper, together, first as friends and later as co-authors. We both noted, not only the absence of mothers in senior positions in the Higher

Education institutions in which we had worked, but also the hidden nature of the presence of motherhood — the lack of any recognition or reference to people's private responsibilities and pleasures in the family context. 'Surviving in the institution' for us meant not only developing our own academic skills and knowledge, but making decisions on the status of our motherhood roles. The aim of this chapter is to explore the experiences of women academics who are also mothers, to name the reality of the struggle and resistance that these dual roles involve, and to suggest strategies for surviving *and* celebrating the possibilities that occupying these two worlds offers.

Although there are differences between us, our many talks around the fact of our motherhood with our location in academic life have revealed several overlapping areas of identity. We will explore these experiences through the use of seven concepts which reflect our major concerns. These concepts are: silence and isolation; the public/private divide; sexuality and the body; choice; power; intellectual space and play. The contributions of the workshop participants were also invaluable in providing a sense of community of experience, and these are included in the text.

Silence and Isolation

Being a mother in academic life is a predominantly silent experience. The facts of this motherhood — the personal individual struggles, compromises and solutions to the daily problem of attempting to combine being a good mother and a competent, productive academic — are largely unvoiced at work. This silence reflects what Hoschchild (1989) has termed *the cultural cover-up*, promoting the idea that it is perfectly feasible to easily combine a career with having children. Any traces of stress or need for compromise are 'kept underground' (Aisenberg and Harrington, 1988), and children are rarely given by women as reasons why deadlines are not met or meetings are unattended. Mothers find themselves, 'already suspect in the academy, their seriousness questioned, [and] compelled to exclude reference to their personal lives in the workplace' (Aisenberg and Harrington, 1988). This feeling of silence was reflected in the experiences of workshop participants: 'I really don't share my personal life with my colleagues — my children — I rarely take them into work or even mention them. Yet I know I work just as hard . . . but I just don't talk about it'.

Academic women are thus struggling to perform within the traditional male model of having someone at home, quietly erasing the problems caused by childraising responsibilities. Arlie Hoschchild describes this as, 'the very clockwork of a career system that seems to eliminate women not so much through malevolent disobedience to good rules, but through making up rules to suit half of the population' (1975: 59).

Both the male dominated establishment and culture of Higher Education silence women's motherhood. Yet the mother identity may also be problematic between women — especially those who identify themselves as feminist, constraining the one area of academia where women may wish to feel more liberated. As Wilkinson and Kitzinger (1993) note, the apolitical nature of the heterosexuality identity may lead women to feel almost guilty about it. Heterosexual mothers may further sense that 'the idea of being a mother [is] seen as second rate' (Ree, 1990), revealing a collusion with men as partners and sons. Although, undoubtedly, to be heterosexual and/or a mother may enable a woman to enjoy 'many of the privileges and rewards of the establishment' (Jacklin, 1993), a prioritization of identities exists in some feminist contexts which renders the mother identity too unsound to be admitted. Silence may thus become a survival strategy.

Mothers in Higher Education may be not only silent, therefore, but also isolated. As one workshop member articulated:

Where are the mothers in academia? Plenty of students are mothers, but what of the full-time appointments? Where are the children? Is it true that all senior academic women seem to be single and childless — is it so impossible to have them both — the career and the babies?

Other participants commented on the support and strength gained from being a mother in their private domestic life. This celebration of the world of children, the relishing of the neighbourly support of other women who share the horrors and pleasures of the mothering experience, becomes a personal survival strategy. 'We may be silent at work, but we are noisy at home. After work, after school, the house is full of mothers, children, laughter, television, toys and junk food.'

Thus, just as women are silent about the problematic aspects of mothering, they are also silent about the joys: the giggling, the cuddles, the pride and the warmth that children bring. Yet as Aisenberg and Harrington (1988) ask, if acknowledgment of the importance of relationships outside the workplace is unacceptable within it, how are women or men ever going to achieve integrated lives? By denying the reality of combining children with academic contexts, women are part of the collusion and compromise that Rosalind Coward (1992) identifies as resulting from women trying to follow unrealistic ideals. Perhaps the time has come for academic women to stop colluding with a male system through their silence and compromising by finding complicated individual solutions. To be more open and communicative about the realities of being an academic mother, and to demand recognition of the differences which people bring with them to academic life are strategies which may help to shatter the silence in which academic mothers are presently situated.

The Public/Private Divide

Different approaches to feminism, diverse and complex as they are, have shed light on the importance of, and interconnections between, the public and private spheres in explanations of women's oppression. These notions provide an important discourse in women's lives. The idea of the private and the public — the world of work and home — shapes women's everyday lives and experiences. As Rosalind Edwards notes in her research with mature women students,

> The public/private split can be used in a revealing way . . . provided it is recognised that the divisions and boundaries between the two are not only not constant, but are to some extent different for each peson according to structural and other factors operating on or in their lives.
>
> (Edwards, 1993: 28)

The notion of the public world as associated with paid work, politics, formal education and the exercise of power and authority has led to the association of this sphere with maleness. Conversely, the private world has been discussed in terms of the domestic, the family arena, the home, children, the site of nurturing, and as such has been associated with femaleness. The presumed unemotional, competitive and mercenary, in opposition to those in the private being altruistic, affective and non-goal oriented (Edwards, 1993).

Academics who are mothers find themselves differentiated within an already minority group (Bagilhole, 1993). This can be a double-edged experience. In one sense, these women may become special women who are placed on a pedestal by men and other women. This misplaced flattery can deny the woman a chance to speak of the tense reality of trying to be an academic as well as a mother. Given this credit it is difficult for women to shatter the illusion of their success. However, Rosalind Coward has forcefully argued that,

> Living an illusion is uncomfortable and often women hover on the point of exposing the illusions of their lives. But most back off, preferring the illusions to the difficulty of personal change. And this is what I mean by complicity. Complicity is about not telling the truth — to other women or to ourselves — and not confronting men about the

areas of our lives that don't fit the illusions. This complicity means that women don't pass on information and knowledge about their condition, and disparage those who try to do so.

(Edwards, 1992: 194)

However, on the other hand, women may feel denigrated by their motherhood, as one workshop participant said:

I feel like an alien with women who have chosen to stay full time in the home with their children. It is as if I have chosen the opposite camp to them. With [most] colleagues I must deny and conceal my 'otherness' which is about being a mother.

Workshop participants, as well as the authors, described and made sense of their experiences with constant reference to the categories, public and private. The energy and tensions involved in maintaining a clear divide between home and work spheres were stressed by women working in Academe. Stories told by women academics who are mothers contain accounts of the joys and struggles in both spheres. As one woman described, her academic work has provided a welcome escape route from all that is domestic. Despite the stress of living between two worlds, some women felt liberated by their position. Articulating hidden aspects of the divide between the public and private may be viewed as tentative steps forward for women academics who are mothers.

Sexuality and the Body

One aspect of being a mother is that it is usually a public fact — and one that is interpreted to be a statement about a woman's sexuality. It is assumed that there has been a period of heterosexuality, and when a woman is pregnant — a fat, visibly sexual being — the recency of the activity is there for everyone to contemplate.

Joanne Martin (1990) describes how images of pregnancy and infant care carry connotations of intimacy, sexuality and nurturance: a context in which organizational norms of efficiency and predictability seem less appropriate. Pregnancy can be threatening for men in organizations. The fact that sexual intercourse has occurred becomes salient. Pregnancy thus helps to reveal organizational taboos — the unstated sexual ideology that undergirds current norms of organizational functioning.

One of the principal themes of this sexual ideology is the public denial of any sexuality. However, because a pregnant woman's belly typically becomes visible, denial and invisible absorption into the usual ways of 'doing business' in a male dominated organization are not possible. Pregnancy removes the option of ignoring a woman's gender: honorary men do not become pregnant. Pregnancy makes men acknowledge a woman's sexuality and the consequences of it. It allows her to take up more space, for her body to become more dominant. These feelings are reflected by one of the workshop participants:

> My colleagues' attention was no longer on my work, or my ability but rather on my growing belly, my clothes, my plans for managing/coping with the baby and finally how I would return to my pre-pregnant body shape. I felt as if I could be either a mother or an academic but not both at the same time.

Another theme of the sexual ideology in organizations is that sex is okay for men but not for women. Men are expected to be married, to have families and pictures of their children (displays of their fertility or their sexual competence) on their desks. Yet women are subject to different, stronger taboos. A pregnant woman upsets the sexual status quo in the organization. Joanne Martin claims that the sexual taboo that the pregnant employee violates is that, 'sex is happening and the high ranking male is getting none of it' (1990).

A theme within this sexual ideology particularly pertinent to the world of Higher Education is that sexuality is irrelevant to academic work. Many women are challenging this by bringing into their work writing on

> women's bodies, their bodily processes, their feelings, their relations with each other, their attitudes towards the male world, and men's attitudes towards women.
>
> (French, 1986: 490)

One of the aims of this chapter is to confront the ideology of higher education with the full spectrum of sexuality, which includes gay and lesbianism, but also women as mothers, and women who wish to become mothers. Motherhood is a legitimate function of the female body and as such it should be less surprising, less stigmatized than it is at present.

Choice

Polarized positions of womanhood, the *altruistic mother* and the *career woman* are unacceptable and limit women's visions of their potential in life. Existing models of motherhood demand a splitting of ourselves (Rich, 1977). We believe these oppositional images of motherhood offer choices that place women in a strait-jacket.

Workshop participants noted how these powerful stereotypes force women to make choices on an either/or basis. This rigid dichotomy unfairly demands the impossible for women. Such charged concepts haunt women academics precisely because whichever choice we have made has been turned against us. The workshop debate surfaced the notion that underpinning the discussion on choice may lie a false assumption that if a woman academic remains childfree then this 'advantage' will provide her with a successful track with in Academe. However, a recent study found that being single often constituted a barrier to women's productivity (Davis and Astin, 1990).

It seems that women feel forced to make decisions based on a male modelled career pattern which ultimately denies them the full range of choices in life. Women can feel castigated for wanting the same opportunities open to men. One woman in the workshop said the following: 'The right to choose has been taken away from women in so many areas. This either/or choice is yet another male-created conflict between children and women's selfhood'.

Refusal to perform social and psychological gymnastics in pursuit of prevailing ideals of womanhood (Coward, 1992) ensures considerable discomfort for those women involved. When considering this, we are mindful of Adrienne Rich when she notes that

> A female child needs to be told, very early, the practical difficulties females have to face in even trying to imagine 'what they want to be' . . . 'You can be what you really want to be' — if you are prepared to fight, to create priorities for yourself against the grain of cultural expectations, to persist in the face of misogynist hostility.
>
> (Rich, 1977:248)

The right to be successful at work, in academia, ought not to foreclose the reproductive possibilities of female members of staff.

Power

To be the mother of children is to be powerless in many respects. They create the type of mother you are, the type of mood you are in, the type of day you will have. Plans are set awry, work is shelved, good feelings turn to despair. The incessant self-centredness of small children is captured beautifully by Adrienne Rich:

> It began when I had picked up a book or began trying to write a letter, or even found myself on the telephone with someone toward whom my voice betrayed eagerness, a rush of sympathetic energy. The child might be absorbed in playing, but as soon as he felt me gliding into a world which did not include him, he would come to pull at my hand, ask for help, punch at the typewriter keys. And I would feel his wants at such moments as fraudulent, as an attempt to defraud me of living even for fifteen minutes as myself . . . I could love so much better, I told myself after even a quarter-hour of selfishness, of peace, or detachment from my children.
>
> (Rich, 1977:23)

Yet at the same time, mothers are also powerful. With younger children, just *sometimes* they can be controlled. In one area of life a mother receives unquestioning love and respect — the experience of being central to someone's life. Mothers of older children in the workshop talked of the tremendous enrichment provided by children in understanding the world. When older children achieve in ways a feminist mother may feel proud of — one participant told of her son who is the only male member of a gender course at his university, a daughter who is gloriously self-confident and assertive — this gives a great sense of personal achievement and power.

This power — and the responsibility that accompanies it — gives women personal power at work. For the job has to take its place amongst competing priorities. This demands a critical appraisal of, for instance, the amount of time mothers want to be away from home, in comparison with some colleagues who do not have caring responsibilities. Mothers may be less wrought up about work, less bruised by the politics, less likely to sit about in rooms late at night agitating about who said what to whom. Quite simply, they haven't got the time. The wearing, grinding aspects of work may be left behind, because emotionally, there is not enough space for them. Children enable some women to get things into perspective as the limits they set on their time are not all bad.

Thus academic mothers may look at their colleagues and decide that, as they can't compete with them on their terms any longer, they are not going to even try. This may also be strangely empowering. This was reflected by the words of a workshop participant:

> There is something about starting ten yards behind everyone else at the starting line, and you're the only one pushing a double buggy. It's almost that you've put yourself in a different race, and so, consequently, to some extent, new rules can be made up: the cards are so stacked against you that you might as well be in control of your own life and live it in the best way that you can.

Rosalind Coward (1992) describes how, for many women, the prospect of starting a family is an enormous relief, not just because they can escape from a competitive environment but because they can also escape from their own competitive feelings. This escape is a persistent legacy of motherhood, and is also a survival strategy — yet could it also be something more, is it a way of going foward, to strive for an alternative to the male competitive ideology that is so pervasive in academia?

Intellectual Space

Families are, as Louis and Rose Coser (1974) argue, 'greedy institutions' for women, requiring constant availability and commitment, to cater for all the physical and emotional needs of the members. These authors assert that many women accept the cultural mandate of committing selflessly and fully to the family, even when engaged in paid work outside the home. Such women are available psychically if not physically. Alongside this, Acker (1980) contends that Higher Education can also be viewed as a greedy institution. Adrienne Rich encapsulates the endless task of patching fragmented needs within greedy institutions when she states that,

> It is difficult to imagine unless one has lived it, the personal division, endless improvising and creative and intellectual holding back that for most women accompany the attempt to combine the emotional and physical demands of parenthood and the challenge of work. To assume one can naturally combine these has been a male privilege everywhere in the world. For women, the energy expended in both the conflict and the improvisation has held many back from starting a professional career and has been a heavy liability to careers once begun.
>
> (Rich, 1980: 147)

As highlighted, significant pressure in the lives of women academics as mothers derives from the issue of time management. The double workload (waged work and domestic work) raises the fundamental question of which part of women academic's lives is prioritized at any given point. A number of competing demands may be felt by combining teaching/family/relationships. While the primary responsibility for the physical and emotional welfare of the children and of the partner remain in the hands of women alone, then as Dorothy Dinnerstein (1978) suggests, 'women will inevitably be pressed into the dual role of indispensable quasi-human supporter and deadly quasi-human enemy of the self.' The strain of managing increasing teaching and publishing demands with that of the role of carer and lover mean that exhaustion levels amongst such women are high. Achieving a sense of balance was seen as a constant tension and aspiration by workshop participants. In one woman's words:

> I wonder if there are enough hours in the day. I am torn, stretched between what I want to do for myself as an individual and what is the minimum I can get away with before someone complains and/or before someone misbehaves publicly and I am pulled up as a bad and neglectful mother.

For feminist academics living with men and families, the idea of disclosing the reality of their partners' lack of support threatens to expose contradictions too stark and painful. Thus men are often conferred with an idealized image of the perfect 'new' man (Coward, 1992). Academics with children can find themselves silenced once more as their partners take credit for being exceptional.

Academic life has been viewed as an ideal arena of work for women (Adler *et al.*, 1993). As Simeone (1987) has noted,

> what may seem to others as a preponderance of free time should in fact be used for the solitary activities of thinking, reading, and writing for a faculty member to achieve success. Faculty men with families may be more able to do so, not only because they have fewer domestic demands on their time, but also because their home lives are constructed in such a way as to support these scholarly activities.
>
> (Simeone, 1987: 137)

Schedule-juggling women academics and mothers have to search for creative ways in which to honour the scholars in themselves. Finding space and time to engage in that journey is a duty to be taken seriously.

Play

> Play has a tendency to be beautiful . . . The play-mood is one of rapture and enthusiasm . . . A feeling of exaltation and tension accompanies the action, mirth and relaxation follow.
>
> (Huizinga, 1971: 154)

One of the reasons why play, generally associated with the activities of children, has remained a hidden aspect of our lives is described by Bohm and Peat (1987) as a 'work ethic which does not consider the importance of play and suggests that work itself is noble while play is at best, recreational and at worst, frivolous and non-serious' (in Henry, 1991: 6).

From our discussions we realized that this unacknowledged element of our lives contained much of our source of replenishment and creativity as academics. Recognition of the impact of play on our working lives, teaching and writing, has led us to reconsider the rewards of keeping in touch with our curious and excited child-selves. Our time with our children, fraught as it often is, has provided us with surprises we believe derive from playtimes we experience as mothers. In addition to this, support and explorations of our own humour with the like-minded women remain a wonderful source of energy. Importantly, our children have revealed and reminded us of the power of laughter and play in our lives. As Mary Daly (1993) points out so well, women's laughter is one of the powers that rocks the world. Letting go of our seriousness and bringing laughter into our work with students and colleagues has become a vital survival strategy.

Endnote

We have attempted to voice the collective feelings and concerns of mothers involved in academic life.[2] These are revealed to be inevitably complex and contradictory, combining the immense pleasure and joy of being a mother with the satisfaction and sense of fulfillment which is derived from succeeding in academia. One of the main conclusions that has emerged is that women could attempt to be more open about the realities of motherhood, and not to collude with the male model of life which dominates Higher Education. All women attending the workshop talked about their personal and individual solutions to their struggles to negotiate time to work and play, solutions which usually remain hidden from the institution.

Yet, as Simeone points out, 'institutions do have a role and a responsibility in creating environments and policies which are supportive of women's attempts to combine career and family' (1987). Perhaps the time has come for British academic women to challenge the supposed incompatibility between the academy and the family.

Another conclusion which embraces everything which has been expressed is the love and strength that children produce — emotions which need to be celebrated. Jean Elshstain (1981) summed this up when she wrote,

> Mothering is a complicated, rich, ambivalent, vexing, joyous activity which is biological, natural, social, symbolic, and emotional. It carries profoundly resonant emotional and sexual imperatives. A tendency to downplay the differences that pertain between say mothering and holding down a job, not only drains our private relations of most of their significance, but oversimplifies what can or should be done to alter things for women.
>
> (Elshstain, 1981: 243)

All the mothers who shared their experiences within the workshop were immensely rewarded by their children. To keep silent about them is thus to deny the importance of their place in our lives.

> o i want to do it all i want
> to drain my tortured mind i
> want to hold yr thin body
> i want to love the children all
> the time, all the time
> (Alta, 1983: 128)

Notes

1 Although we quote studies which use 'marriage' as a description of a legally defined relationship between women and men, we ourselves understand this term in a broader sense to encompass cohabiting and non-cohabiting relationships.
2 We are indebted to all those women who shared their personal experiences with us so generously at the Women and the Higher Education Curriculum Conference.

References

ADLER, S., LANEY, J. and PACKER, M. (1993) *Managing Women: Feminism and Power in Educational Management*, Buckingham: Open University Press.
AISENBERG, N. and HARRINGTON, M. (1988) *Women of Academe: Outsiders in the Sacred Grove*, Amherst, MA: University of Massachusetts Press.
ACKER, S. (1980) in EDWARDS, R. (1993) *Mature Women Students: Separating or Connecting Family and Education*, London: Taylor & Francis.
ALTA (1983) 'o i do want it all i want' in CARTERET, A., VINER, F. and JONES-DAVIES, S. (1983) *"In the Pink"*, London: The Women's Press Ltd.
BAGILHOLE, B. (1993) 'Women academics: Survivors in a male preserve', Workshop presentation at the *Women and the Higher Education Curriculum* Conference, November 1993, University of Central Lancashire.

BLACKSTONE, T. and FULTON, O. (1974) 'Men and women academics: An Anglo-American comparison of subject choices and research activity', *Higher Education*, 3, pp. 119–40.

BLACKSTONE, T. and FULTON, O. (1975) 'Sex discrimination among university teachers — a British American comparison', *British Journal of Sociology*, 26, pp. 261–75.

BLACKSTONE, T. and FULTON, O. (1976) 'Discrimination is the villain', *The Times Higher Education Supplement*, No. 246, 9th July 1976.

BOHM, D. and PEAT, D. (1987) 'Science, order and creativity' in HENRY, J. (1991) *Creative Management5*, London: Sage.

COSER, L. and COSER, R. (1974) *Greedy Institutions: Patterns of Undivided Commitment*, New York: Free Press.

COWARD, R. (1992) *Our Treacherous Hearts: Why Women Let Men Get Their Own Way*, London: Faber and Faber.

DALY, M. (1993) *Outercourse: The Be-dazzling Voyage*, London: The Women's Press.

DAVIS, D. E. and ASTIN, H. S. (1990) 'Life cycle, career patterns and gender stratification in Academe: Breaking myths and exposing truths', in STIVER LIE, S. and O'LEARY, V. (Eds), *Storming the Tower: Women in the Academic World*, London: Kogan Page.

DINNERSTEIN, D. (1978) in ADLER, S., LANEY, J. and PACKER, M. (1993) *Managing Women: Feminism and Power in Educational Management*, Milton Keynes: Open Univerity Press.

EDWARDS, R. (1993) *Mature Women Students: Separating or Connecting Family and Education*, London: Taylor & Francis.

ELSHSTAIN, J. B. (1981) *Public Man, Private Woman*, Princeton, NJ: Princeton University Press.

FRENCH, M. (1986) *Beyond Power: On Women, Men and Morals*, London: Jonathan Cape.

HENRY, J. (1991) *Creative Management*, London: Sage.

HOSCHCHILD, A. R. (1975) 'Inside the clockwork of male careers', in HOWE, F. (Ed.) *Women and the Power to Change*, New York: McGraw-Hill.

HOSCHCHILD, A. R. (1989) *The Second Shift: Working Parents and the Revolution at Home*, London: Piatkus.

HUIZUNGA, J. (1971) in STOR, A. (1972) *The Dynamics of Creation*, London: Penguin Books.

JACKLIN, C. N. (1993) 'How my heterosexuality affects my feminist politics', in WILKINSON, S. and KITZINGER, C. (Eds) *Heterosexuality: A Feminism and Psychology Reader*, London: Sage.

MALINA, D. and LEONARD, P. (forthcoming) 'Just push a bit harder, luv: Birthing an academic career', in MORLEY, L. and WALSH, V. (Eds) *Feminist Academics: Creative Agents for Change*, London: Taylor & Francis.

MARTIN, J. (1990) 'Organisational taboos: The suppression of gender conflict in organisations', *Organisation Science*, 1, pp. 334–59.

REE, J. (1990) in WANDOR, M. (1990) *Once a Feminist*, London: Virago Press.

RICH, A. (1977) *Of Woman Born: Motherhood as Experience and Institution*, London: Virago.

RICH, A. (1980) *On Lies, Secrets and Silence: Selected Prose 1966–1978*, London: Virago.

SIMEONE, A. (1987) *Academic Women: Working Towards Equality*, Bergin and Garvey.

WILKINSON, S. and KITZINGER, C. (1993) (Eds) *Heterosexuality: A Feminism and Psychology Reader*, London: Sage.

Chapter 3

Ivory Towers and Ebony Women: The Experiences of Black Women in Higher Education

Millsom Henry

Introduction

Universities were founded upon elitist values which have flourished throughout an historical process of partriarchy, colonialism and capitalism. These institutions soon became associated with the image of ivory towers, as it depicts a place where prestigious groups of wise, usually white, men pontificated about society away from the pressures and harsh realities of life. Although stereotypical, this image of universities has become quite pervasive. Ironically, universities were also perceived to be liberal institutions, a perception which is still held today and which goes some way to explaining why they have only just begun to grasp the notion that certain groups face discrimination in higher education. Unfortunately, the equal opportunities legislation of the late seventies has, in general terms, failed to stop the discrimination both within and outside the ivory tower. Black feminists have argued that black women, in particular, have suffered from ineffective equal opportunities legislation. Primarily due to their unique status in society then, black women are said to often encounter triple discrimination in terms of their gender, race and class position. Certainly when looking at Higher Education, it is evident that, as members of the staff or the student body, or as subjects within the academic curricular, black women's experiences have largely been rendered invisible. The central aims of this chapter are, therefore, to examine the image of universities as ivory towers; to define who the ebony women in Higher Education are; to document some of their experiences; to stimulate a debate and to call for research into this neglected area of analysis.

In order to describe the experiences of black women in higher education, the structure of the paper follows the same framework as the WHEN

Conference workshop.[1] First, the image of universities as ivory towers is examined, followed by a brief but critical appraisal of the term ebony women. Examples of black women's actual experiences in higher education are then considered alongside an assessment of equal opportunities legislation and policies. Finally, a number of suggestions for future research and action are outlined.

Ivory Towers?

Underlying the declaration 'education is a right, not a privilege' are fundamental ideas that date back to legislation of the nineteenth century which advocated free public education for all. However, these ideas have traditionally referred to the primary and secondary educational sector. In stark contrast, the higher education sector has always been regarded as a privilege. This was primarily due to the fact that universities emerged out of the private sector and, as a result, they quickly became associated with being elite institutions. Although held in high regard, universities were also perceived to be ivory towers. This notion stereotypically portrayed a place where brilliant scholars created and applied 'unbiased knowledge' to the world outside. Those who lived between its walls tended to be white, male and privileged and many believed then (as some still do now) that universities were liberal instititions which selected individuals on an objective notion of ability. The fact that certain groups underachieved in education terms was interpreted as a fault of the individuals themselves and not in the system of selection. Universities were also structured around a rigid division of status which inevitably became a breeding ground for profound snobbery and today, despite the demise of the binary divide and the recent shifts away from an elite to a mass Higher Education system, universities continue to be fundamentally hierarchical organizations which unconsciously (and at times consciously) discriminate against certain groups in society.

Participants at the workshop were asked to examine the image of universities as ivory towers in their groups. Many recognized the traits associated with the stereotype and talked about the overwhelming nature of universities which appeared to thrive on creating and maintaining an intellectually superior and aloof atmosphere, keeping both staff and students in their respective places. For example, one workshop participant comments, '. . . as a mature and usually very confident black woman, walking into the university grounds for the first time was a very intimidating experience . . .' Students (and some members of staff) have often described the difficulty of approaching members of academic staff, especially those who have written the key textbooks and/or journal articles. The workshop participants also referred the process of mystification within universities whereby everyday procedures and practices were perceived to be deliberately obscured. A student recalled her feelings when assessing whether or not to apply to do a doctorate, 'I felt very apprehensive about asking my tutor if I could do a PhD . . . am I supposed to automatically know if I am good enough or should I wait until I get invited to apply?' The processes surrounding the doctorate were, therefore, seen to be part of the mystique and exclusivity of universities. Admittedly, there have been efforts recently to create more positive images, especially by the new universities (Jewson *et al.*, 1991, 1993), but the majority of the workshop participants felt that the negative image of universities as ivory towers was valid.

Ebony Women

The term ebony was deliberately employed in the title of this chapter to highlight the sharp contrast with the ivory image of universities. It is a term used synonymously with the term black throughout this chapter to refer politically to all women of African and Asian descent. Recent debates have highlighted the problematic nature of the term black (Aptheker, 1982; Charles, 1990; Hill-Collins, 1990; hooks, 1981, 1989; Lorde, 1984; Smith and Stewart, 1983 and Spelman, 1988). However, it is utilized here in the sense that it attempts to encompass and not ignore the diverse nature of a group of people facing oppression. The expression ebony women was employed here to acknowledge black women's distinctive position in society and is referred to in a context of appreciating the diversity between black women and recognizing that they actually occupy a variety of different identities simultaneously in terms of their ethnicities, sexuality, religious beliefs, physical abilities, socio-economic status and so on. As June Jordan eloquently put it,

> I think there is something deficient in the thinking on the part of anybody who proposes either gender identity politics or race identity politics as sufficient, because every single one of us is more than whatever race we represent or embody and more than whatever gender category we fall into. We have other kinds of allegiances, other kinds of dreams that have nothing to do with whether we are white or not white.
>
> (Parmar, 1989: 61)

Set in this context, the phrase black/ebony women was accepted by the participants as a practical working definition for the purposes of the workshop.

Distinctive Experiences?

The racist, sexist and elitist ideologies in society continue to be reflected and reinforced in the higher education system which tends to ignore black women's experiences. These experiences are distinctive because they represent multiple forms of oppression rather than simple sexual oppression. A workshop participant recalled a period from her secondary schools days where her schoolteacher informed her that she 'had two great disadvantages in society, being black as well as female'. She was actively encouraged to use them both to her advantage. There is, however, an implicit danger in some of the arguments which suggest that black women are extraordinary beings; this is epitomized in the concept of triple discrimination (Lykes, 1983; Parmar, 1989; Weston, 1993). This concept implies that one form of discrimination can merely be added onto the other, but the process of discrimination facing black women is much more complex. The fact is, black women experience racism, sexism (and classism) interactively and as Smith and Stewart (1983), state 'racism and sexism must be understood not merely as independent parallel processes, but as processes standing in a dynamic relation to each other.' Consequently, racial *and* sexual discrimination (and someti nes classism) are inseparable issues for black women in higher education whether they are members of staff and/or the student body or the subject of analysis.

Educational research has pointed out that individuals experience the benefits of education differently due to a number of factors, for example, their gender, ethnicity and social-class position (Jewson and Mason, 1986a, 1986b; Mirza, 1993). However, the overriding emphasis has been upon the under-achievement of black and white working-class males. Consequently, educational researchers have consistently failed to examine the one group affected by a combination of discriminatory factors, namely black women. With a few exceptions (Wilson, 1978; Bryan *et al.*, 1985; Mirza, 1993), black women appear to constitute a group not worthy of collective analysis, and researchers are left with the unenviable task of having to pull together data from at least three separate fields of study: class, gender and ethnic studies. Nevertheless, by using this diverse statistical and also anecdotal evidence it is possible to document some examples of black women's actual experiences in education.

In school

Black women are constantly aware of their disadvantaged position in education; this stems from the primary right through to the higher education sector. Recent research of black girls' experiences in the United Kingdom school system by Mirza (1993) found that they had tended to have poor access to a wide range of careers advice and spent a lot of their time and energies avoiding the effects of racist and negative teacher expectations. To quote one of Mirza's schoolgirl respondents, 'You feel the discrimination, they try to hide it but you can see through it; They try to say "We're all equal", but you can tell: they talk to you more simply . . .' (Mirza, 1993: 55)

As one of only two black pupils in primary school, one of the workshop participants recalled an episode that occurred around Christmas . . .

> The school was auditioning parts for the nativity play and I was told by my teacher that I would play one of the three wise men, primarily because he was black. I enjoyed acting and felt that I should have a stronger part and I asked if I could play Mary, the mother of Jesus. My teacher kooked at me with amazement, but I stood my ground and refused to play any other role. I could see no reason why I should not play the part, after all who said Mary has to be white? My stance caused quite a stir, but eventually due to the intervention of another teacher who was more senior, I was allowed to play Mary. I knew then that I would be continually fighting to be heard . . .

Black girls therefore learnt about their disadvantaged position in education at an early age. However, many also realized that education itself could be the vehicle of self-fulfilling prophesy. On paper, the new universities do potentially offer black women a number of opportunities, but getting into higher education is not an easy option, and for black women in particular, the obstacles still appear to be quite daunting.

Getting into Higher Education

The significance of role-models has been stressed throughout educational research as a crucial factor in encouraging non-traditional groups into certain areas (Mac an Ghiall, 1988; Mirza, 1993). Black women in academia therefore, have an important role to play. One of the workshop participants stated that her reasons for entering higher education were three-fold, 'for my mum, who worked hard in the hope that I could achieve a better life, for my own self-esteem and to show other black women that academic professions can be a worthwhile career option for them too'. There are, of course, a variety of reasons why black women enter Higher Education, as another workshop participant pointed out, 'from birth I was expected to go to university and do postgraduate study. I felt pressurized and decided to resist this expectation by not registering for a doctorate.'

The empirical evidence on gender and ethnic minorities in higher education, although traditionally kept separate, does shed some useful light on black women's educational position in relation to black men as well as the white population. For example, at times the media and others have attempted to use the slightly better performances of black women in education to further oppress black men. As Mirza (1992) found, suggestions that black women '. . . unlike their male counterparts, have special powers of endurance that enable them to overcome the racism and sexism they face daily' were being used to divide black men and women. The reason for these differences between black men and women are, according to Mirza, largely due to the wider social, political and economic constraints as black men tended to enter occupations which did not given them access to educational mobility.

In terms of ethnicity, the concentration on black male underachievement in educational research led to claims that ethnic minorities were under-represented in the higher education sector. It was not however, until the early nineties that both Polytechnics Central Admissions System (PCAS) and the Committee of Vice-Chancellors and Principals (CVCP) (1991) began to look at data relating to ethnic minorities in Higher Education. The working group set up by the CVCP (Taylor 1992) to analyse Universities Central Clearing and Admission (UCCA) monitoring data revealed that Afro-Caribbean and Bangladeshis were significantly under-represented in the UCCA sector. In addition, this working group found that ethnic minority applicants had distinctive patterns with respect to class, geographical origins, educational background, qualifications, subject preferences and institutional choice. The UCCA Statistical Supplement Report (1991–2) stated that these patterns were due to the fact that there was still a tendency for home Asian and black students to apply for courses with high entrance requirements, to prefer to study in their home region and to have taken resits ('home' is used to distinguish between Asian and black students living in the UK and international/overseas students). With regard to sex, only the figures from PCAS distinguish between sex and ethnicity. In 1992, more women overall applied to the polytechnic sector — 51.4 per cent compared to 48.6 per cent of men. However, more men were accepted — 52 per cent compared to 47.8 per cent of women. In terms of ethnicity, 86.6 per cent of applicants were white men and women compared to 13.4 per cent of men and women of African and Asian descent and 85.6 per cent of all admissions were to white men and women compared to 14.4 per cent of those of African and Asian descent. The male to female ratio was broadly similar for all main ethnic groups.

According to Tariq Modood (1993) the overall PCAS and UCCA figures refute claims of under-representation of black and Asian groups, but they confirm that there are differential rates of selection. The investigations into St George's Medical School (1988) by the Commission for Racial Equality (CRE) aptly illustrates this point. The CRE found evidence of systematic and long-term discrimination against women and ethnic minorities throughout their medical training. Despite the fact that the figures for black female students in higher education are small, the issue is more complex than simple representation in terms of numbers, it is the combination of individual and institutional levels of discrimination that black women have to face in order to stay in higher education.

Staying in Higher Education

Once admitted, black women have stressed the importance of establishing good support networks within and outside the ivory tower. The diverse positions of black women in terms of their personal, professional and/or student status has a direct effect on these support networks. For example, one of the workshop participants described how powerless and defenceless her position was as a first year undergraduate, 'I felt isolated when I complained about an incident of racial abuse . . . Although, I followed the appropriate procedures, it was not taken seriously by the female head of department . . . Eventually, I felt I had no option but to drop out of university . . .' Unfortunately, accounts like this are far too common and send the wrong signals to black women who simply want an opportunity to study and work in a mutually supportive and stimulating environment free from discrimination. Members of academic staff are not exempt from these situations. A colleague protested about the lack of support from her peers;

> I complained about a student who racially abused me verbally. I received very little support as my white colleagues in the department were surprised that I could be racially abused because of my 'light' complexion. Comments were made about the fact that I did not look black which begs the question, what does a black person actually have to look like?

Unlike the figures from PCAS for black women students, there are at present no direct figures about black women as members of academic staff and there are no immediate plans to rectify this position. However, work is currently underway to compile these figures from the 1991 Census by cross-checking responses on ethnicity, gender and type of occupation. Until then, anecdotal evidence suggests that black women tend to be concentrated at the lower end of the academic/administrative scale and on short-term temporary contracts. Furthermore, there is an assumption that black women in academia represent all black women, which can sometimes be a burden as well as a blessing. Far too often, black female academics are sent to represent their institutions or departments for public relation purposes. These positions, however, leave black women vulnerable and open to exploitation. As one of Morley's (1993) respondents put it

> As a black woman, nothing surprises me anymore. I am on a temporary, part-time contract in a poly with a clearly stated equal opportunities policy . . . We attract a lot of black students, and I am used as a selling point. But if a fall in recruitment threatens, I am told by my head of department, who is a white woman, that my contract might not be renewed
>
> (Morley, 1993: 16)

Figures from the Association of University Teachers (AUT, 1993) assert that less than one in 20 of the UK's top academics are women, even though women make up nearly half the student population and over one-fifth of the total academic workforce. Only 4.9 per cent of them are promoted to the rank of professor, a slight increase of 1991 figure (3 per cent), but once professors, women are paid on average £1500 less than their male peers. However, the current campaigns waged by the AUT and other professional associations for women in higher education have tended to focus upon white middle-class women.

The recent calls for promotion to professorships have dominated the current debate, sometimes to the detriment of needs of other women, such as campaigning for a more radical and total transformation of university procedures. Instead, it tends to tinker around the edges and, as Weston points out, '. . . the "glass ceiling" debate . . . essentially addresses the problems of the already privileged.' (1993) This is not to deny the importance of getting more women, both black and white, to the top of the profession, but this does not get away from the more fundamental need to restructure the institutional practices and attitudes that have become entrenched in the ivory tower. Until this issue is addressed, it is possible for all women to become part of the problem as they can occupy both the 'dominant' and 'subordinate' groups in academia. In this regard, the ivory tower becomes both a paradox and a contradiction for women whose position is bound up with a 'weave of criss-crossing threads or matrices of discursive practices and a complexity of social identities . . .' (Morley, 1993: 11). Both black and white women who go into academia, therefore, face a dilemma — they must decide whether to become part of the ivory tower and accept its terms, to 'play the game', to directly challenge the very structure from which their special status is derived or to leave. These decisions are also dependent upon a variety of factors, namely their socio-economic background, their occupational status, their ethnicity, their parental status, their sexuality, their disability, as this gives them differential access to the corridors of power.

There are significant historical differences between black and white women in terms of access to key structures in higher education. The relationship between black and white women has become part of a wider debate about feminism. In the late seventies, feminism was described by Adrienne Rich as, 'white solipsism' — the tendency to think and act as if whiteness described the world. The differences between women were ignored and, consequently, issues of racism were exempt from scrutiny (Bourne, 1983; Carby, 1982; Christian, 1985; hooks, 1981). Researchers such as Cockburn (1991) have already pointed out how gender blind universities are, but they are also colour blind and, for black women, this has meant that barriers have become virtually monumental. The lack of recognition of black women's distinctive position in higher education culminates in resentment for both the system and white women, especially those who claim to be feminists;

> We [black women] get tokenised and exploited by white women too . . . many of whom would describe themselves as feminists . . . I have lost count of how many times I have been asked to contribute to books and conferences at the eleventh hour, that is, when they've suddenly realised the 'black perspective' is missing.
>
> (Morley 1993: 16)

Most gatekeeping positions — in terms of research funding, publications and so forth in the UK — have gone to white men and white middle-class women whose priorities tend to exclude and denigrate the work that many black women can offer. The recent controversy about Toni Morrison's prestigious Nobel Prize award illustrates this point well. Critics complained that Morrison's work was not in the same league as the 'great classics' and implied that she only got the award because of her gender and ethnicity. The profound snobbery about the use of a certain style of academic language and writing must stifle not only black women but all other women and men. If black women are visible or permitted to take part, it is often seen as a token gesture. This negative form of representation implies that individuals are placed in certain positions for demonstration purposes only.

The debate on black women in society should, however, now move onto a more positive footing by acknowledging that change has to start from somewhere. Black women cannot afford to wait for the right social, political and economic constraints to disappear before they feel empowered to make their own valuable contributions to society. According to Morley (1993), women felt that challenging the barriers head-on was a waste of time and instead concentrated upon using the university as a site for empowerment and liberation outside the traditional centres of power because they were perceived to be boring, petty, amateurish, patriarchal, crisis-driven and essentially disabling. For black women, coping strategies have always been a fundamental feature of their lives and the literature that refers to how black women have survived centuries of struggle (Clark-Hine, 1985), may provide useful insights into how they persevere in Higher Education.

The University Curricula

When looking at both the structure and the content of the academic curriculum, it becomes apparent that there has been little awareness of the fact that existing bodies of knowledge and whole disciplines have not developed neutrally. In fact, they often reflect a western, white, male perspective (Kelly, 1985; Van Djik, 1992; Sargant, 1993). Individuals or groups who shift away from traditionally accepted academic disciplines and dare to question the *status quo* are essentially ostracized. For example, a colleague once recalled an episode as an under-graduate at a well-known university;

> While in a lecture on American slavery, I had to sit there amongst a white audience and listen to a white male lecturer use negative stereotypes to describe the slaves. When I approached him, he claimed he was using 'authentic' language as part of an attempt to be realistic. He failed to appreciate my feelings and I made a formal complaint. Needless to say this was a huge step and I ended up getting the worst deal as I was treated as a trouble-maker with an immense chip on her shoulder . . .

This failure to reassess the content of disciplines in line with the changing staff and student populations is indicative of the conservative nature of universities. Williams *et al.* (1989), found that many academics were convinced that universities were fundamentally objective and unbiased. These individuals still saw themselves as liberal and, therefore, found it difficult to conceive that there were indirect or institutional forms of discrimination. Within the university curricula, traditional divisions of status and gender emerge. The make-up of staff and students in the natural sciences have tended to be white and male, consequently, black women who enter this arena feel that they have to justify their presence. As one participant put it, 'I am one of those rare oddities, I am black, a woman and a scientist and I have to constantly prove that I am worthy of the title "scientist". In fact, I have to be triply better than my white male and female colleagues.' This situation is slightly better in the Social Sciences, at least they have attempted to acknowledge the position of women and ethnic minorities. However, only a tiny proportion have recognized the distinctive experiences of black women in society. Women's Studies and Ethnic Studies still tend to treat black women as unusual oddities to be tolerated or added on, although some courses are making serious attempts at foregrounding the experiences of black women.

Nevertheless, Women's Studies and Ethnic Studies have been successful in at least challenging the status quo by questioning the belief that knowledge is neutral and objective. However, as new disciplines, both have suffered serious setbacks in terms of recognition and status and as a result tend to be marginalized. One workshop participant remarked, 'I have purposely avoided doing work on ethnicity and gender for fear of becoming ghettoized, yet I longed to work in this area and felt I had something positive to contribute.' Not supporting capable black female academics to fully utilize their skills is a damning indictment on the current state of the United Kingdom Higher Education system.

Equal opportunities

In the United Kingdom, the legislative framework covering equal opportunities includes The Disabled Persons (Employment) Acts 1944, 1958; The Equal Pay Act 1970; The Sex Discrimination Act 1975; The Race Relations Act 1976; The Equal Value Amendment 1984, Disabled Persons Act 1986 and the Further and Higher Education Act 1992. Nearly all the legislation concentrates on measures to ensure there is not direct or indirect discrimination in employment matters. But there is legislation which goes beyond employment matters.

> The Sex Discrimination Act and Race Relations Act make it unlawful for an educational establishment to discriminate directly or indiretly in a number of respects: . . . in the way in which it affords access to the benefits, facilties and services of the institution . . . [which essentially means] . . . ensuring everyone is treated the same regardless of disability, sex, race or socio-economic background . . . a recognition that members of certain groups have to face particular barriers when they try to gain access to Higher Education and that it is necessary to take positive steps to ensure they will be in a position to gain equal access to the point of selection . . . genuine equality of opportunity requires

institutions to take responsibility for what happens to such people when they have succeeded in gaining access.

(Anderson, 1988: 19–20)

Unfortunately, although equal opportunity policies have become commonplace in higher education, resources have not been made available to change practices to any great extent. The answer is not only about having more black women in higher education, it is also about overhauling the processes of institutional discrimination that remain a crucial feature of Higher Education. To paraphrase the AUT (1987) statement

to point out that there are aspects of the university system that result in inequality of opportunity and racial [and sexual] prejudice is not to accuse universities of direct or intentional discrimination: to do so would be to misunderstand the nature of racism [and sexism] and the way it manifests itself in education. [Rather, the] . . . 'colour-blind' [and 'gender-blind'] approach, perpetuate[s] inequality and prejudice . . . institutional racism [and sexism] must [therefore] be judged by its consequences, not by people's intentions.

(AUT, 1987: 1)

Equal opportunities issues are rarely on universities' agenda in any meaningful way and in fact, the recent drives towards quality and efficiency are actually making the situation worse. As Morley claims 'notions of quality are being used to reinforce institutionalised inequality and discrimination . . .' (1993: 12). The language of progress then, is being used to further curb ebony women's contributions to higher education.

The time must now be ripe for change, and as Jewson *et al.* state

Now that old polytechnics have disappeared and the newly created universities are seeking to find their identities, it is of vital importance to preserve and enhance the best practices with respect to equal opportunities. Moroever, reorganisation and redesignation represents an opportunity to review and enhance policies in the Higher Education sector as a whole

(1993:5)

By undertaking 'equality proofing', that is the analysis of all processes, procedures and services to ensure they do not work to the detriment, intentionally or unintentionally, of particular groups of people (Bhatti-Sinclair, Henry and Rafferty 1992), universities will be well on their way to 'comply[ing] not only with the letter, but also the spirit of the law' (CVCP, 1991). It has become far too easy for universities and other organizations to jump on the equal opportunities bandwagon without understanding its emancipatory nature and the need for on-going commitment. Until this is acknowleged, more realistic statements from universities which emphasize that they are 'working hard or striving to become an equal opportunities employer' would be more genuine.

The Way Forward?

The recent push towards a mass higher education system is long overdue and, in general terms, it is welcomed from an equal opportunity perspective. However, there are genuine concerns as procedures have not been revised and resources have not been delivered. In addition, the fact that equal opportunities legislation has failed to stem the tide of discrimination both inside and outside the ivory tower should not come as a complete surprise as the legislation is weak and there is a lack of political will to improve the situation. Furthermore, it should be acknowledged that legislation is only part of the solution, attitudes and values need to change, but after the long period of patriarchy, colonialism and capitalism in the United Kingdom, the prospects look bleak. Black women's experiences of staff and students and even within subject-specific areas have consistently been silenced even though they make valuable contributions to society. Future plans must take into account a commitment to a rigorous and ongoing equal opportunities programme linked to at least four key areas of university life: (i) recruitment and selection (ii) choice of subject and curriculum development (iii) career development and (iv) support and welfare services. For ebony women in Higher Education, this type of programme would involve addressing their diversity, strengths and weaknesses. To date, these needs have not been met and as a result, black women feel a tremendous sense of alienation and disenchantment with higher education.

Conclusion

This chapter has described the relationship between the ivory towers and ebony women. It is evident that universities are still perceived by black women to be ivory towers as the structures and culture fail to acknowledge or value their contributions to society. As a colleague stated, 'I do not consider myself to be more intelligent than other black women for getting and staying in University, I just happened to be lucky enough to be in the right place at the right time. What is disappointing is that despite the positive contributions of black women to Higher Education, there are still too few of us working in academia.' Universities need to critically examine their procedures and practices. This could be done in part by reviewing their equal opportunities programme. In order to deconstruct the image of Universities as ivory towers, there also needs to be a fundamental change in attitudes and a recognition that black women's experiences in higher education are not only distinctive but also dependent on a number of interrelated factors. It is essential that future research attempts to document these experiences, quantitatively and qualitatively, through perspectives that encourage the analysis of the diverse and interactive nature of black women's experiences within academia.

Notes

My sincere thanks to all the workshop participants for their contributions: Veronica Cairns; Jan Sethi; Lin King; Parneet Scinota; Beverley Burke; Shabana Hamid; Keith Wright; Deb Barnes; Helen Peters; Louise Allen; Paula Asgill; Fiona Dennis; Keiko Ishimaru; Rahni Binjie; Rebecca Priestley-Leach; Dawn Whittle; Yvonne Lornea; Melody Mtezuka; Sue Ottway.

1 This chapter represents an amalgamation of a formal paper with contributions from participants of an interactive workshop given at the Women in Higher Education Network (WHEN) Conference at the University of Central Lancashire in November 1993.

References

ANDERSON, B. (1988) 'Action for access: Widening opportunities in higher education', *National Advisory Body for Public Sector Higher Education Report*, pp. 19–20.

APTHEKER, B. (1982) 'Strong is what we made each other: Unlearning racism within women's studies', *Women's Studies Quarterly*, **9**(4), 13–16.

ASSOCIATION OF UNIVERSITY TEACHERS (AUT) (1987) 'Ensuring equal opportunities for university staff and students from ethnic minorities', June.

ASSOCIATION OF UNIVERSITY TEACHERS (AUT) (1993) Update Issue No. 8, 7 June.

BHATTI-SINCLAIR, K., HENRY, M. and RAFFERTY, J. (1992) 'Report back from the Equal Opportunity Workshop', unpublished paper, Oxford: Computers in Teaching Initiative Support Service (CTISS).

BOURNE, J. (1983) 'Towards an anti-racist feminism', in *Race and Class*, Summer, 25.1.

BRYAN, B., DADZIE, S. and SCAFE, S. (1985) *The Heart of the Race: Black Women's Lives in Britain*, London: Virago.

CARBY, H. (1982) 'White women listen! Black feminism and the boundaries of sisterhood', in *The Empire Strikes Back: Race and Racism in 70s Britain*, London: Hutchinson.

CHARLES, H. (1990) *Womanism: Recognising 'Difference': One Direction for the Black Woman Activist*, Occasional Paper No 21: University of Manchester.

CHRISTIAN, B. (1985) *Black Feminist Criticism: Perspectives on Black Women Writers*, New York: Pergamon Press.

COCKBURN, C. (1991) *In the Way of Women: Men's Resistance to Sex Equality Within Organisations*, London: MacMillan.

COMMISSION FOR RACIAL EQUALITY (CRE) (1981/1991) Economic and Social Research Council (ESRC) Local Census Database.

COMMITTEE OF VICE-CHANCELLORS AND PRINCIPALS (CVCP) (1991) 'Equal opportunities in employment in universities, Feb, London: Committee of Vice-Chancellors and Principals (CVCP).

HILL-COLLINS, P. (1990) *Black Feminist Thought: Knowledge, Consciousness and the Politics of Empowerment*, London: Unwin/Hyman.

hooks, b. (1981) *Ain't I A Woman: Black Women and Feminism*, Boston, MA: South End Press.

hooks, b. (1989) *Talking back: Thinking Feminist: Thinking Black*, Boston, MA: South End Press.

JEWSON, N. and MASON, D. (1986a) 'The theory and practice of equal opportunities: Liberal and radical approaches', in *Sociological Review*, 34(2), pp. 307–34.

JEWSON, N. and MASON, D. (1986b) 'Modes of discrimination in the recruitment process: Formalisation, fairness and efficiency', *Sociology*, 20(1), pp. 43–63.

JEWSON, N., MASON, D., BOWEN, R., MULVANEY, K. and PARMAR, S. (1991) 'Universities and ethnic minorities: The public face', in *New Community*, 17(2), pp. 183–99.

JEWSON, N., MASON, D., BROADBENT, J., JENKINS, S. and THANDI, H. (1993) 'Polytechnics and ethnic minorities: The public face', University of Leicester Discussion Papers in Sociology No. S93/4, July.

KELLY, A. (1985) 'The construction of masculine science', *British Journal of Sociology of Education*, 6, pp.133–54.

LORDE, A. (1984) *Sister Outsider*, Trumansburg, NY: Crossing Press.

LYKES, D. (1983) 'Discrimination and black women', *Journal of Social Issues*, 39(3), 79–99.

MAC AN GHAILL, M. (1988) *Young, Gifted and Black*, Milton Keynes: Open University Press.

MIRZA, H. (1992) 'Superwoman shot down', *The Guardian*, 27 May.

MIRZA, H. (1993) *Young, Female and Black*, London: Routledge.

MODOOD, T. (1993) 'Subtle shades of distinction' *THES*, July 16, Synthesis: pp. iv.

MORLEY, L. (1993) 'Glass ceiling or iron cage: Women in UK academia', paper presented at the 1993 Women's Studies Network Conference, Northampton: Nene College.

PARMAR, P. (1989) 'Other kinds of dreams', in *Feminist Review*, Spring, 31, pp.55–65.

SARGANT, N. (1993) 'Learning for a purpose' — Department of the Environment (DoE) and University of East London Report.

SMITH, A. and STEWART, A. (1983) 'Approaches to studying racism and sexism in black women's lives', *Journal of Social Issues*, 39(3), pp.1–15.

SPELMAN, E. (1988) *Inessential Woman: Problems of Exclusion in Feminist Thought*, London: The Women's Press.

TAYLOR, P. (1992) 'Ethnic group for university entry', Project Report for CVCP Working Group on Ethnic Data, The Centre for Research in Ethnic Relations, University of Warwick.

VAN DIJK, T. A. (1992) 'Discourses and denial of racism', in *Discourse and Society*, 3(1), January, 87–118.

WESTON, C. (1993) 'Women, discrimination and work', October, **195**, Association of University Teachers (AUT) Bulletin.

WILLIAMS, J., COOKING, J. and DAVIES, L. (1989) *Words or Deeds? A Review of Equal Opportunities Policies in Higher Education*, London Commission for Racial Equality (CRE).

WILSON, A. (1978) *Finding a Voice: Asian Women in Britain*, London: Virago.

Additional Sources

ASSOCIATION OF UNIVERSITY TEACHERS (AUT) (1993) *Update*, No. 8, 7 June.

ASSOCIATION OF UNIVERSITY TEACHERS (AUT) (1987) 'Ensuring equal opportunities for university staff and students from ethnic minorities, June.

COMMISSION FOR RACIAL EQUALITY (CRE) (1981/1991) Economic and Social Research Council (ESRC), Local Census Database.

COMMITTEE OF VICE-CHANCELLORS AND PRINCIPALS (CVCP) (1991) 'Equal opportunities in employment in universities', February, London.

UNIVERSITIES CENTRAL CLEARING AND ADMISSIONS (UCCA) (1991–2) Statistical supplement to 13th Report.

Chapter 4

Fighting Back or Biting Back? Lesbians in Higher Education[1]

Chris Corin

This chapter is written largely from my personal perspective as a lesbian academic who has worked in England and Scotland in university-level politics departments and within Women's Studies. The linkages I make to debates in this area are principally from a social science perspective. Concentration is on lesbians as teachers and researchers in higher education. While my strength is in political analysis I recognize that this perspective is just one dimension. I have tried to avoid making this an exclusive discussion in terms of social science jargon. Women working in law, medicine or maths, engineering and elsewhere in higher education are very much involved in debates about sexuality and gender. Social science and arts departments tend to provide more forums for discussion than do science, law or medical departments where the numbers of women are generally fewer and men more often set the agendas. Issues within science concerning debates on reproductive technology and problems of law regarding equal opportunities are being closely argued by feminists. Yet the overall context of how to break down the barriers within the *status quo* is not common to all women working for change. Lesbians are generally very isolated within a higher educational context which is deeply anti-lesbian. Within an academic ethos which apparently is concerned with the questioning of knowledge and with assessing popular opinion, lesbian oppression does not appear to be questioned. The organizational culture of higher educational institutions is also deeply embedded with prejudice against lesbians.

At the outset it is good to stress that lesbians do not form a homogenous group. Various issues including class, different ability, race, ethnicity and political alignments cause differences among lesbians. Linkages are apparent between the oppression lesbians face within society and in higher education. What is different about lesbian oppression in higher education? Three aspects stand out in this context. In the first place, aspects of organizational culture present within higher educational settings include the strong normalizing aspect of public and social spaces in terms of discussion of heterosexual lifestyles and interests. It is often here that issues of 'coming out' or not, and acceptance or non-acceptance of lesbian lives become apparent and problematic. Second, the ethos of higher education *per se*, given the traditional elitist ethos, is that higher education is there to challenge received wisdom and to formulate discussion on popular opinion. The question here is why, within higher education generally and within women's studies in particular, issues concerning lesbians and lesbianism are not being considered and discussed more widely.[2] This challenging of opinion and discussion of popular views is not happening, so there is an apparent failure. A third aspect of concern within higher education is the pedagogical aspect. What are the implications of being a woman, feminist and lesbian in higher education? How can lesbian oppression be talked about and theorized? Do such discussions raise particular problems for lesbian teachers and lesbian students? What expectations are aroused when lesbians are 'out' within their institutions?

Institutional Heterosexism and Anti-lesbianism

Almost a quarter of a century ago Abbot and Love (1972) described a situation in the USA in which:

> Being gay is *ipso facto* a challenge of sex-control/sex-denial . . . Being naively, openly, gay is punished with ridicule, public condemnation and loss of job . . . Authorities usually suggest that the only way out of their pathetic state is personal cures.
>
> (Abbot and Love, 1972: 186)

How far have things really changed in this regard in the UK in the last 25 years? In some contexts it can be said that great strides have been made, yet in other ways instances of heterosexism and lesbian oppression are certainly alive and growing. As Ruth Magnani says in *Women Like Us*:

> I believe that on the surface things have changed, quite a lot. There's a lot going on in the media about us, and people discuss it more. But it's very different when it's near home. On your doorstep! I still think parents are very shattered if they find out their children are gay or lesbian.
>
> (Magnani, 1992: 89)

This sums up the anti-lesbianism apparent within society in terms of 'not wanting our daughters to become one'. The political climate in the UK in late 1994 is one which includes continuing attacks against single mothers and pretend families and the failure to gain equality for young gay men. Coupled with the lack of flexible and open sexual education at schools, real social distress is being caused by the after-effects of the introduction of Section 28. Lesbian mothers are not considered real mothers. Our families of close friends and loves are not viewed as real families.

What is different about this situation within higher education? Is the Academy more heterosexist or oppressive or is it simply indicative of a wider atmosphere? Given the earlier point regarding higher education as a site for promoting discussion and questioning knowledge, the issue of institutionalized heterosexism raises several contradictions. Heterosexism can be viewed as the unquestioning and unambiguous presumption of heterosexuality as the 'normal', 'natural' way of being. Such a universalizing presumption can silence lesbians before we even begin to speak — especially when all discussion in staff rooms and elsewhere centres on this presumption. Anti-lesbianism on the other hand can be defined as discrimination against lesbians through prejudice, fear, bigotry or something other. The perceived taboo on lesbianism within societies underpins much lesbian oppression. As Adrienne Rich shows:

> Lesbian existence comprises both the breaking of taboo and the rejection of a compulsory way of life. It is also a direct or indirect attack on male right of access to women . . . an act of resistance.
>
> (Rich, 1981: 21)

As such lesbian existence is a basic attack on the presumption of heterosexuality. Rich uses Kathleen Gough's eight characteristics of male power as a framework for analysis (Gough, 1989). This schema forms a 'pervasive cluster of forces, ranging from physical brutality to control of consciousness, which suggests that an enormous potential counterforce is having to be restrained'. (Rich, 1981: 12). Such lesbian attacks on institutionalized heterosexuality are often resisted by active prejudice. In this context the ethos within higher education can be viewed as not just heterosexist but rampantly anti-lesbian.

Out-in/visibility in Higher Education

As all lesbians know, 'coming out' is a series of processes. Some lesbians find the hardest step is coming out to oneself, yet after that it does not get easier as barriers constantly have to be faced. For many of us who choose to come out at work there are many different situations involved in the processes of disclosure/ non-disclosure of lesbianism. Not being able to talk about our lives openly within a supportive framework can be a crushing experience. As Clare Sullivan points out:

> As I sit round the table of young, 'lefty' and unmarried teachers excluded from the social chit-chat of the summer holiday, no one knows that I am on the verge of ending a long-term relationship; a month later, off work with a supposed virus no one knows that I am in fact falling apart at the seams; . . . People remember not to mention the name of divorcees, 'other halves', ex-boyfriends, etc. For me that doesn't happen.
>
> (Sullivan, 1993: 96)

Many women have written of precisely this trap that we are caught in concerning the dangers of institutionalized anti-lesbianism and how this affects our possibilities of interacting with other staff members. In her work 'Dyke in academe (II)' Paula Bennett writes of those:

> Caught between silence on one side and fear on the other, the typical closeted gay academic spends his or her professional life in a state of constant duplicity, internally and externally divided by a lie that is not spoken, by an act of deception that is never acted out . . . Sometimes the ability to communicate on both sides becomes warped beyond recognition. Then the failure to speak becomes in itself another form of oppression.
>
> (Bennett, 1982: 5)

I give these examples because I believe that heterosexual colleagues, even the most ardent feminists, totally underestimate the oppression of compulsory heterosexuality. Where heterosexism and anti-lesbianism coalesce with racism, black lesbians' lives become even more complex in terms of the choices to be made. In an excellent recent work *Challenging Lesbian and Gay Inequalities in Education*, Akanke speaks of choosing not to come out:

> Being 'closeted' is not a choice I wish to make. Nevertheless because of the pervasiveness of racism it is one that I choose to make. Being black, however is not a choice. As a black woman my colour is my most obvious feature, not my sexual preferences. Within British society, black people's lives, sexuality and culture are regarded negatively. Our

61

colour often dictates our level of income, housing and educational attainment.

(Akanke, 1994: 102)

As black lesbians raising black children in a 'white, racist, sexist, homophobic society' Akanke and her partner Terri recognize that they are 'fighting a system that threatens to devour "our" children' (ibid: 102). Akanke relates that, being out holds no attraction as it is another potential weapon to be used against their children. The complexities for many lesbians of various layers of loyalty, to oneself, children, family (pretend or otherwise) coupled with self-preservation, make very difficult choices necessary. One woman scientist recalls a conversation regarding such choices:

> I remember a conversation with a feminist scientist in the US, in which I commented that it was a pity in some ways that she did not stay in physics; after all, I stressed, we haven't exactly got many feminists working in physics . . . After a long pause she looked at me levelly, and said, 'listen, I was doing physics at Harvard, I'm black and a lesbian: something had to go.'

(Birke, 1994: 186)

Survival has to be a priority for all women within higher education and certainly for lesbians choices are often stark.

The intersections of gender/sexism, race/racism, class/class oppression and disability/ablism with compulsory heterosexuality and institutionalized lesbian oppression can certainly cause some 'mind-blowing' complexities and layers of oppression and reaction. As lesbians, whether we are able to be out at work (in whatever form) or whether we are prevented from sharing our existence with colleagues, each of us develops various coping mechanisms for everyday life in our institutions.

In her work on lesbians in organizations, Marny Hall writes of the development of coping strategies. Although she is discussing corporate structures, there are parallel conditions and situations within many higher educational institutions. In terms of disclosure and promotions, 'Though no respondent thought her homosexuality had any impact on work performance, most felt their future options limited by their lesbianism' (Hall, 1989: 134). Some claimed not to be ambitious, others were planning to work outside of organizations in the future. Some of the coping strategies mentioned by Hall could have signficance for lesbians.

The neuterized/neutralized strategy is concerned with minimizing gender. 'Femaleness is the discredited and visible side of one's lesbianism' (Hall, 1989: 135) so that computer-related work was popular in terms of neutralizing sexuality and sexual preference. Non-disclosure strategies highlight the ways in which lesbians can pay intense observation to details, such as wedding rings, use of personal pronouns, which are less important to heterosexuals. For lesbian interviewees who chose non-disclosure many used strategies to avoid feeling that they were betraying themselves and their communities. Such strategies included denial and dissociation, which can include not telling but not necessarily denying, or differentiating between 'dykey women' and those 'who handled their gayness discreetly' (Hall, 1989: 136–7). Avoidance strategies meant avoiding personal situations and social interactions with co-workers. Some respondents used distraction such as being openly feminist or liberal to distract from being identified as lesbian. Finally, Hall notes token disclosure such as relating outings with a room-mate (who was also a lover) and partial disclosure such as discussing their lesbianism only with those who could be deemed 'safe' and would keep this knowledge to themselves.

The implications of lesbians using various strategies to move through the conflicting cultural and subcultural imperatives certainly show that:

> the old reductionist notion of 'coming out' is not an act, but rather a never-ending and labyrinthine process of decision and indecision, of nuanced and calculated presentations as well as impulsive and inadvertent revelations — a process, in short, as shifting as the contexts in which it occurs.
>
> (Hall, 1989: 137)

In this context, it is important to consider whether or not heterosexual colleagues are aware of the complexity of lesbian existence. Additionally, when we consider coalitions, it will become important to find out in which ways heterosexual women colleagues wish to work together to resist the heterosexist and anti-lesbian conditions which give rise to the need for lesbians to indulge in such complex strategies.

One obvious aspect of the institutionalized heterosexism that needs to be challenged within higher educational institutions is the strong normalizing aspect of social and/or public places. It is generally in the coffee room or at social events that lesbians feel particularly vulnerable to anti-lesbianism, be this targetted or accidental. This normalizing pressure can affect how lesbians live their lives. In her work on Anti-monogamy Becky Rosa points out the pressures on lesbians to become or stay monogamous partly as this fits in with wider presumptions and pressures of a heterosexual world:

> As lesbians individually and collectively we have to invent our own relationships — we are not shown how these should be as we grow

up . . . lesbians face extra pressure to be monogamous because of anti-lesbianism. Many lesbians stay in monogamous relationships for the support they provide from an anti-lesbian world . . . there is also pressure on lesbians to be as 'normal' as possible. Many lesbians and [probably more] gay men take the line that we are just like hetero-sexuals except for the sex of our lovers.

(Rosa, 1994: 114–5)

This says a good deal about how lesbians are viewed. It has certainly been my experience that when colleagues at work can see that I have a permanent friend/girlfriend/lover/partner or whatever label is attached to two people involved in a sensual, emotional and sexual relationship, they appear more relaxed about my lesbianism.[3] It seems that having a partner makes me and my lesbianism more 'knowable' within a heterosexual context. When no such partner is apparent I seem to become something of a dangerous or suspicious element. If, in between discussions of family holidays or heterosexual dinner-parties I chance to mention something like a lesbian disco or a Pride March, this is often taken as somehow threatening or embarrassing and definitely not very sociable! Yet it is being able to discuss such aspects or our lives that allow us to 'be ourselves'. There is much joy in being lesbian. Not being able to share this is sad. Lesbian lives are clearly too counter-cultural for some of our heterosexual colleagues.

In terms of institutional prejudices there are many examples of lesbian invisibility and oppression. Who counts as a partner to be notified in emergencies, to benefit at our death? How many UK universities and colleges have sexual orientation included in their equal opportunities policies? What does the term sexual harassment mean for lesbians? Can we include blatant heterosexist behaviour as harassment of lesbians? In their work, *The Sexuality of Organization*, Hearn *et al.*, point out that most organizations are dominated by heterosexual men:

Such heterosexual hegemony tends to construct lesbians and gay men as isolated exceptions, so that they and their sexuality come to be seen, by many heterosexuals at least, as private and individual, even as personal 'problems'.

(Hearn, *et al.*, 1989: 23)

Such institutional prejudices are deeply embedded within our higher educational institutions. It will take a good deal of work both in terms of changing people's minds and various long marches through the committees to change some of these prejudices and the damaging practices that they entail.

Thinking about Changing our Ideas in Practice?

Change can be associated with social movements, political activities and discourses, and ideas. What are we concerned with in higher education? Many feminists are concerned with all aspects of change. Most of us who are involved in teaching see one of our principal roles as educators in terms of re-viewing intellectual discourses and challenging certain opinions. We also consider and assess popular views on various issues and debates. The question here concerns why these debates and challenges appear not to be happening with regard to institutionalized heterosexism and anti-lesbianism.

The wider political context in the UK around discussion of Section 28 reinforced arguments about the social construction of sexuality by highlighting particular situations such as education, the media, leisure activities, which could be instrumental in reproducing sexual identities. With education in its broadest context viewed as a site of promotion of homosexuality it is important for feminists to consider something of the underlying assumptions of this debate. This is especially the case in terms of what this means for teaching about lesbianism and the possibly changing circumstances of lesbians being 'out' in their institutions.

Lesbian academics generally recognize the importance of challenging anti-lesbian ideas in all areas of study within higher education. As someone involved in teaching politics, my work raises issues concerning the political significance of my intervention and the role higher education can play in wider political change. Questions about the ways in which politics are discussed within higher education centre on whether or not our discussions and assessments become part of wider change processes. How we define politics is vitally important with regard to what and how we study. Functionalist definitions emphasize external male-dominated activities, whereas feminist analyses look at political relations. For feminists, studies in the politics of housework are viewed as being core issues equal with electoral studies. In my European politics course I include lesbian and gay rights, and I consider lesbian feminism in the Feminist Thought course. It is impossible to know how I would teach these if I were heterosexual but it is an area that would be worthwhile to consider with colleagues.

Most feminists in higher education are familiar with such debates through-out various areas of study or disciplines. Within Women's Studies these disciplinary boundaries are being broken down. A brief look at strategies for feminist intervention within Women's Studies highlights at least four such strategies: being 'token' women in male schools and departments, showing that we exist; caucusing within the institution through intellectual networks outside our own departments; establishing interdisciplinary research and discussion seminars and developing Women's Studies teaching programmes (Aaron and

Walby, 1991). Certainly within Arts and Social Sciences faculties Women's Studies is a rapidly growing area and is taught at over 50 institutions in the UK.[4] In their work *Making Connections* Kennedy *et al.*, note that:

> Through the development of consciousness and activism, women have turned subordination into knowledge, weakness into strength, vulnerability into power. As pedagogic and scholarly practice, Women's Studies can activate new ways of being in the Academy, new ways of knowing, new ways of organizing.
>
> (Kennedy, 1993: xiv)

Given the possibilities within Women's Studies for challenging old ways of being why have many heterosexist and anti-lesbian notions remained unchallenged? Certainly the institutional emphasis on creating demarcations and working within fixed categories is a major barrier, but given that Women's Studies is breaking through these, why are lesbian issues and analyses still marginalized within Women's Studies.

Out on our Own?

Is there a reason for lesbians to become more visible in higher education? What purpose is this to serve? What are the consequences of being an 'out' lesbian academic? These are but a few of the questions that need to be considered when thinking about the complexities of lesbian visibility within higher education. One consequence of active prejudice within higher education can be precisely that the 'perceived' problems are considered in such as way that they become 'other' and outside general academic discourse. This highlights one barrier to be overcome in potential alliances amongst feminists in terms of Lesbian Studies and its acceptance within Women's Studies. Examining the political nature of lesbian studies both in further research and in teaching about sexuality is one choice open to us in higher education. Considering lesbian academics carrying out research on homosexuality Celia Kitzinger notes that:

> While accusations of collusion with the forces of oppression may succeed in eliciting a guilty sense of our own privileged position as academics, many of us are aware of how much more privileged that position could be had we not chosen lesbianism as our research topic, or had we not made our lesbianism obvious to our 'superiors' in the academic hierarchy.
>
> (Kitzinger, 1987: 180)

Some time ago two lesbian colleagues and I wrote about lesbians working in education in Scotland (Marchbank, *et al.*, 1993). On re-reading this it still seems crazy that my Head of Department actually put in writing to me that my 'political commitment' to feminism might mean that I would not be able to teach 'a course in feminist theory in a completely neutral manner, such as those on Facism [!] and Liberalism'. He suggested that if this were the case then perhaps I should 'disqualify' myself! To call this double-speak would be an understatement. My political commitment to feminism could just as easily read 'dangerous lesbian'. The language used of 'neutrality' — 'objective' social scientists or as in war-time? 'Disqualify' sounds as if someone [the lesbian] has cheated in terms of the rules of the academic game. There seemed to be a coalescence here between a deep personal prejudice on the part of this particular professor and the anti-lesbian culture within the institution. This not only enabled such a letter to be sent but gave it a force of impact that meant my changing aspects of the particular course, i.e. my teaching practice. Such incidents indicate that often when lesbians are visible within the Academy they are perceived as only being able to represent a small set of minority interests — lesbian interests. Additionally, 'out' lesbians are viewed as people who will proselytize. Perhaps there is a fear of conversion in such prejudices.

Certainly group discussion with students on sexuality and other topics within Women's Studies allow for reflection on experience and theorizing from this. In her case study of a Women's Studies module provided within Community and Youth Work Training, Louise Morley emphasizes: 'how feminist theory can inform liberatory pedagogical practices and group process' (Morley, 1993: 118). Women's Studies is a context in which students learn about experiences of oppression and in which they can be empowered to 'work towards change whilst simultaneously understanding and resisting the limitations, structures and processes of disempowerment' (ibid: 120). Care needs to be taken from the point of view of group dynamics. When studying lesbian feminism I know from discussion that some of my students have felt silenced by their heterosexuality and the knowledge of my lesbianism — seeing me as expert and themselves as unknowing. It is useful to be able to discuss this with students, but embarrassment and shyness often preclude such possibilities. Sensitivity to group dynamics is also essential to avoid misunderstandings and mistrust.

The need for recognizing a collectivity amongst women before emphasizing difference is highlighted by Morley in her example of a session on heterosexism early on in a group:

When the session took place, tension levels soon rose as some women related to the subject as a 'special need', i.e. what information did they need to have about lesbians and gays in order to provide a non-discriminatory professional service. They were unable to see how heterosexuality as an institution and as ideology upholds female oppression. This refusal to examine their own implication in the information blocked the development of dialogue and resulted in lesbians in the group feeling objectified and pathologized by heterosexual women.

(Morley, 1993: 126)

In such situations it is an important part of the process to let people express a wide range of their feelings — not just anger but vulnerability too. This example highlights the strength of Women's Studies teaching to empower women but also the potential dangers of such explorations within student groups. Much careful thought needs to go into such teaching and Morley's work is certainly a good example.

Just as exploring certain issues can be threatening for students and heterosexual women colleagues, we again realize the implied 'threat' of lesbianism, often as a political challenge. In her work Celia Kitzinger points out the dangers of liberal gay affirmative work which tends to depoliticize lesbian lives (Kitzinger, 1987: 178). Again, the emphasis is on lesbianism as a political challenge. In this context Sheila Jeffreys reiterates the need for recognizing heterosexuality as a political institution. If, as was noted earlier regarding lesbians who want to be viewed as similar to heterosexuals, research on heterosexuality and homosexuality views each as equally valid, anti-lesbianism could be seen as 'just' an irrational prejudice. One step on could see homosexuals as: 'a harmless minority who should be tolerated and indeed assimilated into main stream heterosexual culture' (Jeffreys, 1990: 220). It is in such arguments that the understandings of lesbian feminists and heterosexual feminists need to be discussed, clarified and further developed. Until we are clear about the nature and context of oppression against lesbians, forming coalitions and alignments is problematic.

Lesbian/feminist Alliances and Resistance

What sorts of alliances can we make amongst ourselves as lesbians, lesbian feminists, feminists in Higher Education generally and/or lesbian/feminists involved in Women's Studies in particular? As feminists our way of making politics differs markedly if we are lesbian. Above all the difference lies in the *politicized* nature of our lesbian identities. We do see things, situations, oppressions, differently because of this. Our experiences of oppression within higher education often makes us want to 'get out':

> The one thing we are all aware of battling against is being 'sucked into the system' in terms of relaxing our vigilance to question, attack and discredit outmoded and prejudicial notions. To stay in academia, be it formal or community, for the money and the holidays, would not be a soft option for any of us. It would at best be a sign of defeat, but more importantly it would be a living hell.
>
> (Marchbank, Corrin, Brodie 1993: 165)

Having to retaliate in exchanges with prejudiced colleagues in an anti-lesbian environment makes life hard. Few lesbians are in secure positions from which to resist such attacks.

Lesbians in higher education face varying levels of oppression and have differing opportunities for change. Sometimes we can fight back in various creative ways. Sometimes we have to bite back our responses out of fear, for ourselves and/or others or out of economic necessity, not to lose our jobs, homes or other important elements in our lives. Serious questions are raised about remaining within such blatantly repressive institutional settings. Knowing that I enjoy teaching makes me recognize my own needs regarding student feedback. Yet, teaching in higher education generally is being squeezed into more limited time frames with more students per group and fewer resources. Above all, having to deal with day-to-day prejudice is tiring and oppressive. It would be wonderful to have supportive networks of lesbians and feminists within our institutions with whom we could share our possibly shocking and/or hilarious, accounts. Some such networks are being set up both within individual institutions and within wider groupings. Both the Women's Studies Network (UK) Association and the British Sociological Association now have lesbian sub-groups.

One aspect of sharing in such discussions would concern our own strength of identity. There is generally a strong identification apparent within lesbian groups to which I have belonged. This, for me, is generally less the case amongst women's groups, especially academic women's groups. Could this have something to do with the instability of heterosexual identities? Stacey argues that the introduction of Section 28 'can be read as a sign of the impact of [feminist and lesbian and gay] movements and indeed of the instability of the patriarchal discourses on sexuality' (Stacey, 1991: 297). It is important also to consider the instability of heterosexual feminist's identification with their sexuality.

In their work, *The Precariousness of Heterosexual Feminist Identities*, Kitzinger and Wilkinson point out that while lesbianism is a politicized identity there are no corresponding heterosexual feminist identities which are 'political *by virtue* of their heterosexuality' (in Kennedy, *et al.*, 1993: 33). For some heterosexual feminists 'the contradictions between political ideology and lived personal experience are acute and painful and involved constant compromise' (ibid: 33). What is important here for any alignments of lesbian feminists and heterosexual feminists is that theory and practice do not coalesce. 'Many women find their own feminist analyses of heterosexuality difficult to reconcile with their heterosexual life styles' (ibid: 20).

For these authors it is clear that the tenaciousness of lesbian identity contrasts with the precariousness of heterosexual identity. Perhaps because heterosexual women never had to confront otherness by facing fears and 'discovery' of one's identity (often hated) and then naming oneself. Heterosexual identity is assumed by default so heterosexual women have not made a commitment to heterosexuality which parallels lesbians' commitment to lesbianism.

> 'Default' identities like these, which constitute the 'normal, natural way to be' [white, able-bodied, male, etc.] are always less well theorized, less articulated, less self-conscious, than are oppositional or oppressed identities; lack of reflectiveness is the privilege of power.
>
> (Kitzinger and Wilkinson, 1993a: 32)

In this context Kitzinger and Wilkinson disagree with the idea of Rich's continuum because in trying to assimilate the term lesbian into a heterosexual-lesbian continuum these meanings are lost:

> 'Heterosexual' and 'lesbian' are *not* opposite ends of the same continuum. Because 'lesbian' is an intrinsically politicized identity, and heterosexuality is not, the two terms are not commensurate, do not belong in the same conceptual space. Lesbian feminists have available a whole set of explicitly political meanings (cf. Onlywomen Press, 1981).
>
> Kitzinger and Wilkinson, 1993a: 33)

Many issues are raised by the above recognition, not least that the status of compulsory heterosexuality as the unproblematized and apolitical norm oppresses lesbians in many ways. As the lesbians stated earlier, having to suppress themselves and their lives within the workplace has meant that their lives take on an unreal quality. When major changes happen in lesbians' personal lives they cannot be acknowledged. These issues, both in further theorizing and in resisting prejudice and bad practice, could certainly form a core around which lesbians and heterosexual feminists in Higher Education could coalesce.

When considering why women choose to enter coalitions with other women Bernice Johnson Reagon argues that there is no place any more where people can hide; there can be no space that is 'yours only' or just for people who want to be there. Black women have highlighted this within women's politics (Reagon, 1983). Reagon stresses that coalition work is hard — it is some of the most dangerous work we can do. There are dangers for lesbians/feminists in facing our challenges which cannot be minimized. For heterosexual feminists it is a dangerous enterprise to ask political questions of heterosexual relations and identification. For lesbians dangers abound in enabling ourselves to further politicize our identities. As Audre Lorde recognizes:

> To assess the damage is a dangerous act. I think of how even as a feminist lesbian, I have so wanted to ignore my own homophobia, my own hatred of myself for being queer. I have not wanted to admit that my deepest personal sense of myself has not quite 'caught up' with my 'woman-identified' politics. I have been afraid to criticize lesbian writers who choose to 'skip over' these issues in the name of feminism.
>
> (Lorde, 1982: 33)

Again the combined oppression of heterosexism and anti-lesbianism bite deep. If we as lesbians/feminists are to begin to overcome some of the worst aspects of lesbian oppression some forms of alliances will become important. But what forms and for what ends are crucial questions. When recently asked about the value of coalitions and alliances between different groups of women June Jordan responded:

> I would say about coalitions what I said about unity, which is what for? This issue should determine the social configuration of politics. I am not going to sit in a room with other people just to demonstrate black unity, we have got to have some reason for unity. Why should I coalesce with you and why do you want to coalesce with me, there has to be some reason why we need each other.
>
> (Pratibha, 1994: 263)

This illustrates a great deal in terms of recognizing that as lesbian feminists and heterosexual feminists in the world of academia we need to recognize our reasons for alignment. Being feminists involved in higher education is not enough. Recognition of the need to politicize the identity of heterosexuality is important. Lesbian feminists come to any group or project with politicized perspectives.

Nonetheless, whether we are 'out' or not we take our lesbianism into every area of our work, just as we take our personal politics, our personal histories, and every other aspect of ourselves. This does not prevent us from being rigorous and professional but perhaps we are more aware of our own standpoints, as feminists, as women and as lesbians, than are some of our colleagues.

(Marchbank 163)

We are not about to de-politicize ourselves. As Kitzinger and Wilkinson point out this would not be at all in our interests:

Categories of oppressed people are not well served by denying the existence of the categories to which they belong: at the very least, such denial refuses a name for the oppressed and militates against effective collective resistance.

(Kitzinger and Wilkinson, 1993b: 31)

One way in which feminists can work together in further theoretical work with practical teaching implications is within Women's Studies and Lesbian Studies. By its potential for interdisciplinarity Women's Studies can be open to all feminists in some way — conference attendance, group meetings, teaching, researching, learning, talking. Tamsin Wilton has emphasized the failure within Women's Studies to take account of lesbianism and lesbians:

The particular 'problem' of lesbianism is that recognition of lesbian possibility obliges non-lesbian women to recognize not only their own anti-lesbian feelings but also their own positioning as the sexual partners of men. Until non-lesbian feminists begin deconstructing the heterosexual imperative, and developing a radical heterosexual feminist politics, lesbianism will continue to face denial, ghettoization and rejection within Women's Studies, and this denial is costing feminism dear.

(Wilton, 1993: 171)

Here again we are returned to the question of 'why do we need each other?' We need each other if we wish to work together to resist the many oppressions we face as lesbians and feminists. We need each other if we are to be able to teach and research in ways that develop our understandings of ourselves as lesbian or as heterosexual. We need each other to develop our understanding of what prejudices such as anti-lesbianism mean in the context of developing knowledge, in all areas. We need each other if we want to continue to develop and disseminate feminist ideas and empower ourselves and students to recognize and resist prejudice and oppression. We need each other if we want to move beyond our partial knoweldge of each other and our misunderstandings. I have certainly learnt much in writing this chapter and, hopefully, it can become another useful building block in furthering our lesbian/feminist resistance.

Notes

I would like to thank Jenny Kitzinger, Louise Morley, Monika Reinfelder and Lorraine Stefani for very helpful comments on a draft of this paper.

1 This title centres on the opportunities and lack of them that lesbians have within higher education to challenge our oppression. Sometimes we can fight back against lesbian oppression but often we have to bite back our words, precisely because of the repercussions.

2 There has been and continues to be questioning of lesbian oppression and issues affecting lesbians by academics such as Jeffreys, Kitzinger, Wilkinson, Wilton, Rich and many others. The point here concerns the lack of questioning from feminists regarding issues such as heterosexuality as a political identity.

3 This has been my experience, particularly with heterosexual women, as I choose to have very little day-to-day social contact with heterosexual male colleagues.

4 For full details see Women's Studies Network (UK) Association Handbook of Women's Studies courses in UK, 1994.

References

AARON, J. and WALBY, S. (1991) *Out of the Margins: Women's Studies in the Nineties*, London: The Falmer Press.

ABBOT, S. and LOVE, B. (1972) *Sappho was a Right-On Woman: A Liberated View of Lesbianism*, New York: Stein and Day.

AKANKE, 'Black in the closet' in EPSTEIN, D. (Ed.) (1994) *Challenging Lesbian and Gay Inequalities in Education*, Buckingham: Open University Press.

BENNETT, P. (1982) 'Dyke in Academe (II)' in CRUICKSHANK, M., *Lesbian Studies: Present and Future*, New York: The Feminist Press, pp. 3–8.

BIRKE, L. (1994) 'Interventions in hostile territory', (conversation with Evelyn Hammonds, March 1992) in GRIFFIN, G. HESTER, M., RAI, S. and ROSENEIL, S., *Stirring It: Challenges for Feminism*, London: Taylor & Francis, pp. 185–93.

CORRIN, C. (1994) 'Women's politics in "Europe" in the 1990s' *Women's International Studies Forum* Special Issue 'Images from Women in a Changing Europe', Oxford: Pergamon, pp. 289–97.

GOUGH, K. (1975) 'The origin of the family' in RAPP, R. (Ed.) *Toward an Anthropology of Women*, New York: Monthly Review Press.

HALL, M. (1989) 'Private experiences in the public domain: Lesbians in organizations' in HEARN, J., SHEPPARD, L., TANCRED-SHERIFF, P. and BURRELL, G. (Eds) *The Sexuality of Organization*, London: Sage, pp. 125–38.

HEARN, J., SHEPPARD, D. L., TANCRED-SHERIFF, P. and BURRELL, G. (Eds) (1989) *The Sexuality of Organization*, London: Sage.

HOAGLAND, S. L. (introduction) (1988) *For Lesbians Only: A Separatist Anthology* London: Onlywomen Press.

JEFFREYS, S. (1990) *Anticlimax*, London: The Women's Press.

KHAYATT, M. D. (1992) *Lesbian Teachers: An Invisible Presence*, New York: State University of New York Press.

KITZINGER, C. (1987) *The Social Construction of Lesbianism*, London: Sage.

KITZINGER, C. and WILKINSON, S. (1993a) 'The precariousness of heterosexual feminist identities' in KENNEDY, M., LUBELSKA, C. and WALSH, V. (Eds) *Making Connections*, London: Taylor & Francis, pp.; 24–36.

KITZINGER, C. and WILKINSON, S. (Eds) (1993b) *Heterosexuality: A Feminism and Psychology Reader*, London: Sage.

MAGNANI, R. (1992) 'Ruth Magnani' in NEILD, S. and PEARSON, R., *Women Like Us*, London: Women's Press.

MORAGA, C. and ANZALDUA, G. (1981) *This Bridge Called My Back*, New York, Kitchen Table: Women of Colour Press.

MORLEY, L. (1993) 'Women's Studies as empowerment of "Non-traditional" learners in community and youth work training: A case study', in KENNEDY, M., LUBELSKA, C. and WALSH, V. (Eds) *Making Connections*, London: Taylor & Francis, pp. 118–29.

PRATIBHA, P. (1994) 'Other kinds of dreams' (including interview with June Jordan) in GITHENS, M., NORRIS, P. and LOVENDUSKI, J. (Eds) *Different Roles, Different Voices: Women and Politics in the United States and Europe*, New York: Harper Collins College Publishers, pp. 259–64.

REAGON, B. J. (1983) 'Coalition politics — Turning the century' in SMITH, B. (Ed.) *Home Girls — A Black Feminist Anthology*, New York: Kitchen Table Press, pp. 356–68.

RICH, A. (1981) *Compulsory Heterosexuality and Lesbian Existence*, London: Only-women Press.

ROSA, B. (1994) 'Anti-monogamy' in GRIFFIN, G., HESTER, M., RAI, S. and ROSENEIL, S. (Eds) *Stirring It: Challenges for Feminism*, London: Taylor & Francis.

SILVERA, M. (anthologized by) *Piece of My Heart: A Lesbian of Colour Anthology*, Toronto: Sister Vision: Black Women and Women of Colour Press.

STACEY, J. (1991) 'Promoting normality: Section 28 and the regulation of sexuality' in FRANKLIN, S., LURY, C. and STACEY, J. (Eds) *Off-Centre: Feminism and Cultural Studies*, London: Harper Collins Academic Press.

SULLIVAN, C. (1993) 'Oppression: The experiences of a lesbian teacher in an inner city comprehensive school in the United Kingdom' in *Gender and Education*, 5,(1), pp. 93–101.

Chapter 5

Women in Higher Education: 'What are we doing to ourselves?'[1]

Breda Gray

Introduction

Feminist academic literature over the past ten years has analysed how women academics are responding to the patriarchal nature of institutions of higher education (Culley *et al.*, 1985; Ramazanoglu, 1987; Klein, 1987). Less attention has been paid to how patriarchy in the academy and mainstream definitions of academic success affect women's relationships with each other. The ways in which we work with other women have implications for our lives, our experiences of higher education and our constructions of knowledge. Similarly, the processes by which we make other women 'Other' have the potential to provide important sources of learning about how the patriarchal academic system affects women's experiences as staff and students.

This chapter focuses on three issues affecting women's experiences of higher education; first, women's relationship with *academic* knowledge; second, the ways in which *procedures* in higher education support and maintain dominent definitions of *academic* success; and third, what Mary Evans (1993) calls *the success ethic* in higher education. I explore these issues with reference to relationships between women in higher education from my own experience and with reference to the discussion that took place amongst women in the conference workshop.

Definitions of *academic* knowledge and the procedures that support these are not value free, but reflect dominant interests within the academy. These interests relate to the preservation of particular ways of producing and disseminating knowledge which mainly serve to reinforce patriarchy and capitalism. Procedures play a crucial role in defining both practice and knowledge within the academy. Some examples of procedures in higher education include the ways in which examination boards operate, employment is handled and the ways that students and staff are selected for membership of various committees. Although procedures constantly influence decisions and behaviour in higher education, it is often only when a crisis arises, or when I feel unjustly treated, that I become aware of their existence. This may reflect the individualistic nature of much academic work and the lack of collective attention to procedures and their implications. The individualistic nature of academic work depends on established notions of success and the rewards that this brings. There appears to be a widespread acceptance of particular definitions of success and a silence about the personal and academic costs involved. This chapter is motivated by my interest in exploring how I, and other women in higher education, can recognize and respond to procedures that impact on the academic environment, and how we might create different definitions of success that are meaningful in our lives.

In a recent article, Mona Wasow (1992) asks academics 'What are we doing to ourselves?' Her concern for staff and students in higher education arises from the pressure 'to produce quickly' which she sees as discouraging 'the careful development of original or complex ideas'. Although she is commenting upon the North American academic system, her views seem relevant to the current situation in British universities and colleges. She goes on to suggest that

> Most original, complex ideas evolve over many years and develop out of passions, beliefs, and dreams, as well as rigorous scholarship. All this takes time . . . constant compromise can do a lot to destroy a person's self confidence, desires and dreams . . . There has always been pressure for excellence, for getting publications out, and for making a name for oneself. It is a question of degree.
>
> (Wasow, 1992: 486)

Mona Wasow's article interests me because her question, which seems an obvious one, is rarely posed by academic writers. Although there is an increasing emphasis on reflexivity within some academic circles, this reflexivity seems to exclude any critical reflection on academic trends and procedures and how these impinge on the production of and definitions of knowledge within the academy. While women in higher education, and particularly in Women's Studies, have done much to question and expand definitions of *academic* knowledge, this questioning appears to have taken place mainly in theory and in isolation from everyday practice and work within the academy. For example, few articles include a reflexive approach to the structural position of the author, the process by which publication is achieved or the choices made in the process of writing and publication. In the group discussion that arose after the presentation of this conference paper, we noted the extent to which the focus invariably returns to men and their behaviour. By focusing on men we avoid facing our own choices, activities and behaviour as women. As long as notions of what is academic are being questioned only on epistemological grounds, while not denying the importance of these debates, dominant notions of what constitutes academic knowledge will remain well insulated from change.

Women's Academic Lives

The word *academic* has many associations — books, men, knowledge, brains, writing, ideas, questions, abstract, non-practical, cold and logical. While the abstract, logical and non-practical hold some attraction for me as they allow me to escape from some of the practical, confusing and emotional aspects of my life, I am constantly troubled by the recognition that something is missing, that this perception of knowledge cannot be the whole story. Knowledge or activity that does not take account of the practical and the emotional, that remains cold and unaffected by the complexitities of human experiences is, in my view, sterile and, therefore, can have unhelpful implications in practice. Events and experiences become constructed in coherently theorized and abstract ways within the academy. These constructions often do not reflect the individual's intuitive and emotional responses to different experiences. If higher education excludes experiential learning and emotional responses to events, then, I repeat Mona Wasow's question 'What are we doing to ourselves?' While some Women's Studies courses have attempted to incorporate experiential learning into the academy, current academic priorities around publishing and increasing numbers of students leave little of the extra time, commitment and support that are essential for experiential learning. Traditional definitions of *success* in Higher Education exclude the experiential, the spiritual and the emotional, and procedures within the academy serve to maintain these rigid boundaries.

The academic career, like most careers, follows the traditional linear track. The student with a first class Bachelors degree registers for a PhD and with adequate support from the 'right' academics obtains the necessary funding. Through an ongoing process of academic justification, the successful postgraduate student becomes a lecturer or researcher and has some chance of moving up the hierarchy, if she aspires to do so. Students who enter the academy later in life, or those with a disrupted pattern of academic achievement, find that the procedures within higher education are not designed to respond to their circumstances. Often the contacts and support necessary to guide one through and around the procedures are not there. In addition, students with non-traditional backgrounds are often ineligible for particular sources of funding and other resources. Previous jobs and life experiences fall outside the realm of the academic and therefore count for very little.

Having recently moved into higher education as a part-time lecturer and PhD student, I am interested in the contributions that feminism can make to higher education, to learning and the creation of knowledge. One way of finding out about these contributions and assessing the ways that I may engage in academic work is to look to established women academics for role models and different ways of being a woman in the academy. My experience so far has highlighted the constraints that the academy places upon the potential contributions that women might bring to academic life.

My first impressions are that in order for women to develop their presence in higher education, a life of dedication is required. The focus of this dedication varies among women, but the high level of commitment seems to apply to all women academics. Increasingly high workloads mean that even those women for whom academic work is 'just a job' feel overwhelmed with work, and see their employer as demanding more and more commitment. Some women compete within the academic system on its terms, attempting to attain success via research ratings, publications, committee memberships, delivering conference papers and so on. Some women dedicate their lives to challenging the system and traditional definitions of knowledge. Most women probably find themselves falling somewhere between these categories, making compromises and struggling with the inevitable contradictions encountered by feminists working in higher education. In my limited experence of higher education, I have found myself shifting from one of these categories to another, often within the same day. Teaching, reading and writing are rewarding activities and there is always the wish to do each of them better. However, it can sometimes feel as if life *becomes* these activities. In an effort to prevent work from encroaching on so much of my life, I often revert to seeing it as just a job, and try to allocate more time to outside activities. Maintaining boundaries and the energy to address feminist agendas within the academy is a difficult task. Our group discussion highlighted the need for support within the broader network of institutions of higher education and outside the academy in order to maintain perspective.

An Ambivalent Academic

As a student in higher education, I have learned to adopt an approach to my thinking and writing that emphasizes abstract theory, logical argument and balanced critique. These are the things I have learned to do reasonably well and, for which I have been rewarded by academic qualifications. There is, therefore, a part of me that has an investment in defending the academic requirements and the procedures that accompany them. Yet there is another part that recognizes ways in which academic institutions and their procedures help to sustain patriarchal, heterosexist, imperialist and racist ideologies.

I write, as what Gillian Rose (1993) would call an 'ambivalent academic'. In her recent discussion of women and space, she suggests that women never participate wholly in the academy. She explains her ambivalence when she says 'I . . . feel too complicit with my discipline's forms of and claims to knowledge to be able to map . . . new spaces' (p. 72). She goes on to warn that it is dangerous for women academics to emphasize their ambivalence because ambivalence and uncertainty are represented as feminine and, therefore, of lesser value in academic discourse of knowledge,

> it matters that I'm a woman advocating ambivalence, able only to say, with Julia Kristeva, 'that's not it, that's still not it' and having nothing more certain, more prescriptive to add.
>
> (Rose, 1993: 79)

Given this warning how do I deal with my ambivalent feelings about the academy? On the one hand, my ambivalence operates in a seemingly positive way by allowing me to accommodate a range of views and to remain open to ideas. Yet, it also means that I can maintain some distance rather than compromise, and thereby, avoid coming face-to-face with my own power and that of other women. By remaining ambivalent I can keep my investment in the academic at a safe level and remain a semi-outsider. However, to partici-pate more fully in the academy would involve the following options; to accept the rules and procedures; to resist these; or to engage in constant personal and professional negotiation, making some compromises along the way. These dilemmas echo my earlier characterization of women academic's experiences of higher education. I think that a further option might be to maintain the position of ambivalence. This option foregrounds ambivalence as a source of knowledge and engagement. While acknowledging Gillian Rose's warning about representing oneself as ambivalent, I think ambivalence is more than a shield from one's own power and that of others. It represents the dilemmas and questions that feminism raises about learning, knowledge and how we live our lives. It allows for reflexivity, negotiation, movement and communication. Either complete acceptance or rejection of academia involve the dangers of reinforcing positions and a closing down of possibilities. This theme of ambivalence re-emerges many times throughout this chapter. Having explored some of the issues relating to women and academic work, I move on in the next section to look at the role of procedures in higher education and the extent to which women staff and students engage with procedural influences on their work.

Procedures in the Academy

Dominant perceptions of academic knowledge as theoretical, justified argument and abstract analysis are perpetuated by well-established academic procedures. These procedures gain their authority from tradition, precedence and the implicit ways in which they operate. When I speak of academic procedures, I include procedures such as the ways in which one gains entry to higher education, promotion within academia and the rules and regulations governing the allocation of research funding. The everyday lives of staff and students in higher education are structured around these procedures. They provide the frameworks within which we judge our progress and our performance. They institutionalize ways of behaving and are often critiqued on the basis that they interfere with academic freedom. But, what does academic freedom mean? Procedures are seen as neutral, independent and abstract, but in practice, they exclude and devalue some behaviours and experiences while including and valuing others. It is for this very reason that they require greater scrutiny.

Procedures lead to what Robin Morgan (1989) calls the genius of patriarchy, i.e. 'compartmentalisation, the capacity for institutionalising disconnection'. Catherine MacKinnon (1983), refers to procedures as 'impersonal processes' in her discussion of the ways in which the state sustains men's interests. She goes on to assert that impersonal procedural norms are never neutral. The very notion of objectivity, upon which these procedures rely, excludes experiences that cannot be defined in an objective manner and in relation to a particular procedure or rule.

For example, staff in higher eduction might ask themselves the following questions: To what extent do I rely on procedures to prevent awkward questions being asked: to justify prioritizing research over teaching: to provide answers where there are none or where the answer may be only a partial one: to disguise ambivalence: to simplify or ignore some aspects of a complex situation? How often do students in higher education, because of fear of the consequences, go along with procedural requirements even when these are in conflict with how they want to present their work, or how they want it to be assessed? What kinds of knowledge, questions and dilemmas are crushed by the heavy hand of procedural practice?

Academic knowledge is constantly being constructed by academic procedures. This point is emphasized by Suzanne Franzway *et al.* (1989), who suggest that procedures bring about beliefs that justify a particular pattern of practice, and persuade us to regard that pattern as just or efficient. Procedures also help us to know where we stand, and facilitate the smooth operation of organizations. However, the operation of impersonal procedures has the effect of reducing people to roles, stages in a process, and levels of achievement. We can probably all identify times when objective procedures have robbed us of the personal meanings of our experiences. For example, the presentation for approval of a course curriculum that bears little resemblance to the experience of running the course, or a research report to a funding body that excludes many of the more emotional, messy or experimental aspects of the research process. Procedures create systems of shared meanings that influence organizational cultures. If procedures can be made more visible then they may become more open to question. In this way their operation as impersonal processes might be undermined. It is only by demystifying procedural processes that 'flexibility and capacities for creative action . . . [may] become more important than narrow efficiency' (Morgan, 1986: 35).

I am not suggesting that procedures in themselves are bad. Without some procedures, those in positions of power would be able to dictate practice as they went along. Procedures can be empowering to those at lower levels of the hierachy as they provide tangible position statements that can be challenged. They represent attempts to make the work and behaviour of large groups of people more predictable and manageable. Some procedures can benefit women such as those designed to ensure safety at work and equal opportunities procedures. However, my argument is that procedures serve particular interests and exclude other interests and that challenging them inevitably upsets the *status quo*.

What are the implications of this discussion about procedures for women's relationships with each other within higher education? Procedures can be used by women to perpetuate their own interests within organizations. For example, if I have achieved certain qualifications by keeping to procedures, I may find it hard to question these procedures even when it is obvious that they are working in opposition to the interests of other women. Procedures also serve to simplify or disguise the complex power relations between women. When women invoke the procedures of the institution and suggest to other women that they must be adhered to, power is being portrayed as residing in the institutional procedures. In such cases the power residing in the position or role of the woman using the procedures is disguised. Procedures can serve to disguise power dynamics within relationships between women. The power of one woman to implement procedures potentially against the interests of another women is not addressed. However, the negotiation of power between women (however painful it is at times) is an important source of empowerment for all women. Although honesty may not be a very politically astute strategy, it seems to be the only way in which we can interact positively with academic structures and procedures and with each other. The questioning of both the procedures themselves and how we use them might reveal some of the contradictions that underly our relationships with each other. Honesty makes these contradictions and inconsistencies more visible. This can be a frightening prospect in a context where one is supposed to know where one stands.

Procedures also function to maintain an objective and reasonable organizational culture. Mary Evans, in a recent article, highlighted the

> unwillingness which many women have to make a fuss. Making a fuss involves upsetting the order of the workplace, becoming a trouble-maker and questioning not just an abstract system of authority but a real everyday one.
>
> (Evans, 1993: 20)

She goes on to point that 'many universities function by doing much to disguise authority and hierarchy.' This often means that the individual is shocked when she confronts 'the realities behind the facade of democracy and consultation'. Hierarchical relationships between women are complex and raise issues about power and difference that are often painful and difficult to address. Procedures often act as a protective shield against engagement with the realities of power relations between women. Failure to address power relations as openly as possible maintains the reasonable organizational culture of academic work and disguises the ways in which hierarchies work. By avoiding making a fuss, by trying to be reasonable, and by following procedures unquestioningly, there is a danger of perpetuating unaccountability in the use of power and authority between women.

How women academics engage with the operation of procedures in higher education is related to academic success which is often the reward for recognizing and implementing procedures. However, if keeping to procedures is the only way that women can succeed in Higher Education, then the compromises involved may eventually rob many women of the passions, desires and dreams that Mona Wasow speaks about. In the next section of this chapter I discuss the ways in which academic success is constructed and its implications for relations between women.

The Success Ethic

Mary Evans (1990) suggests that western capitalism is best served by the widespread acceptance of 'the success ethic' that is based on individual achievement and rewards for hierarchical success. Within the academy of the 1990s, this means, amongst other things, scoring a research rating of five for lecturers, and a first class degree or a distinction for students. If these kinds of achievements are not at the top of our lists of priorities, success in conventional terms will probably elude us. Achievements such as developing different learning approaches, creating a supportive learning environment within Higher Education, or challenging procedures within the academy rarely contribute to success and gain little external recognition. The only sources of possible recognition for these activities will be from people with similar interests (rarely at high levels in the hierarchy), or from oneself. As this kind of recognition is not so publicly visible, women pursuing these objectives need more affirmation and support. In our group discussion, women emphasized the need to maintain networks through trade unions and other women's groups in higher education that challenge the *status quo*. Yet these groups also involve explicit and implicit hierarchical structures which operate in exclusive ways. It is important to recognize exclusionary practices within women's groups and the fact that these groups do not exist in a vacuum untainted by dominant values and practices.

While the recognition and approval that go alongside conventional success are seductive, the criteria that must be met in order to achieve academic success are hard to accept. The personal costs involved in attempting to achieve success are very high. As for those striving for success in other professions these costs include the development of many instrumental relationships and little time for non-work oriented relationships and activities. The following quote from Culley *et al.* (1985) drawing on Simone de Beauvoir's *Second Sex* helps me to understand some of my ambivalence towards traditional definitions of success:

> the correspondence between the idea of female virtue and the image of the mother tends to work against our capacity to achieve, or even to aspire to, such professional success. As mothers, we are expected to nurture; as professionals we are expected to compete. The context in which our nurturing is to take place is in the patriarchal context in which we teach . . . In our culture the role of nurturer and intellectual have been separated not just by gender, but by function; to try to recombine them is to create confusion.
>
> (Culley *et al.*, 1985: 12)

Although I am not a mother and do not identify greatly with the role of nurturer, I want to maintain caring and friendship relationships at work and outside work. However, values relating to care and relationships do not fit easily with current priorities within the academy. Time is required for more productive activities such as marking, teaching and research.

Mary Evans (1990) shifts the focus of the discussion about women and success from mothers to fathers when she points to the high number of women who identify with their fathers. 'The problem with this identification with men', she suggests, 'is that the very strengths that men often possess are acquired at a cost to women' (p. 60). The women secretaries and caterers that support our work in the academy and the other (mainly women) helpers, whether family or paid workers in the home, who support our academic lifestyles are a rarely acknowledged aspect of the production and dissemination of knowledge in higher education.

The rewards for success in the labour market are such that men learn to maximize their chances of promotion in professional hierarchies (Evans, 1990). While the rewards of hierarchical success are high for women too, Mary Evans (1990) warns feminists of the 'need to be aware (not to say suspicious) of the pervasive, and seductive appeal of maximizing individual success'. The implication of Mary Evans' discussion seems to be that the maximization of individual success, whether justified as necessary to make a living, or on other grounds, involves cost to others as well as ourselves. While she warns against the appeal of individual success, Mary Evans does not suggest any possible ways in which women might be able to obtain recognition for collective or different types of activities. I am not sure how Mary Evans' views connect with Simone de Beauvoir's suggestion that internal images of the mother make it hard for some women to pursue achievement and thereby accept their own power, strengths and abilities. Although many women in Higher Education struggle with value conflicts between care, relationships and achievement, reflection on personal priorities and values is often forced to take second place to the constant pressure of work. These value conflicts are hard to resolve and the prospect of resolving them (if it is possible) seems overwhelming.

Evelyn Fox Keller and Helene Moglen (1987) in their discussion of competition, feminism and academic women, suggest that

> feminists inherited a mythology of sisterhood that fits poorly into a world of scarce material and emotional resources, we have found that sisterhood itself — real or mythic — is often inappropriate to our circumstances. Sometimes we are mothers, sometimes daughters, sometimes lovers, sometimes friends . . . None of these relations can be cleansed of the threatening feeling of envy and resentment — even of the aggression — that we associate with competition.
>
> (Keller and Moglen, 1987: 495)

Competition, they suggest, creates special problems for feminists:

The fact is that women seem to experience different, deeper and more painful forms of competition with one another than do their male peers.

(Keller and Moglen, 1987: 495)

The depth of these feelings may be related to the women's movement's 'emphasis on mutuality, concern and support', which Keller and Moglen suggest are 'tremendously difficult to implement in the real world situations of the current academic marketplace' (1987). Feminist scholarship is now part of the academic marketplace and the conventional reward system which emphasizes competition, rather than mutuality and collectivity (Keller and Moglen, 1987). This leads to considerable conflicts between women and within women themselves about priorities, values and principles. While Keller and Moglen put forward the view that 'it seems more sisterly to struggle than to be successful' (1987), they appear to justify the inevitability of the success of a few when they follow this comment with the following questions:

And how could we expect academic rewards to be evenly distributed? Is everyone's work of equal value and has public recognition ever been an adequate indication of quality?

(Keller and Moglen, 1987: 505)

These are crucial questions to pose, but also to continue to struggle with. It is unlikely that they will go away, but it is important to continue to problematize these realities if we are to expose underlying interests and power dynamics at work in Higher Education.

The subject of success in the sense of traditional notions of achievement or accomplishment that brings wealth, fame and/or position, raises questions that are difficult for women to resolve. These include questions such as: How do women respond to women who have achieved prestige and power in the conventional way? How do women who have become successful respond to other women who have made different choices in their lives? Do the behaviours of individual women have implications for other women? Marie Maguire puts forward one solution to these kinds of questions:

We need to become more able to accept the ways in which we are different from other women, to realise that we have our own unique resources and disadvantages, and that in order to be honest about who we are, and what we think, we may have to risk conflict.

(Maguire, 1987: 150)

One Question Leads to Another

A first order question at this stage is whether women in higher education are able or willing to pause for long enough to try to answer Mona Wasow's question of what we are doing to ourselves, and to respond to her plea for time to develop complex ideas and to allow our passions and dreams to influence our work. If we paused to consider these questions we would then be faced with further questions about which academic structures and procedures are blocking our potential contribution to knowledge and learning in Higher Education.

If we are to be honest about our feelings and desires then it may be necessary to expand the range of discourses available to feminists within higher education. Further questions emerge such as: Does an ideology of mutuality and cooperation amongst women disguise women's engagement with dominant competitive ideologies within higher education? What makes different priorities, competition and conflict so difficult to face and negotiate amongst women in Higher Education? If competition is recognized and discussed, then, ironically, it may be easier to foster cooperative and supportive relationships between women in the academy. The denial of competitive feelings and behaviour can lead to defensiveness that might not otherwise be necessary (Keller and Moglen, 1987). I am not suggesting that women in Higher Education explore their deepest feelings about competition or success in public or even in private. Rather, it seems important that there is space and permission to acknowledge competition amongst women. The relative silence about competition and the emphasis on sisterhood and mutuality can lead to high levels of disappointment and disillusionment. By acknowledging the range of feelings and relationships we engage in we may be able to reduce current high levels of disappointment amongst women in Higher Education. Power relations, communication and patterns of behaviour change and develop with learning and negotiation. Helene Cixous (1979) suggests that our potential to change lies in our power to transform the here and now. She calls this a process of learning how to inhabit time humanly. While her advice seems relevant to today's academic women it is hard to achieve alone. As the discussion in our workshop emphasized, women in higher education have to overcome the predominantly individualistic culture within the academy in order to communicate with each other and develop support networks.

A further question relates to how women negotiate the academic, the material and the personal. An academic career may be seductive for some women because it offers the possibility of transcending the everyday experiences of negotiating life in a patriarchal society through abstract theorizing. Yet most women are also aware of the dangers of unaccountable and ungrounded theories. Responses to this dilemma can be to withdraw from the academy or take an anti-theoretical stance. The latter option is a worrying one because an anti-theoretical or anti-intellectual approach to feminist thinking and activities could degenerate into a rejection of the complexity of women's lives and fundamentalism. Self-consciousness and reflexivity about practice is a necessary safeguard for feminists within Higher Education.

Given the many significant changes in policy in higher education over the past five years and the extreme implications of these for women, it is surely time to pause and reflect on where we are going and what we are doing to ourselves in the process. However, when we do ask 'What are we doing to ourselves?' the answers will not be clearcut. The choice for women academics may not be simply between the 'success of conformity' and the 'lonely grandeur of a principled outsider' (Bammer, 1991). A central theme throughout this chapter has been that of ambivalence. Although this might be seen as representing a stage in a woman's academic career out of which more clarity or resigned cynicism might emerge, I think that there is much to be gained from maintaining a state of ambivalence. It is positive in the sense that it reflects the gap between ideals of mutuality and equality and the realities of hierarchical relationships between women in the academy. By engaging with ambivalence, speaking it, exploring it with other women in Higher Eduction, it may be possible to agree some joint goals. Despite recent postmodern, poststructuralist and feminist trends, and their apolitical emphasis on difference, fragmentation and individualism, it may still possible to harness women academic's ambivalence to organize politically to effect changes within higher education that will enable each of us to develop our ideas and to realise our dreams. Jane Miller summarizes this point in the following quote:

> Women must allow themselves complexity, doubleness, the strength of uncertainty . . . Only truthfulness to the diversity of women's experience and to the problems of thinking and talking and writing about these things will bring real change.
>
> (Miller, 1990: 164)

Note

1 I use Mona Wasow's article title 'What are we doing to ourselves?' as part of my title for this chapter.

References

BAMMER, A. (1991) *Partial Visions Feminism and Utopianism in the 1970s* London: Routledge.

CIXOUS, H. (1979) *Vivre l'orange/To live the Orange*, trans. CORNELL, S. with LIDDLE, A. and CIXOUS, H., Paris: des femmes.

CULLEY, M., DIAMOND, A., EDWARDS, L., LENNOX, S. and PORTUGES, C. (1985) 'The politics of nurturance' in CULLEY, M. and PORTUGES, C., *Gendered Subjects: The dynamics of Feminist Teaching*, London: Routledge and Kegan Paul, pp. 12–13.

EVANS, M. (1983) 'The teacher's tale: On teaching women's studies' in *Women's Studies International Forum*, **6**(3), pp. 325–30.

EVANS, M. (1990) 'The problem of gender for women's studies' in *Women's Studies International Forum*, **13**(5), pp. 457–62.

EVANS, M. (1993) 'A faculty for prejudice' in *Times Higher Educational Supplement*, 12 November, p. 20.

FRANZWAY, S., COURT, D. and CONNELL, R. W. (1989) *Staking a Claim Feminism, Bureaucracy and the State*, Cambridge: Polity Press.

KELLER, E. F. and MOGLEN, H. (1987) 'Competition and feminism: Conflicts for academic women', *Signs*, **12**(3), pp. 493–511.

KLEIN, R. D (1987) 'The dynamics of the women's studies classroom: A review of teaching practice of women's studies in higher education', *Women's Studies International Forum*, **10**(2), pp. 187–206.

KRISTEVA, J. (1981) 'Women can never be defined' in MARKS, E. and DE COURTIVRON, I. (Eds) *New French Feminisms*, Brighton: Harvester.

MACKINNON, C. A. (1983) 'Feminism, marxism, method, and the state: Towards feminist jurisprudence', *Signs*, **8**(4), pp. 635–58.

MAGUIRE, M. (1987) 'Casting the evil eye' in ERNST, S. and MAGUIRE, M. (Eds) *Living with the Sphinx Papers from the Women's Therapy Centre*, London: The Women's Press.

MILLER, J. (1990) *Seductions: Studies in Reading and Culture*, London: Virago.

MORGAN, G. (1986) *Images of Organisation*, Newbury Park, CA: Sage Publications.

MORGAN, R. (1989) *The Demon Lover: On Sexuality of Terrorism*, New York: W. W. Norton.

RAMAZANOGLU, C. (1987) 'Sex and violence in academic life or you can keep a good woman down', in HANMER, J. and MAYNARD, M. (Eds) *Women, Violence and Social Control*, Basingstoke: Macmillan Press Ltd.

ROSE, G. (1993) 'Some notes towards thinking about the spaces of the future' in BIRD, J., CURTIS, B., PUTNAM, T., ROBERTSON, G. and TICKER, L. *Mapping the Future Local Cultures, Global Change*, London: Routledge.

WASOW, M. (1992) 'What are we doing to ourselves?', *Social Work*, **37**(6), pp. 485–7.

Part II

The Empowerment of Women in Higher Education

Chapter 6

Commonality and Difference: Theory and Practice

Mairead Owen

It seems to me that one of the most contentious, persistent and rewarding debates within the feminist movement is that of commonality/difference, at the level of both theory and of practice. However, I also feel that that debate is becoming splintered, the various aspects are becoming separated when it is essential that they are conceived as interrelated and interdependent. At the beginning, understandably, it was women's common oppression which was the main focus. Gradually, and again understandably, women who felt on the margins of the initial movement stressed their differences, and the movement has been towards difference. Moreover, the same drive which seems able only to contemplate commonality or difference seems able only to stress this in theory *or* in practice. Difficult as it may be I feel that it is imperative that we hold both commonality and difference within an integrated concept of feminism and that we see these two conceptualized and actualized as feminist theory and practice. We need to attempt the admittedly difficult task of holding these four aspects of women's situation in an integrated whole. I cannot suggest any simple way to achieve this. I have few answers. I suspect that it is a feature of the commonality/difference debate which I find so interesting that the more one thinks about the issue the more it shifts and slides.

The analogy which stays with me when I think about commonality/difference is that of a pattern of black and white squares, where, at one moment one sees the black squares on a white background and at another, white squares on a black background, or those optical illusions where there is sometimes an old hag, sometimes a pretty young women. (An ironic coincidence that the examples are about colour and age?) When we enter theory and practice into this picture, the situation becomes even more complex. Commonality/difference: theory/practice. Each of the four is sometimes foreground, sometimes background, and each one permutates with the others.

But the essential factor is that, whatever our perceptions of the situation, at any one moment *all* the aspects are actually there together. I'd like to suggest that it is our perception, as with optical illusions, that is lacking. In this chapter I shall try to look at, in turn, commonality in theory and difference in theory then commonality in practice and difference in practice.[1] However, I do this only because of the linearity or writing and speaking. My contention is that we should be constantly and vividly aware of their combined and interactive presence.

Commonality in theory

Even when I try to separate theory from practice in order to consider the concept of commonality, it seems to me that, as feminists and academics we actually operate with a concept of commonality underlying the very circumstance that we are offering courses on Women's Studies. Beyond the not-always-so obvious biological fact of female bodies, there is implicit in our practice a concept of 'womanness', some sort of common quality that we share. The very philosophical question arises then of how to define a category. Even though there has been a great deal written and talked about this, I am not sure if we have quite grasped the nettle. What is this commonality, this womanness? Wittgenstein in his *Philosophical Investigations* (1953) has pointed out how difficult it is to define a category, how difficult to pin down what is common. He tries to resolve the difficulty by offering a consideration of the concept of *games*. I am rather dubious about this. Is it playing straight into the hands of absolute male chauvinism to equate women with games? 'Consider for example the proceedings that we call "games" . . . for if you look at them you will not see something that is common to *all* but similarities, relationships, and a whole series of them at that . . . a complicated network of similarities overlapping and criss-crossing.' (Wittgenstein, 1953: 31) (Italics in original). Could we compare womanness to games? Could we see commonality as that complicated network of similarities? Does this enable us to steer clear of the hazard of essentialism with all its dangers or the rocks of biological determinism and the ideologies from which we are trying to escape — women are naturally caring, naturally maternal, therefore their role will always be, and has to be, the angel in the house? I would like to suggest that, in spite of the dangers, we should still hold on to Simone de Beauvoir's idea first expressed in 1949 that woman '*is* defined and differentiated with reference to man and not he with reference to her; she is the incidental, the inessential as opposed to the essential. He is the Subject, he is the Absolute — she is the Other' (de Beauvoir, 1949: 16) [Emphasis added].

It was insights such as this, illuminating the situation of women, which led so many women to realize that their personal dissatisfactions were part of a larger, structured inequality or oppression. 'The problem with no name' became objectified, politicized and the general coming-out as a women unfulfilled, socially, politically, sexually, was a heady experience. The emphasis was on that 'otherness' of women, the marginality and/or oppression suffered by half the human race at the hands of a stronger half. There were divergences. At first there was a stress on androgyny, the fact that all women could be, and were, mostly like men, that women were capable of taking their places with men in all walks of life. Womanness was socially constructed within a patriarchal society. This view came to be identified with feminism by many people; an attitude of social constructionism and androgyny was the goal. But the new orthodoxy of social constructionism in its turn was questioned. A more woman-centred argument arose. Writers like Adrienne Rich (1977) pointed out that it is part of the old patriarchy, the recurring dichotomies of nature/culture, male/female, sacred/profane, to oppose body and mind. We do live in our bodies and cannot separate from them. The French feminists, too, urged that we 'write the body'. We must accept and celebrate our femaleness and our female bodies. Adrienne Rich talks of the need for awareness of 'the diffuse, intense sensuality radiating out from clitoris, breasts, uterus, vagina: the lunar cycles of menstruation; the gestation and fruition of life which can take place in the female body' (Rich, 1992: 31). Of course we can still hold to commonality whether we embrace essentialism or social constructivism. However derived, we can share that common womanness.

Commonality as a theory is, therefore, a shifting concept. In the United Nations report on the decade of women (1975–1985) the researchers concluded that 'instead of defining just one difference between men and women, women's ability to bear children is used to define their entire lives' (Taylor, 1985: 3). Perhaps in that statement is the thread of Wittgenstein's 'similarities, relationships and a whole series of them at that'. Could we use a minimalist theory of commonality with two interdependent strands, a female body though of different colours, length of wear, in different states of ability, etc., linked with a continuum of disadvantage: disadvantaged in some societies, oppressed in others, tortured because of our womanness in others? Surely this is the background assumption of standpoint theory, that we are capable of a greater understanding and awareness of the world because we are oppressed. We experience patriarchy (and capitalism) from both sides, aware of both men's history and our own.

It seems to me that there is a certain feeling that we have moved on from commonality. Been there, done that, got the T-shirt! I wonder if the project of exploring the theory of commonality does not have more to offer than this. Can we not, as I have suggested, hold on to that theory at the same time as we move on?

Difference in Theory

Recently as we know, women have questioned this commonality. Black women blazed the trail when they called attention to difference by reference to their own experience and the fact that the mainstream stress on commonality belied that experience. Other women in hitherto marginalized groups like lesbian women, working class women, disabled women, women of minority religions, followed. This triggered not just a change in practice but a change in theory. I saw this very clearly in my experience of teaching for the Open University. I taught in 1991 the last year of the old half course, 'The Changing Experience of Women', which was almost completely about the subordination of all women, about their difference from men and the way their experience of life was shaped by this fact. The new course in 1992, 'Issues in Women's Studies' had shifted the focus to the problems and the possibilities of difference. There has been a deconstructing of the concept of womanness and overarching theories to explain our common experience and oppression. There has been a necessary questioning of an assumption of commonality. We have queried the possibility of any universalistic answers, of sharing another's space, of a consistent subjectivity and the humanistic idea of the Subject. We have suggested that the very discourse of commonality, of feminism, may not be a contradictory, subversive discourse but another falsely universalizing power code. From the point of view of post-modernism, post-structuralism and post-feminism, the very enterprise of feminism is suspect. The background becomes the foreground. The theorising becomes even more complex. Are we talking sister or stranger?

Commonality in Practice

The shifting meanings of the debate I find enormously stimulating, if often perplexing, at a theoretical level and, of course, that theory derives from lived experience. Commonality and difference can be, and often are, gut reactions. It is exhilarating and supporting when we reach out and feel a oneness in our experience with other women. When there is a presumption of oneness and we find that our experience does not resonate with that of other women we feel jarred, upset — angry? Surely it is the lived experience of these feelings which we try to understand and put into some sort of coherence, to see the pattern which is theory, these patterns, these abstractions which we order and explore and put into context and conceptualize in the academic world.

But perhaps far more immediate and practical than the epistemological problems and debates is the fact that these *are* lived experiences. The movement to a stress on difference grew from practice. Politics and power are implicated in those experiences of groups who feel themselves marginalized. Audrey Lorde had pointed out that when 'white women ignore their built-in privilege of whiteness and define woman in terms of their own experience alone, then women of colour become other, the outsider whose experience and tradition is too alien to comprehend' (Lorde, 1992: 49). Similarly lesbian woman have railed against the assumption of heterosexuality so endemic in feminist writing, feminist practice, in women's studies itself. As Adrienne Rich says, 'The assumption that most women are innately heterosexual stands as a theoretical and political stumbling block for many women. It remains a tenable assumption, partly because lesbian existence has been written out of history or catalogued under disease' (Rich, 1984: 177). Working-class women have felt that the feminist movement is a movement of the middle class, part of the ongoing hegemony of the ruling class. Latterly women who are disabled, who are old, who are members of minority religions, any women who do not feel part of the commonality, the sisterhood, have pointed to the tensions of difference. And, as Audrey Lorde has said, that probably includes more of us than was at first thought. 'Somewhere on the edge of consciousness, there is what I call a mythical norm, which each one of us within our hearts knows "that is not me" . . . white, thin, male, young, heterosexual, Christian and financially secure' (Lorde, 1992: 48).

At the same time as we are teaching and researching these ideas I think many of us, and certainly this is my experience, are seeing those dilemmas actualized in front of us. It seems to me that more than any other subject, students of Women's Studies come to university or college with the most intense hopes and fears. I think this makes the subject unlike other parts of curriculum. Other subjects excite and interest students but I would argue that our students come so often with a personal agenda. I think these feelings about commonality and difference were highlighted and framed by our experience at Liverpool John Moores University of putting on a new Women's Studies degree, which started as a complete degree programme in October 1992. Many of the courses had been running in other degree programmes, as there had been a tradition of gender consciousness from the women who eventually set up the degree. However, perhaps there is something about a degree labelled Women's Studies which formalizes ideas and concepts about 'what women want', to quote Freud. Many writers have discussed the high expectations that women bring to a Women's Studies Degree (e.g. Aaron and Walby, 1991; Hinds *et al.*, 1992; Richardson and Robinson, 1993). I think this is a tremendously important area for discussion. Until I had experience of teaching Women's Studies I just had not realized the hopes and dreams that women have from this degree.

I am aware of commonality and difference day-to-day. I find the classes are more stimulating and enjoyable than mixed sex classes. I feel a commonality; students feel a commonality. Students come to me and say that in other courses they don't speak. In the Women's Studies courses, they gradually start to take space for themselves and hopefully that will empower them to speak in mixed sex classes. Research, such as Coates (1986), reports on the differences between women's conversation and men's: the turn taking that is important for women, the hierarchy that is established in a group of men, the supportive work done by women in conversation with each contribution being taken up in turn, the way in which points are scored by men to establish the extent of their knowledge. All these qualities show up in lectures, tutorials, workshops. Women's way of learning is exploratory, tentative, searching, they look for support in this. Men tutors tend to believe that students should be challenged and confronted in their ideas, tested and made to defend their propositions. Very often this type of pedagogy can be completely destructive of women's ideas. And the latest ideas of innovative teaching (which seem often to re-invent the wheel. Montessori proselytized most of them in the thirties and they were not new then) tend to suggest that for either sex women's way of learning is actually more effective. *Co-operative, experiential, group* are the buzz words. Giving out *facts* in a hierarchical way may accord with a patriarchal ideology but is not actually effective.

Difference in Practice

However, this paints perhaps an over-rosy view. There are differences in the lecture room as well. In John Moores University, because of the system of modular degrees, there are, to begin with, three broadly different groups of students. One group has elected to do Women's Studies as the main part of a degree, one group would be doing it as a minor component and one group would be taking a particular course as an elective, a one-off where they might never do any Women's Studies again. So the background, the political orientation, the strength of interest varies. The groups are very disparate, naturally in a gathering of that size of (mainly) women from different parts of the country and from overseas, too. During the course of the year it emerges that we have women from various ethnic minorities, of different sexualities, different classes, of degrees of disability, different religious beliefs and practices, different ages.

One of the most basic difficulties concerns the nature of the course itself. From an institutional point of view a Women's Studies degree is an area of knowledge like any other. As academics we are interested in theories, concepts, the exploration of information, research, methodology. The degree has to be validated and must stand or fall by rigorous standards of academic research/ exploration. Yet there is the feminist argument from some women that this is a patriarchal institution with partriarchal ways of thinking and that by setting up a Women's Studies course according to these standards we betray feminism. If we feel that logical thinking, the excitement of research, of exploring the world we live in in a comprehensive and thoughtful way are valid aims, have we just been socialized into our patriarchal society? A Women's Studies degree which does not conform to the standard academic pattern tends to give further ammunition to our male colleagues, male employers, men in general and, we have to keep reminding ourselves, many women.

An important difference in my experience is between those who already 'speak feminism', who are interested in, or who have already done some Women's Studies and those who are new to feminist ideas. A certain amount of heat is generated by that difference! There is the interesting pedagogical challenge of understanding and encouraging radical thought on the one hand but at the same time respecting the views of women to whom these ideas are very new, challenging and worrying. Women with untroubled family histories can feel that 'men have a rough time too' and sometimes find the anger of women who have had personal experience of domestic violence threatening in itself. While similarly the view that men also get anorexia, have stressful lives, can be raped or at least similarly abused can seem a betrayal of women's suffering. These views cannot be unproblematically ascribed to those who have experience of oppression and those who have not.

From the very inception of a Women's Studies degree, there can be radical debates about what that degree should be. The implication of commonality in the setting up and running of a Women's Studies degree appears to be predicated on an assumption that we have our womanness in common. Yet it seems to me that the aim of quite a proportion of the students is a recognition of their difference, their ontology, their being in the world. Some Women's Studies students are just interested because the areas we discuss are relevant to their lives yet many have a more personal agenda which they hope to explore in the classes. More than that, I think many hope for solutions to problems. I think also that as the course progresses and previously apolitical women explore the dis-advantages and oppression of women they often become politicized.

The fact that Women's Studies draws from across the disciplines can compound the differences. Women's Studies is one of the few truly inter-disciplinary courses and I think, because of that, has a tremendous role to play in challenging the conventional, arbitrary divisions of knowledge in a really radical way. Other disciplines may lament the fact that students tend to keep knowledge in separate boxes labelled politics, science, technology, literature, etc. In Women's Studies we really do integrate that knowledge and look for the similarities and differences between the theories and concepts adopted by different philosophies.

On the other hand, to use as examples some of my own courses, in a Women and the Media course where some are committed feminists and some are media buffs, the jargons can talk past each other! In Equal Opportunities, the conventional lawyers and the radical feminists are only rarely the same people.

The different expectations of the course can be a problem. We do have an academic degree. We discuss theory, we do assignments and examinations. We try to make them as innovative and user friendly as possible. We continually try different approaches but we are, at the end of the day, assessing other women. A small but vocal group of students reminded us that in really radical Women's Studies courses such aspects as Indian dancing have been incorporated. We did find somewhere on the University elective programme a module on fencing with foils and one on psychology for tennis players. But the curriculum is academic. The shape of the courses echoes sociology, politics, education studies, media studies and all the disciplines from which we ourselves come. Academic credibility is an inescapable criterion. I know that many women academics have had to fight to put on a Women's Studies course at all. The hazards of including dancing or aromatherapy or relaxation need not be spelled out.

It is not, though, the academic differences which are most salient but the experiential and existential differences. Those very differences of class, sexuality, colour, disability and so on, make up the lived experience of our students' lives.

One of the assignments we asked for, rather tentatively, at the the end of our first year was that the students do some field research to complete a module on Introduction to Feminist Research. We had some doubts about doing actual research so soon and asking for feminist research into the bargain and I know the students had many reservations. But in the event they did excellent and very valuable work. Many of them chose to actualize the aphorism that the personal is the political and worked on aspects of life that reflected their own difference. Here we really felt difference — the pain that difference can make. Students described the situation of lesbian women who cannot share their trauma when partnerships break up. Family, friends from childhood, colleagues at work, are sometimes not even aware of their lesbianism. At the end of another piece of research was the bleak statement, 'Black lesbians have to seriously consider separatism as ultimately the only way to live their lives.' This student pointed out how there is not even much writing about British black lesbians. The material is mostly American, and we are divided by a common language. The student talked of a black lesbian who had a white partner and how the white partner would use common phrases or ideas that were derogatory to black woman. 'To her it really was just a phrase. But it was so constant, that to me it was just a knife every time she said it. This was someone I was trying to get close to and trying to share my deep emotions with and she was like obliterating my very existence.' An Irish student interviewed an Irish woman, who had lived here for 60 years, and who asked the student to put a quote in her project because it conveyed her feelings. 'I can't say it as long as we live in this country. I can't feel that way. You, you know I'll never go back to Ireland, but my spirit is there. That's how I feel about Ireland.' When she first arrived in Britain she was told not to speak to anyone in case they realized she was Irish. This reminded me of a recent experience of my own. I come from an Irish background though I have lived in England most of my life. When I went to a relative's funeral in Northern Ireland, those of us from England were warned not to go to pubs or restaurants in the evening without someone resident in Ireland — with an Irish accent. It is sobering to find oneself suddenly the enemy or the outsider.

Two of the projects focused on bisexual women. This seems to be an area very much in need research. Bisexual women appeared to be rejected by both straight and gay women. 'It's a cop-out', said one gay woman, 'I believe that bisexual women would always in the end opt for heterosexual respectability and go back to men.' In a very different mode, one student wrote a project with the title, 'If only I could lose weight my life would be different: fact or fiction', and produced compelling evidence of the way in which it would be different, the way people change their attitudes to fat people, of how in our society it feels to be outcasts, outside of the heterosexually-based small change of day-to-day conversations and meetings, of the completely different attitudes towards fat and thin women who are otherwise similar. One student wrote of the deeper effects of domestic violence. Beyond the obvious trauma was the pain of alienation, the feeling that women who have suffered domestic violence were outside the norm. One woman spoke of looking at other families and feeling how different she must be, wondering what was wrong with her, that her family was the way it was while other families projected the cosy, nuclear family image.

Perhaps the most useful final word about difference and those who have been marginalized by feminism was contributed by a student who felt all the feminist doubts about using a group for research until one woman said, 'I feel really good that I'm saying all this and someone's writing it down.' The student found this statement completely changed her attitude and she then reported in her project how moved and disturbed she had been by the stories she had heard. 'We must listen to women and tell their stories or we will let them shrivel unheard and go on weeping in the darkness.' In the students' written work (and I feel enormously grateful to them) I have been made aware of that weeping in the darkness, seen the real pain of difference.

Conclusion

I feel in their work that the students demonstrated what they want from their courses and more than that the way forward for feminism. They want recognition of their difference which is not just observation but a real openness to their life experience. They also want a commonality which can accept that difference, which encompasses that complicated network of similarities and relationships of which Wittgenstein spoke. They want to be able to live their difference and at the same time, with Sojourner Truth, that indomitable black woman of nineteenth century America, pose the question, 'Ain't I a woman?', and receive the unequivocal answer, 'Yes!' This debate needs to continue to be thought through and explored theoretically, to contribute to that very sophisticated and radicalizing growing body of feminist theory and at the same time practised in the 'everydayness' of our lives.

It has seemed to me that we have tended to leave behind the concept of commonality as we moved towards difference, opted for theory while we neglect practice or eschewed thought for action — seeing them as separable. Surely, it is essential to remember that while it is difficult for us to focus on the different aspects at the same time, like those optical illusions commonality and difference, theory and practice are each and all ontologically present in the lives of women and somehow we must combine them in one integrated whole.

Note

1 Since this collection of papers is dealing with women in higher education and especially Women's Studies, I would like to illustrate the discussion by reference to the experience of students on Women's Studies courses in my own institution.

References

AARON, J. and WALBY, S. (1991), *Out of the Margins*, London: Falmer Press.

COATES, J. (1986) *Women, Men and Language*, London: Longman.

de BEAUVOIR, S. (1949–1988) *The Second Sex*, London: Pan.

HINDS, H. PHOENIX, A. and STACEY, J. (1992), *Working Out: New Directions for Women's Studies*, London: Falmer Press.

LORDE, A. (1992), in CROWLEY, H. HIMMELWEIT, S. *Knowing Women*, Cambridge: Polity.

RICH, A. (1977) *Of Woman Born*, London: Virago.

RICH, A. (1984), 'Compulsory heterosexuality and lesbian existence', in SNITOW, A. *et al.* (Eds), *Desire: The Politics of Sexuality*, London: Virago.

RICH, A. (1992) in CROWLEY, H. and HIMMELWEIT, S. *Knowing Woman*, Cambridge: Polity.

RICHARDSON, D. and ROBINSON, V. (1993) *Introducing Women's Studies*, Basingstoke: Macmillan.

TAYLOR, D. (Ed.) (1985) *Women: A World Report*, Oxford: Oxford University.

WITTGENSTEIN, L. (1953) *Philosophical Investigations*, Oxford: Basil Blackwell.

Chapter 7

Postgraduate Students: Empowering Ourselves

Deryn Rees-Jones, Rebecca D'Monté, Joanne Winning and Sally Kilmister

Introduction: Producing this Paper

We think that it is a bad mistake for women to pursue deliberately the puppets, tinsel, and formulae already worn out by men. If, in the same context, some women . . . perform their tasks in the same manner as the men do, these women will only be adding to the monuments of incompetence . . . We find such a rat race uninteresting and totally without benefit for women.

We think that women must offer other forms of social systems, other forms of creation, other goals, other directions, and by 'other' we mean 'better': we mean those that stress the value of human beings as a whole, that truly liberate them . . . Why, you will ask, would women succeed where men have failed? Why not? Let us try, it is well worth the effort.[1]

The aim of this account is to document one attempt to find other and better directions for ourselves as women in higher education. In this context we feel that existing power structures, critiques of those structures and our own empowerment are intermeshed concerns which need to be addressed. We take as our starting point for this paper our experiences in founding the Women's Research Network (WRN) at Birkbeck College, University of London.[2] The Preston Conference presented us with an opportunity to focus our ideas, to share with others our successes and failures, and to enter into a dialogue with other women facing similar challenges.

The Preston workshop was structured in the following way. We spent the first part of the session introducing ourselves and discussing how and why the WRN came into being. We then split into four groups to address specific problem areas, before reconvening to discuss our findings and to conclude the session. Our written account follows a similar structure: our appraisal of the main problems encountered in setting up the WRN, a summary of the group discussion and concluding remarks.

Producing a paper from a workshop session in which we thought it important to stress the interconnectedness of the problem areas has been a difficult task. What has emerged is a polyphonic text, in which each of our voices registers its experiences and its appraisal of those experiences. However, this polyphony leads, at times, to a certain repetition of ideas and a retelling of events. Initially, we were unsure about the editing out of these repetitions. After deliberations about the effect upon the reader, we decided it was important to incorporate the repetitions as they occurred, and to view them creatively, as indications of a sharing of experience and, also, as markers for the most frequent and urgent insights with which the WRN has presented us. If this is the nature of polyphony then we are eager to work with it, and we would ask the reader to do the same.[3]

Deryn: How can we counter the replication of power hierarchies when organizing our women's group?

The Women's Research Network and the spin-off Women's Theory Group were established in 1992 in response to the feeling that as women postgraduates our development was compromised by power structures that acted to stifle and inhibit our intellectual exploration and expression. In particular, we felt that there was no place for us to query, or express doubt, or even, on occasion, to admit to ignorance. We felt there were few places for us within the institution that were non-judgmental and did not expect us to perform intellectually. A consensus of silence around which hierarchies of knowledge operated in a self-perpetuating way, acted to exclude those unwilling or unable to engage with particular and privileged modes of discourse.

After deciding to establish a place for ourselves which did not replicate these unacceptable structures, but was a place where we could interact in what we saw as more positive ways within the institution, we faced the day-to-day practicalities of organizing ourselves as an alternative, women-only group. This involved a range of activities: building up mailing lists of women postgraduates from across the disciplines both in Birkbeck and London University more generally; designing and displaying posters to ensure that our meetings were sufficiently well-publicized to attract women from diverse intellectual backgrounds; booking rooms; establishing programmes which reflected the broad interests of our regular attenders; as well as facilitating meetings. Obviously these were, and still are, very time-consuming and expensive tasks. At present we manage by a system of informal rotations with women volunteering to design and circulate posters, to stuff and mail envelopes, to make photocopies of material for discussion available for particular meetings; and so far, this seems to have worked quite effectively.

The way we organize ourselves on a practical level obviously has important implications for the core purpose of the network — finding new ways of talking about issues which circumvent the possessive, and often possessing methods of the institution. Faced with the problem that such a willingness to relinquish control might result either in chaos, or in inertia, we have ended up as a nominal steering committee. We have put a great deal of effort into stressing that we are open to all suggestions and contributions, that we are a group which serves rather than dictates. In renegotiating combative strategies of communication, we hoped to make our meetings more hospitable to all women, encouraging the participation of postgraduates from a variety of intellectual, ethnic, cultural or class backgrounds.

In WRN meetings there is now a strong sense that we are there to be supportive to each other. Women have been encouraged to be alert to the needs of others, and we have propagated an ethos which depends on really listening so that dialogues result in real exchanges, rather than taking place as a series of rhetorical swoops and manoeuvres. What we are aiming to achieve is an atmosphere in which all women present are given a sense of their own authority, where the inevitable theoretical disagreements take place in a way which gives space to others. This, we hope, leads not to weakened arguments but rather gives us a series of positions from which to negotiate difference in a fruitful, respectful and imaginative way. In practice, this seems to have come surprisingly easily, and has heralded for many women a new intellectual freedom. We are, however, also painfully aware that the very freedom which the WRN has provided for us may well, at some time now or in the future, be at the expense of other women within the Women's Research Network, and we hope that we are all sensitive enough to be aware of the subtle ways in which power can restructure itself insidiously.

Rebecca: Finding Common Ground

Once we had decided to set up the Women's Research Network, it seemed but a small step to put this into operation. However, there were two important and related issues which first needed to be addressed: why might we need to find common ground as women, and how can we talk to each other across the disciplines? The first of these questions is one that appears prominently on the feminist agenda at the moment, incorporating, as it does, the idea of woman as an historically gendered subject and the problem of whether gender should be isolated from other elements that possibly have equal bearing on one's social, economic and political position, such as race, class and ethnicity. In other words, is it possible for women to come together simply because they are *women* and, if so, what exactly would bind them together? Indeed, our very first session explored what we all meant by the term woman and how we could usefully define gender. There seemed to be no easy answers to these questions: we only knew that it was important for us to remain aware that the idea of gender was constantly in flux and to realize that, although we felt the need to redress the power balance within the institution by providing a female-only open space, we could not rely solely on our gender being the only constitutive point which would draw us into a cohesive whole.

Again, although we all believed in the importance of this open space, it became increasingly apparent that everyone had her own ideas about what form this should take. Some wanted a literary group while others wanted to create a more politically active force. Alternatively, there were those who considered that the group should operate mainly as a network or exist primarily to provide social interaction. There were even rumblings about a throw-back to the 70s-style consciousness-raising groups, attractive to a few but off-putting to many.

It was difficult to work with all these equally valid ideas and, inevitably, a compromise was reached. Out of approximately 3–4 sessions per term, we scheduled a formal meeting (usually consisting of a tripartite forum) and try to provide a balance with an informal session, often with an academic base so that people can swap tips, pool information, etc. These are then augmented by various other events, such as film showings, outside visits, and a study weekend. Again, the setting up of spin-off groups, such as the Women's Theory Group (involved with close analysis of theoretical texts particularly relevant to women), has been a successful way of providing something for everyone. Because a planning meeting is held at the beginning of each term, an egalitarian approach is hopefully maintained through consultation, and this meeting also provides a useful feedback session on what has happened during the previous term. This is very much in keeping with what we see as one of the basic tenets of starting a women's group, as outlined in the first UK edition of *Ms Magazine*:

> There is no leader. Part of the purpose is to challenge habits of passivity, dominance, hierarchy, and need for outside instruction. Each woman deserves to become her own leader, and that means she is listened to carefully.[4]

Listening carefully is one way we have tried to counteract the problems inherent in finding a common language, a way that we can talk to each other across the disciplines. Since the group started within the English Department and is still mainly organized by English students, it has been difficult to maintain a multi-disciplinary perspective. Even though the mailing list is composed of around 70 students from a wide variety of disciplines (eg., English, Psychology, Art History, Politics and Sociology, German, History, Philosophy, Applied Linguistics, etc.), this diversity has not been consistently represented at the meetings. Although the topics already covered by the group would seem to preclude such exclusion, with sessions on women and madness, academia, pornography, women and food, and a forum session on interdisciplinarity itself, it was felt that the WRN needed to become more pro-active in seeking out and engaging with students from other departments.

Joanne: Do we need a women-only space and why?

One of our first discussions within the WRN was around the issue of the Network being just that — a *women's* group — that is to say, a group composed of women, and not a mixed group of men and women. In many ways it was our most important formative discussion. I would like to look at the needs we felt promoted us to set up a women's space in our institution and the problems which this space has created.

The needs had to do with the space, or lack of it, that a woman's voice commands in the academic setting and the way in which women are silenced or find speaking difficult in mixed academic groups. All of us, I am sure, have felt that heart-pounding, stomach-turning moment of first hearing your voice in a seminar or question-section of a lecture. This accompanies the heart-stopping decision to make some intervention in this setting at all. There is no doubt that seminars and lectures are scenes of intense competition and performance and that while not all men feel comfortable in this envrironment, it *is* men who have up until now set the boundaries of the discourses used in the academic public sphere and have benefitted from the outcome of the jockeying for position and validation which takes place here. Of course this is more complex than a simple gender divide — there are women who can hold their own and articulate themselves well in this setting, women who, through access to power or other validatory processes, are comfortable with the status quo. However, the four of us, after one session too many struggling with these dynamics, inquired of one another if there was another way of doing things. We concluded that there was. In the thoughts that ensued and the ideals of learning and education that we articulated, we realized that at base what we were looking for was a sense of collaboration rather than competition and an environment in which problems and difficulties could be solved rather than hidden and internalized while the larger momentum of the seminar was leading off into excesses of academic performance, skill and self-promotion.

We didn't feel we could achieve this properly in a mixed setting until women felt empowered enough to carry these things through with each other. So we made the decision to make the group meetings women-only and make a safe space for the women's voice in all its various registers. That means expressing difficulty, pain, anger, encouragement, enjoyment, knowledge and a whole range of emotional and intellectual possibilities which are so often missing from academic interactions. Having made this decision, opportunities presented themselves to us to go back to much of the theory and learning which had created so many difficulties for us in the past. In other words to *share*, rather than *compete*, in our intellectual pursuits and our research.

So that has been the theory, but, of course, women can compete with each other as men can. And this is where the problems begin. The competition I have described is effectively a behaviour pattern most commonly used by men, but not a behaviour pattern used exclusively by men. And through our first year we have encountered concern from women that they were feeling excluded or intimidated by the women's space we had created. This is a hard lesson to learn. Particularly since we have all invested a great deal emotionally in the ideal of our women's space. It suggests that coming together is not enough on its own but that what is needed is a re-learning of the training we have undergone in higher education about the ways in which we share knowledge. It is as much about changing the external as expressing the internal. And this in some senses has been the idea behind building a network, so that we have a sense of ourselves as a larger multi-disciplinary, hopefully multi-institutional group.

As well as this, our women-only space has had to be interrogated — both by women within it and women outside it — about the exclusions it presents. What space is there in the term *women-only* for black women, for lesbians, for women with disabilities? A diversity which allows access to every woman is something with which we are still struggling. The fact is that our space in the Women's Research Network has not been a mixed space in many ways. Dealing with difference is never easy, particularly in an alternative space which has already been idealized by the women who create it. But asking the group what it chooses to focus on for discusssion, and to whom it actively appeals, is essential. In the process of empowering ourselves we must recognize that what we are presented with is a *hierarchy of difficulty* in terms of articulation. White middle-class women have privileges in higher education which black women do not; straight women have privileges in higher education which lesbians do not; able-bodied women have privileges in higher education which women with disabilities do not. And the question must be — where is our women-only space in relation to these realities? Our first year has proved, with its resounding absences, that creating a women-only space is simply not enough. Without a commitment to hard, painful work and self-reflexivity we ourselves can all too easily reproduce the exclusions which necessitated our empowerment in the first place.

Sally: Empowering Ourselves: Institutional Frameworks

In order to make clear our reasons for setting up the Women's Research Network it may be helpful to describe its context. The immediate context for the Network is provided by the institutional framework of Birkbeck College, and I am interested in probing a little more closely the relationship between the WRN and the College. Such an examination does not pertain solely to our own individual case but offers an example of the way in which established and, to some extent, normative power structures can respond to and co-exist with alternative 'others'. Equally important for us is an awareness of the response made by the other to its more powerful partner.

With governmental codification of competition between educational institutions and the jostling for position which has been exacerbated by the funding policies of the late 1980s and early 1990s, it is more necessary than ever that postgraduate students have as clear an understanding as possible of their function in this game of shifting rules. One useful consequence of changing policies seems to have been that the significance of postgraduates to the individual institution is now more generally appreciated. Institutional competition in the area of research could be said, in this respect, to have produced benefits, as in the increased monitoring of research projects. There is, however, also a downside. The pressure placed on established, new and would-be universities can lead to the interests of the institution being treated as paramount at the expense of the individual student. At the same time, our workshop discussion in Preston revealed the ways in which on occasion some new universities and, perhaps even more so, those colleges pushing to achieve university status, are seeking to raise their research profiles without always establishing clear structures within which their newly expanded postgraduate body can work. Uncertainty over the nature of postgraduate work and a lack of clearly-formulated and articulated guidelines and expectations seem, at least on anecdotal evidence, to be not uncommon problems in the new university sector. It is ironic that this should be the case just at the point at which similar failings are beginning to be rectified in the old universities.

The WRN at Birkbeck exists then within this broader context. The institution against which we define ourselves as 'other' can be understood as not only Birkbeck College but — admittedly with a certain lack of precision — the overall educational establishment as it is inflected by government policy. And it is within this context of an already established structure of interlinked power relations, that we need to consider the question of empowering ourselves. This is one reason why the idea of empowering ourselves is, in my opinion, as problematic as it is exciting. In our particular case, we have to recognize that from the moment of our inception as a group, our identities as individual women postgraduates were slightly altered. The WRN gave us a new collective identity which grounded the wishes of the group and gave us a new status in the institution. This is undoubtedly welcome but we need nevertheless to be aware of the risk of appropriation. The insidious co-optation of ideas of self-development and self-help and their translation into the language of entrepreneurship must make us use such phrases as empowering ourselves with care. What, we might ask further, of the danger of playing into the hands of those who impose and implement policies of increased student numbers unaccompanied by an increase in resources? Empowering ourselves is perhaps treacherously near to 'all by ourselves', an exciting initiative of self-organization turned to use by those we might with to criticize.

Birkbeck's attitude to us has been mostly very positive and in this we have been considerably luckier than some similar groups in other colleges. We are certainly luckier than those isolated individuals trying to set up groups in the face of lack of interest and hostility. Indeed, the Preston workshop brought home to us the extent of our good fortune. Nevertheless, we do need to be aware of the fact that the WRN, an organization set up in opposition to many things we found inappropriate and contrary to feminist principles, can simultaneously serve other ends than those intended. The WRN is embedded, existing from its outset as a voice of opposition but also as an already institutionalized critique of the institution. This precarious balance is perhaps symptomatic of the situation in which many academics now find themselves. Compromises must constantly be made in spite of strongly-held principles, and likewise, the WRN must try to function as cannily as possible within existing institutional constraints. In recognizing this shared experience we are led to acknowledge that many people in education are required to mediate between institutional imperatives and personal convictions and that it would be a mitake to regard Birkbeck, our institution, as a monolithic or to allow a 'them and us' attitude to take hold. My words of warning notwithstanding, we have, as Deryn and Joanne have described, established an alternative to the department-organized seminars, we constantly do try to create a genuinely less competitive working space and we hope that we can bring back into the mainstream what we have learned, so as to encourage gradual yet lasting changes. To remain on the periphery is probably to leave problem issues untackled at source and, equally disturbingly, to fulfil a role as official 'other' to the mainstream curriculum which may then be left unchallenged by us.

The Workshop

After outlining our own experiences in setting up a women's group, we moved on to the discussion part of the workshop session. This was run with the objective of discovering how other women were coping in an academic environment, whether anyone had started or joined a women's group and whether this had, in fact, helped them in any way. This was an integral part of the workshop which was designed to examine the four specific areas we had already defined: power hierarchies, finding common ground, women-only spaces and institutional frameworks. Splitting the 15 participants into smaller groups in order to discuss these areas in more detail gave us all the opportunity to move beyond these original starting points and raise further issues. Although each group began by discussing a particular question, the interconnection of the issues soon necessitated broader discussions.

We began by looking at the women's organizations we already belonged to and why. It was interesting to discover that most participants already belonged to a women's group, chosen specifically for the nature of its women-only space. However, we had all chosen our group for different reasons — social inter-action, professional network, support mechanism — and it was considered that all these reasons were equally valid and necessary. From this we moved on to discussing how female students can feel isolated within their institutions, particularly if returning to study or if working as the only woman in a male-dominated discipline or department. It was also noted that it could be very dispiriting to make contact with another woman in the same field, only to find her unapproachable or unsympathetic. This inevitably brought up the problem of how women adjust to working or studying within the hierarchy and, particularly, issues of power and territoriality.

The problems of competition and oppressive hierarchies can and do exist between women and positive strategies must be constantly encouraged to negotiate this reality. For instance, it was suggested that the purpose and ethos of the group should be verbalized at the beginning of each meeting and that in this way a 'contract of attitude' could be set up between participants. In the light of the discussion around issues of exclusion, it was suggested that groups for black women, lesbians and disabled women might be set up to allow the space which the mixed group denies. In order not to lose a sense of unity with all women, these groups could be affiliated to the larger group. From this, we deduced that it was not enough just to *be* women but that all women needed to make a commitment to *being* supportive. Nevertheless, there was agreement that women do share fundamental problems around the nature of research, regard-less of their particular disciplinary background. The act of coming together provides support through the articulation of these issues with each other.

Conclusion

Engaging with issues of empowerment involves inherently problematic dynamics; these were as evident in the workshop session as they have been in the WRN. The participants agreed that there were certain areas of difficulty which must be negotiated in order to create an accessible and open space for everyone.

Both in founding the WRN and running this workshop, we began with a profusion of questions and, perhaps, a certain amount of self-doubt. Although many of these questions remain unanswered and, indeed, may continue to do so, simply voicing these uncertainties has become a step towards empowerment. The workshop was an encouraging sign that, although the problems which we encountered at Birkbeck were also encountered by other women students, these did not have to be a major stumbling block and could, in fact, be part of a learning process. The important point which was reiterated again and again during our workshop — and during the conference as a whole — was that space for the multiplicity of women's voices should and must be made.

The Women's Research Network has been an experiment. We have tried out various ways of structuring our meetings; we have also tried different kinds of topics in order to see what works best, and to provide some variety. This account is, by its very nature, only part of the story. In holding the Preston workshop with other women, and writing it collaboratively, we have been able to experience other forms of co-operation. We need to provide supportive rather than competitive structures. We need to listen to all our voices rather than hearing only one voice. Only through such processes of empowerment, can we address the problems faced by us all in setting our own agendas as women postgraduates in higher education.

Notes

1 Horer, S. and Socquet, J. (1974) *La création étouffée* [Smothered creativity], Reprinted in Marks, E. and de Courtivron, I. (Ed.) (1981) *New French Feminisms: An Anthology*, Hemel Hempstead: Harvester, p. 243.
2 Birkbeck is a college of the University of London, and provides mature students with the opportunity to study part-time in the evenings while being in full-time employment. Postgraduate students form a large percentage of its overall intake. It is possible to undertake research on either a part-time or a full-time basis.
3 We would like to thank all the participants and acknowledge their contribution to this discussion. This chapter in its current form has benefitted greatly from their input.
4 'Starting groups: The basics', *Ms Magazine*, Nov/Dec 1992, **III**,(3).

Chapter 8

Life Lines: Writing and Writer's Block in the Context of Women's Studies[1]

Trev Broughton

I have taught Women's Studies at the University of York for seven years, and I have, in my time, sauntered out of the library with *Exotic Interludes* in one hand and *Macho Sluts* in the other, head held high, defying the librarian to smirk. So researching this paper has been a chastening experience.

> Dear Ms Broughton. We have been unable to trace the item *Free Yourself to Write* and require a photocopy of your reference.
>
> Dear Ms Broughton. Your Interlibrary Loan *Writer's Block and How to Use It* has now arrived and may be picked up at the issue desk.

Scurrying, mortified, from the library with my shameful trophy tucked between two volumes of Proust, I know at last what it feels like to be a dirty old man at the newsagent. 'It's not for me,' I want to shout. 'It's for my students, it's for my research.'

That books about the writing process and writing anxiety should, in an academic library, seem more like pornography than pornography, is to be expected. Cultures, even professedly liberal ones, generate their own taboos, their own magnetic fields of fear, guilt and desire. This happens to be one of ours. Consider, for instance, one of the words heard most frequently on any campus (and the more strongly continual assessment has taken hold, the more you will hear it):

> *Deadline.* 1860. 1. A line that does not move or run. 2. Mil. A line drawn round a military prison, beyond which a prisoner may be shot down. 1868. [Shorter Oxford English Dictionary]

Of course, we all need deadlines; you can't just abolish them. Institutions thrive on them. So do some writers. But there it is: 'Women's Studies Deadline'. A chilling oxymoron at the heart of our undisciplined discipline. A line that will not move or run. Cross it at your peril. My aim in what follows is not to tackle the many challenges and problems besetting academic assessment within Women's Studies, although the issues of writer's block and women-centred pedagogies necessarily, and properly, overlap. My purpose is threefold. I want to argue that we should address in a creative way and as a matter of urgency the fact that many Women's Studies students suffer from writing anxiety; to assess the usefulness of the available literature; and to propose some ways forward.

Contexts

Some time ago I realized I was spending a great deal of time with individual students who were, in various ways, failing to write: failing to get started on essays; failing to translate notes into prose; failing to shape ideas; sometimes even failing to hand over completed work to a reader. So great was their emotional and political, not to say economic, investment in Women's Studies, moreover, that they were experiencing these academic difficulties as assaults on their identities as feminists. Day after day I heard myself making the same reassuring noises, offering the same trite bits of advice, scarcely sounding convincing, even, or especially, to myself. I found that our relationship — a power relationship when all's said and done — rendered my own experience of the problem either irrelevant and self-defeating (after all, I'd finished my degree, hadn't I?) or ineffectual ('lots of people feel like this, honestly'), or simply inadmissible: my student didn't want to know that her tutor felt as she did; didn't want her terror reflected back with a seal of teacherly legitimacy. After struggling for an hour with her, trying to scrape the fear from her guts, and tossing some half-baked pieties at her in exchange, I would return to my own writing nightmare, which had, I would console myself, the virtue of being a proper grown-up nightmare: fear of publication, fear of research ratings, fear of being found out. If all else failed, as it often did, and a temporary setback congealed into a fixed pattern of anxiety and delay, I would send the student along to Dr Caroline Hall, the University Student Counsellor who was, after all, trained and paid for that kind of thing.

After one particularly gruelling session, I made an appointment to see Dr Hall, to discover from an expert how to deal with students' writer's block. Caroline, it turned out, came to that meeting with her own history of involvement in the subject, in many ways different from mine. As a psychologist she had a longstanding professional interest in the mechanics of writer's block, and as a counsellor had a strong empirical sense of the extent, diversity and seriousness of the problem: indeed she was in the throes of writing an article about it (Hall, 1992). She also came with a sense of frustration that her own expertise and experience in the field was being squandered at an institutional level, and that her attempts to suggest a revision of University strategy had so far gone unheeded. In a purely professional sense, the meeting was timely on both sides.

The timeliness, like most coincidence, was overdetermined. Within minutes, we had abandoned our careful agenda about other people's problems and were pouring out our own anxieties, our own fears and frustrations about writing. We amazed and delighted each other with epic tales of procrastination, prevarication, work begun but never finished, work finished only to be buried in obscure journals no-one would ever read. Looking back, we now recognize that our own painful failures to complete projects — mine on women's writing, Caroline's, even more ironically, on writer's block — were intimately and dialectically connected with our perceived failure to help individual students complete theirs. For the moment, however, it was enough simply to admit our fears and laugh about them.

I learned a lot from that meeting: more, indeed, than I had learned from several years of solitary struggle. I learned that many of the techniques I had picked up for helping students were widely practised; that there were others (Flower, 1981; Annas, 1985); but that in isolation problem-solving exercises might not be enough. After all, both Caroline and I between us knew every trick in the (unwritten) book. I also learned that the worst aspect of the problem was the feeling of powerlessness and loneliness it engendered. I learned, in other words, that talking about it helped. I have since come to understand writer's block as, like writing itself, an intersubjective process rather than a condition, as an argument between the would-be writer and some remembered or introjected interlocutor; and to realize that this destructive relationship thrives on the secrecy and mystique of the 'scene of writing'. Finally, Caroline confirmed what I had suspected: that the counselling service saw proportionately more students from Women's Studies than from any other department except Music — up to 20 per cent — and that many of these clients were having problems getting down to writing. While it would be unwise to draw any hasty conclusions from this statistic, since Women's Studies may be a more 'help-seeking' culture than Maths or Engineering (see Bloom, 1985: 127), it is, nonetheless, a worrying phenomenon.

It is important to stress that I am not claiming that women *per se* have more problems with academic writing then men. Writing problems are context-specific, and relate to a wide range of personal, structural and ideological factors as well as to gender (Bloom, 1985). Indeed, in the US, where the writing process has been extensively investigated, most studies seem to demonstrate that insofar as evidence of difference appears, *dispositional writing anxiety*, a generalized fear of writing, occurs more frequently in male students than in female (Daly, 1985: 47–8). There is, however, one relevant exception to this tendency. Among a relatively small sample of returners to college over the age of 22, M. O. Thompson (1981) found significantly higher levels of writing anxiety among women than among men. Since Women's Studies attracts a high proportion of mature students this is an important finding. Certainly it corresponds to my own intuitive sense that, far from being the empowering or liberatory experience we might expect, writing, for many Women's Studies students, is often stressful and even disabling.[2]

We do not have to look far to discover possible reasons for this. If we encourage non-standard entrants; candidates for whom English is a second or third language, candidates returning to education after a long break and candidates with mainly vocational training; we are inviting groups who are structurally disadvantaged in a variety of ways with regard to the demands of so called higher academic writing. If we invite disaffected physicists, zoologists and mathematicians, we should not be surprised to find that academic writing is something of a mystery to them. If we take historians, literary critics and sociologists who have studied nothing but history or literature or sociology for three years or more, it follows that interdisciplinary work will be a frightening, as well as an exciting challenge. If we add to this brew the fact that Women's Studies students are typically highly motivated with correspondingly high expectations of themselves, and are working within complex domestic, financial and political situations, and the fact that feminist knowledge is currently in a ticklish condition and not in the mood to provide easy answers to urgent questions,[3] we have a very volatile constituency: so volatile that it is tempting to devote our energies as teachers to finding productive common ground in seminars and to let writing fend for itself.

One further factor comes to mind, one it is irresponsible to ignore. Teachers of Women's Studies, like all academics, may find themselves caught in a cycle for which 'publish or perish' is rapidly becoming a frozen metaphor. Be published, often, in the right forms and in the right places, or be punished, by having your teaching and administrative loads increased: this is now the reality for many individuals, many departments, many institutions. It is hardly surprising, in these circumstances, that what advice we do offer about getting down to writing has a slightly hysterical edge, since we may be counselling supervisees at the expense of our own research.

The anxieties we might feel, as teachers and students of Women's Studies, are underscored and perhaps even reinforced by feminist folk-knowledge about the uneasy relationship between women and writing: what Gilbert and Gubar (1979) have theorized as 'the anxiety of authorship'. Literary history is punctuated by women's agony over the impropriety, the danger, the certain failure of their attempts to write, while there is a whole industry of feminist literary historiography, and feminist literary theory, committed to analysing women's so-called silence. It sometimes worries me that much feminist theory is unintentionally complicit with the 'graphocentrism' of the academy, even as it appears to assume the inevitability, possibly the desirability, of women's alienation from the pen, and from the symbolic order it inscribes. In these circumstances one can easily slip into equating our academic writing with the phallic patriarchal pen itself. This may be a productive analogy but it may also foreclose debate.[4]

Life Lines: Writing on Writing

Writing anxiety and the writing process turn out to be interdisciplinary issues, and hence promising from a Women's Studies perspective.[5] Advice handbooks, feminist literary criticism, theoretical and therapeutic accounts of writer's block, and pedagogical studies of the writing classroom all have a bearing on the problem. Most departmental and institutional guides offer brisk and cheery advice on note-taking, planning and referencing, and may include a problem-solving section, though they seldom address themselves to the more troubling questions of, for instance, access to a 'voice', motivation, or discipline.[6] More helpful in this respect are the many guides to the creative writing process, which often include material on emotion, overcoming blocks, organizing time, and so on. Works such as those by Pearlie McNeill (1992), Victoria Nelson (1985), and Joan Minninger (1980) are a rich source of writing exercises, and deal extensively and sensitively with the 'genuine fear of reprisals or repercussions' that assail us when we begin to write (McNeill, 1992: 3), although they do so with the assumption of a personal vocation to write, and hence of the need for individual strategies to realize that vocation. These manuals can be both reassuring and practical, though, because they construct an intimate, exclusive relationship between text and reader, they may do little in themselves to dismantle the aura of isolation that is so corrosive a part of writing's mystique.

The other problem with the creative writing literature is that it often starts from the premise that one should literally reverse the rules and habits learned in formal education.[7] Unfortunately, this is seldom the case within the academy, even in the 'progressive' purlieus of Women's Studies. Manuals typically speak of relaxing into the writing process, getting in touch with the child in the unconscious, and respecting creative urges. All this is seductive, but has limited application in an academic environment in which one may have to write to order, on subjects not necessarily of one's own choosing, and to criteria that, however woman-centred, are still critical.

The British literature on successful creative writing is distinguished by its long-standing workshop tradition which, stripped of some of its authoritatian mannerisms, has played an important role in workers' and feminist educational intitiatives.[8] In this respect it has much in common with the significant body of work, encompassing feminist aesthetics, composition pedagogy and psychology, to have emerged in the United States from the writing revolution in the composition classroom. Here, fairly rigid conceptions of 'composition' have coexisted with and are often challenged by politically informed ideals of diversity and equity.[9] The keystone of the North American composition class is the notion of writing as process rather than as product. This stress on 'pre-writing, free writing, rough drafts . . . learning logs, reading diaries, journals, and exploratory essays' (Caywood and Overing, 1987: xiii), maps comfortably on to many aspects of a certain style of feminist theory about female identity and mental health.[10] Though unwilling to explore the limits of its own version of individualism, the New Writing literature offers an inspiring insight into what it is possible to achieve within the context of higher education, provides a vital corrective to the academic obsession with dotted i's and crossed t's, and directly addresses the dilemma facing feminist teachers everywhere:

> Can we teach writing to our students in a way that validates who they are, that allows them to handle their materials confidently and comfortably, with discipline and integrity, and that also gives them the survival skills to write in a way that will be acceptable to the world that we are training them to enter.
>
> (Annas, 1985: 361)

There is, of course, a vast psychological literature on the causes, symptoms and treatments of writer's block[11]. Robert Boice (1985) has put into practice and compared many of the available therapies, and admits, rather shamefacedly that his academic clients seem to respond best to behaviourist strategies: more or less crude systems of externally moderated rewards and punishments.[12] Most practitioners, however, work with either cognitive or psychoanalytic models. At the cognitive end of the spectrum, observers such as Mike Rose (1985) regard writer's block and writing anxiety as signs of faulty ways of controlling the conscious processes involved in composing (premature editing, indecision, self-doubt, etc.). In a Women's Studies context such observations have to be used with caution, as our students may actively dispute the legitimacy of the cognitive strategies available, or the aesthetic criteria on which they may covertly be based. On the other hand, examining our typical patterns of thinking, whether or not we go on to diagnose them as 'maladaptive self-talk', can be helpful and save time.[13] At the psychoanalytic end, theorists such as Leader argue that cognitive errors and technical difficulties:

> while painful and important to solve, are not actually writer's block: writer's block is what is at stake when, knowing the correct procedures, one obsessively returns to bad practices and drives up known dead-ends.
>
> (Leader, 1991: 17–18)

However, the distinction between writer's block as something you can cure and something you can learn your way out of doesn't seem especially helpful to me, and I prefer to see writer's block as a continuum of difficulties ranging from the contextual to the cognitive to the unconscious.[14] It is here, interestingly, that feminist theory comes into its own as a way of negotiating the gulf. Put simply, its dismantling of the boundaries between *inner* and *outer*, private and public, personal and political, allows for a flexible conceptualization of both writer's block and literary production — one that embraces the need for physical as well as psychic space, and that can value, politically and aesthetically, a wide range of strategies of writerly resistance and writerly survival.

A Practical Way Forward?

Drawing on the range of ideas and materials identified here, and on our own conviction that writing anxiety, like writing itself, might more effectively be dealt with collectively than individually, Caroline and I devised a series of workshops based on a mixture of discussion, writing exercises, spoken and written advice. Our aims were to provide new students and returning students with a kitbag of tools for engaging actively with the process of writing and for managing this effectively; to raise consciousness about writing difficulties as a shared problem and a shared responsibility, albeit one involving a vast array of specific difficulties and challenges; and to dissolve some of the intransigent boundaries between speaking and writing, reading and writing, thinking and writing, writing and being read. It seemed to us that the group-based approach has several advantages over individual tutorials or counselling sessions, quite apart from the more equitable distribution of energy and effort it represented. Obviously, like any therapeutic community, it might offer a safe space in which to bring to consciousness and to celebrate the elaborate rituals and the survival strategies implicit in both writing and not writing: a space in which to take risks (to try out how it feels to be read, for instance). A further advantage was the possibility of making the members of the group aware of themselves and each other as a resource: as a potentially user-friendly community of readers and editors. As it worked out, the workshops have the unforeseen benefit of exposing, in a light-hearted way, the often unacknowledged element of competitiveness that, left to itself, can throttle even a Women's Studies class.

Broadly, the workshops cover the themes of getting started, time management, problem-solving and working with a reader. However the format of the sessions is as important to their success as the topics covered. Practical advice about the mechanics of the writing process alternates with diagnostic exercises aimed at uncovering individual and collective strengths and weaknesses, and with more speculative discussion about our attitudes to writing. In practice, these different modes are remarkably compatible. One can, for instance, introduce the protocol of *brainstorming* by collectively generating ideas on the subject of skills involved in essay writing. The resultant list, which will include everything from correct punctuation to working across disciplines, can then be used as the basis for assessing one's own characteristics as a writer. This may lead to a more general discussion of how the resources and needs of the group might be matched to each other. Again, one might suggest as a time-management exercise a daily five minute bout of *free writing* describing the building each participant calls home. Each member will be asked to address the task with a different type of reader in mind: an architect, a photographer, a burglar, a psychoanalyst, or whatever. The resulting writing can then be used in small groups to identify, by analogy, the different kinds of signposts required by readers, and to generate ideas about what a Women's Studies reader might require from an essay.

There is no recipe for a successful academic writing workshop. In a Women's Studies context, the urgent need to establish common ground across disciplines focuses one's mind in a way the creative writing class need not. Furthermore, the design of each session has to take into account a range of factors, from non-negotiable criteria such as institutionally-imposed modes of assessment, the profile and size of the student cohort, to more flexible but equally important considerations such as the spacing and timing of essay deadlines, whether or not the workshops are optional, and so on. In adapting the available strategies and models to the needs of the Centre, I have found it useful to bear in mind the four themes Robert Boice has identified as the 'four p's' of writing block treatment: process, product, productivity and politics (Boice, 1985: 212–4).

Despite the evolution of process-oriented pedagogies, the process of higher academic writing remains one of the best kept secrets of college life. Women's Studies, for historical reasons, has tended to gain its institutional foothold in postgraduate courses rather than, say, in the school syllabus, so it is vital that we set about demystifying the process of advanced essay-writing: by exploring a range of writing practices in the group; by breaking down the process into its composite parts and by sharing ideas for achieving efficiency. A simple first step is to ask each member of the group in turn to describe their own scene of writing: how, when, where, and within what rituals does writing take place? The point is not to prescribe 'best practice' but to allow students to become self-conscious, as individuals and as a group, about the process of composing, about what works for them and about the diversity and sheer innovativeness of the strategies they have at their disposal. Sharing and comparing rituals and practices, they may begin to demystify the process for themselves, and develop a sense of control over it. Analysing what does work may also be the first step towards identifying weakness in current practice: towards spotting the points at which writing typically falters, or stops, or fails to appear at all. As Pamela Annas (1985) notes, 'Sometimes simply knowing that their writing block is there, lurking round the particular corner of the process, makes it slightly less terrifying.'[15] Beginning with a question about current writing practice (rather than about blocks or fears) allows the group to acknowledge that writing sometimes does take place. We have a great deal of information and advice about what goes wrong in the writing process and about ways of correcting it, but comparatively little about the conditions and routines of successful or happy writing. Once the scene of writing has been set, one can suggest new strategies for enhancing the process, such as nutshelling, drawing issue trees, elaborating on key words, etc., (Flower, 1981).

Demystifying the process need not occur at the expense of understanding the product; Women's Studies is ideally about the generation and spreading of new ideas, so it is vital that students communicate effectively to their readers. Workshops should thus encourage students to work with each other to produce reader-friendly work, and to see academic writing as a job to be done, with specific purposes. Incidentally, this goal involves facilitators in some hard thinking about what we really do expect from a Women's Studies essay. For instance, what do we actually mean by *interdisciplinarity*; How do we recognize and reward it? Do we mean ventures in an unfamiliar discipline, or manoeuvres between disciplines? And in what circumstances is *the personal* really appropriate? We need to be able to spell out at least some preliminary guidelines for our students if we expect them to write regularly and boldly.

For excellent reasons, Women's Studies courses tend to be assessed by submission of written work rather than exams. This means our students are usually expected to produce a lot of writing over a long period of time. Time management skills may have to be learned or relearned in order to sustain this level of output in often difficult working conditions. But productivity is important not just because the overwhelming evidence suggests that practice is the key to good writing, but because regular productivity can enhance one's sense of competence and control (Boice, 1985).

Finally, the aim of a writing workshop should be to transform, as far as possible, the relationships of production and consumption within which writing happens. The politics of the Women's Studies writing workshop are explosive and we have to be prepared to see our criteria of assessment tested and even undermined. I would argue that this is a necessary risk. Only if we give students access to the tools available for academic writing, and to a consciousness of their strengths and resources as a group can we expect them to mount a coherent and successful critique of existing paradigms of knowledge, including, of course, our own.

Conclusion

Extensive work exists on how to help students with their writing. The challenges are to adapt models of writing pedagogy developed in the United States Composition laboratory, in the therapist's clinic and in the leftist creative writing movement, to explicitly interdisciplinary contexts and to feminist goals, and to enable Women's Studies teachers from whatever discipline — sociology, history, medicine — to gain access to them. Looking back over the project to date, I should emphasize that there were still students whose writing problems were so intense and complex that our best collective efforts failed to help them — then again, professional conselling and the medical establishment failed as well. My fear is that if we don't address the problem of writer's block in Women's Studies in a considered and systematic way, the history of our endeavour will be strewn with the names of those who, and here I use our official university jargon with all the irony I can muster, 'failed to submit'.

The Getting Down to Writing project is still in its infancy, and we, the students, Caroline, and myself, are continually rethinking our needs and reworking how we can meet them. Anecdotal evidence suggests that we are making some progress. One student wrote to me after an early workshop:

> It was so reassuring to realise that I'm not completely insane/hopeless/
> idiotic, and that it's a difficult process for everyone. It was also a big
> relief to bring it out in the open and laugh at our fears and rituals.
> Of course the writing I have to do this week still looms terrifyingly,
> but I do feel calmer and less isolated, and can see that perhaps it doesn't
> have to be approached as a life and death struggle of epic proportions.[16]

Surveying the range of work on writing in other fields I often feel that we are simply reinventing the wheel. On the other hand, as one student pointed out, some wheels do need reinventing. As teachers of Women's Studies we may easily become so immersed in the richness and variety of our materials, and there is so much we want our students to know that we forget that our job is to enable them to generate their own knowledges for a newer day.

The increased emphasis nationally on skills and training at higher degree level has favoured the development and implementation of projects such as ours, and we now have a writing workshop scheduled as a regular part of our training programme. The university is looking into applying the kinds of model we have developed in Women's Studies elsewhere on campus. How successful the writing workshops have been is not easy to gauge. Last year more students completed the MA on time than ever before, with a large number submitting their work early. I am inclined, however, to attribute this to the fact that students are running out of money earlier than ever, and being forced to move on. Maybe those behaviourists were right after all.

Notes

1 I would like to acknowledge the contribution to this paper of the MA students, past and present, of the Centre for Women's Studies, University of York, especially those involved in the pilot project 'Getting Down To Writing'. The Innovations Fund of the University provided initial funding for the project. Thanks most of all to Dr Caroline Hall for her collaboration, wisdom and friendship.

2 Thomspon found that the returning student has problems with 'finding the right word, getting started writing, imposing organization, and overcoming the panic and avoidance defences' (1981: 8).

3 I have in mind the fact that Women's Studies students are likely to encounter serious challenges to their commonsense assumptions about what it might mean to be a woman; about whether the category 'woman' is philosophically and politically tenable; and about how such challenges can be translated into theory and practice. See for example, Spelman, (1990); Riley, (1988); Fuss (1990).

4 This is, of course, a crude caricature of a huge and diverse body of scholarship. Futhermore, those students trained in the subtle arts of metaphor and paradox will find other bits of themselves to write with. For a Women's Studies candidate intent on a critique of heterosexism in the welfare benefits system, the advice 'write your body' won't butter many parsnips.

5 Maxine Hairston (see Frey, 1987) sees linguistics, anthropology, and clinical and cognitive psychology as contributing to the study of the writing process.

6 An honourable exception here is Caroline's own manual for blocked students (Hall, forthcoming 1994).

7 'My writing belongs to me. No one will collect it, grade it . . . critique it' (Minninger, 1980: 65).

8 Compare, for instance, the approaches of Hobsbaum (1992) and McNeill (1992).

9 'Equity, as we understand it, creates new standards which accommodate and nurture differences. Equity fosters the individual voice in the classroom, investing students with confidence in their own authority. Equity unleashes the creative potential of heterogeneity' (Caywood and Overing, 1987: xi). See also Hilgers and Marsella (1992); McLeod and Soven (1992).

10 Feminist work on writing perdagogy tends to take its starting point from Carol Gilligan, Nancy Chodorow, or Adrienne Rich. See Caywood and Overing, 1987: passim.

11 The terrain is usefully surveyed in Leader (1991) and Boice (1985).

12 Boice cites the work of Nurnberger and Zimmerman (1985), who, beginning with evidence that 'contingency management' might work 'devised a "productive avoidance" technique that virtually ensures writing by having the client write out checks for a meaningful sum to a hated organization (e.g., the Ku Klux Klan) which are to be mailed on any scheduled writing day when the preset number of pages are not completed' (p. 198).

13 Boice cites three examples of what is called the 'maladaptive self-talk' typical of the cognitive processes of a blocked writer: '(a) They question their own performance and worry about the performance of others; (b) they devalue the task or situation and wonder about alternatives; and (c) they are preoccupied with anticipation of punishment and loss of esteem' (1985: 206).

14 In any case, my experience suggest that pratfalls at the level of technique, inappropriately handled, are the swiftest route to giant unconscious blocks.

15 Annas asks her Writing as Women group to perform this exercise on paper, with particular attention to the material conditions of writing (1985: 368).

16 *Private correspondence*, June 8 1992. Comparison between this student's route towards empowerment with that of Cixous is suggestive here: 'I have children, a job, but none of these things ever stopped me from writing. *When it's a question of life and death one always finds time to write*' (Hélène Cixous in Sellers, 1989: 18; emphasis mine).

References

ANNAS, P. (1985) 'Style as politics: A feminist approach to the teaching of writing', *College English*, **47**(4), (April) pp. 360–71.

BLOOM, L. Z. (1985) 'Anxious writers in context: Graduate school and beyond' in ROSE, M. (Ed.) *When a Writer Can't Write: Studies in Writer's Block and Other Composing Process Problems*, New York: Guildford Press, pp. 119–33.

BOICE, R. (1985) 'Psychotherapies for writing blocks', in ROSE, M. (Ed.) *When a Writer Can't Write: Studies in Writer's Block and Other Composing Process Problems*, New York and London: Guildford Press, pp. 182–218.

CAYWOOD, C. L. and OVERING, G. R. (Eds) (1987) *Teaching Writing: Pedagogy, Gender and Equity*, Albany, NY: SUNY Press.

DALY, J. A (1985) 'Writing apprehension' in ROSE, M. (Ed.) *When a Writer Can't Write: Studies in Writer's Block and Other Composing Process Problems*, New York and London: Guildford Press, pp. 43–82.

FLOWER, L. (1981) *Problem-Solving Strategies for Writing*, New York: Harcourt Brace Jovanovich.

FREY, O. (1987) 'Equity and peace in the new writing class' in CAYWOOD, C. L. and OVERING, G. R. (Eds) *Teaching Writing: Pedagogy, Gender and Equity*, Albany, NY: SUNY Press, pp. 93–106.

FUSS, D. (1990) *Essentially Speaking: Feminism, Nature and Difference*, New York: Routledge.

GILBERT, S. and GUBAR, S. (1979) *The Madwoman in the Attic: The Woman Writer and the Nineteenth-Century Literary Imagination*, New Haven, CT: Yale University Press.

HYALL, C. (1992) 'Fear of failure and the writer's block' in *Psychosomatics: Medicine, Metaphor, Myth or Madness*, London: City University, pp. 15–19.

HALL, C. (forthcoming 1994) *Getting Down To Writing: A Students' Guide to Overcoming Writer's Block*.

HILGERS, T. L. and MARSELLA, J. (1992) *Making Your Writing Programme Work: A Guide to Good Practice*, London: Sage.

HOBSBAUM, P. (1992) 'The Teaching of Creative Writing', in MONTEITH, M. and MILES, R. (Eds) *Teaching Creative Writing*, Buckingham: Open University Press, pp. 24–33.

LEADER, Z. (1991) *Writer's Block*, Baltimore: Johns Hopkins.

MCLEOD, S. H. snd SOVEN, M. (Eds) (1992) *Writing Across the Curriculum: A Guide to Developing Programmes*, London: Sage.

MCNEILL, P. (1992) *Because You Want to Write: A Workbook for Women*, London: Scarlet Press.

MINNINGER, J. (1980) *Free Yourself to Write*, San Francisco, CA: Workshops for Innovative Teaching.

NELSON, V. (1985) *Writer's Block and How to Use it*, Cincinnati, OH: Writer's Digest Press.

RILEY, D. (1988) *Am I That Name? Feminism and the Category of Woman in History*, Basingstoke, UK: Macmillan.

ROSE, M. (Ed.) (1985) *When a Writer Can't Write: Studies in Writer's Block and Other Composing Process Problems*, New York and London: Guildford Press.

SELLERS, S. (Ed.) (1989) *Delighting the Heart: A Notebook by Women Writers*, London: Women's Press.

SPELMAN, E. (1990) *Inessential Woman: Problems of Exclusion in Feminist Thought*, London: Women's Press.

THOMPSON, M. O. (1981) *The Returning Student: Writing Anxiety and General Anxiety*, ERIC Document Reproduction Service No. ED 214558.

Chapter 9

The Influence of Feminism on Black Women in the Higher Education Curriculum

Kalwant Bhopal

All black people are subordinated by racial oppression, women are subordinated by sexual domination, and black women are subordinated by both, as well as class.

(Foster-Clark, 1987:46)

Introduction

Black[1] women's experiences in higher education have rarely been discussed. What are the experiences of black women in higher education? How do they differ from the experiences of white women? What differences do colour and culture make to these experiences? How can feminist ideas help us to analyse the process black women go through in higher education? How can the situation be improved for black women?

Black women have been and are entering the arena of higher education and it needs to be recognized that their experiences are different from the experiences of white women in society. Their experiences need to be recognized as not only experiences of women, but as experiences of black women who may suffer racism in society, who have different personal experiences from white women. We need a forum for the discussion of such issues, and must recognize them as fundamental to an understanding of black women's experiences in higher education.

My own experiences as a black woman (of Indian descent) have prompted me to write this chapter. As a black woman I am able to see the experiences of black women both as an academic (a lecturer) and as a student (PhD research scholar). I am able to see both sides of the coin: from the perspective of the student who feels she has no power, and from the perspective of the lecturer who may also feel powerless and vulnerable, as I myself have felt, being the only black female member of staff in an academic institution. In many instances, I have felt very isolated and alone, unable to identify with other members of staff and also with the subject matter being taught. Some areas that need to be discussed regarding the experiences of black women in higher education include: black women's exclusion from higher education, the influence of stereotypes, academic research, language and power. This chapter will examine such issues and explore how the situation can be improved for black women and their position validated.

Black Women's Exclusion from Higher Education

Within higher education, there exists a feeling of isolation and alienation in which black women may experience a lack of empathy and a lack of identity with other students and with staff. There is also some sense of dissonance with the subject matter taught, in which there exists a notion of exclusion. This exclusion takes place on the grounds of culture, difference and the notion of *other*. Culture itself is a complex term, frequently important to people's sense and identity of self. It is diverse. Different communities have different values and different ways of life. The definition of culture is not necessarily limited to religious beliefs, communal rituals or shared traditions. These interactions provide a way of life which define a social collectivity. Culture is not necessarily understood as what expresses the identity of a community, but may refer to the processes and categories by which communities are defined as such, how they are specific and different. The diverse bases of cultural differentiation include ethnicity, caste, class, gender, religion, language, dress. Black women's culture is regarded as deviant as judged in comparison to white culture. Indeed, there exists a notion of superiority/inferiority which reinforces the deviant other. Difference, therefore, is regarded as deviance (Brah, 1992; Lawrence, 1982; Phoenix, 1991).

This is also reflected in the subjects taught within higher education which exclude black women and do not take into consideration the significance of ethnic differences. The subjects taught are usually ethnocentric and disregard the notion of ethnic diversity; there is the assumption that all forms of oppression are supported by traditional western thinking. For example, some white feminists (Finch, 1983; Oakley, 1973) have argued that the family is the key site of oppression for women and we need to abolish the family in its existing form to achieve equality. This suggestion however, is threatening to black women, because many black women find the family to be the least oppressive institution. Indeed, in the family organization, they may experience a sense of dignity, self-worth and security that they do not experience in the outside world. Also, black families are not necessarily composed of a man, a woman and children. There are many black single parent and homosexual families. Re-affirming the importance of the family as a kinship structure can sustain and nourish individuals. Hindu and Sikh cultures, for example, look to the family for the security and comfort they need, to obtain a separate identity which gives them a sense of belonging and a sense of shared empathy. hooks (1984) argues;

> White feminists act as if black women did not know sexist oppression existed until they voiced feminist sentiment. They believe they are providing black women with 'the' analysis and 'the' program for liberation.
>
> (hooks, 1984:10)

hooks argues that feminists do not understand and cannot imagine how black women also live in oppressive situations and she states that black women 'often acquire an awareness of patriarchal politics from their lived experience, just as they develop strategies of resistance' (hooks, 1984:11).

The concentration on cultural differences between black and white people has frequently obscured the fact that cultural beliefs, identities and practices necessarily embody the structural forces that affect people's lives, and that culture is dynamic and not static. For example, Phoenix (1991) argues that the attention given to young black mothers who are devalued helps constitute black women as abnormal mothers and means that they are visible only as members of a stigmatized group. Phoenix argues that contrary to popular belief, some young black women have children, not to rely on state benefits or council housing, but because they want them and do not see their age as a limiting factor. Phoenix considers that moral panics arising from motherhood in the teenage years are unjustified. Women who become mothers in their teenage years do so under difficult circumstances and sometimes because they want to. Indeed, studies that focus on black people have frequently used a narrow definition of cultural influence to explain their behaviour (Watson, 1977; Wilson, 1978). Such explanations are unsatisfactory, because they oversimplify cultural influence and thus reinforce the social construction of black people as deviant from the norms of white British behaviour. Black feminists maintain that the black family is a qualitatively different proposition from the family structures in which white women are involved. The black feminist challenge to the unitary nature of the family as a site of female oppression indicates that the family cannot be easily defined. The black family, like the white family, does not take a particular form.

Another example of the exclusion of black women from the feminist movement is the notion of work. Some feminists have talked about work outside the home as the key to liberation, but have ignored the fact that a vast majority of black women are already working outside the home. Many black women do menial jobs that neither liberate them from dependence on men, nor make them economically self-sufficient. These women are excluded, their experiences are not seen as relevant, they are not seen as important or as making a valuable contribution (Collins, 1991; Davis, 1981; hooks, 1984). Here the term developed by Adrienne Rich (1990), the notion of '*white solipsism*', is appropriate. Rich uses this term as a political term to describe the tendency to think, imagine and speak as if whiteness described the world. White solipsism is not the consciously-held belief that white is superior, but is based on tunnel vision, which simply does not see non-white experience or existence as being significant. Such ideas have served to exclude black women from some feminist analyses. As Lorde states; 'By and large, within the women's movement today, white women focus upon their oppression as women and ignore differences of race, sexual preference, class and age' (1992:48).

Despite the political and theoretical diversity of feminism, feminists have a common recognition of themselves as a social category separating them from and placing them in opposition to others. However, the black female constituency as an object of political analysis is demarcated by the experience of race and gender oppression. Black women bring to feminism lived realities of racism that have marginalized them.

Making the false assumption that the experience of white, middle-class women is universal to all women, black or white, is highly problematic and contentious. At the same time, black women's experiences are not universal, but different, yet all can be considered as equally valid. We need to take into consideration the significant differences in family forms between ethnic groups themselves. Indeed, the experiences of Asian women within society assume no degree of difference. The term Asian itself is very broad and includes individuals who define themselves as; Hindu, Sikh, Moslem and Bangladeshi as well as people of the Orient, such as Japanese, Chinese, Korean, etc., and many others. This indicates we cannot make sweeping generalizations regarding the position of women in society and in the family. The household may have a different place in the experience of women of different ethnic groups in a racially divided society. For example, Asian women's role in the household may be different from that of white women due to cultural and religious influences. Culture and ethnicity are defining and determining factors of black women in society. As Khan (1979) has argued,

We can no longer study cultures in relative isolation or focus on a clearly delimited group of people. An understanding of relations between ethnic groups demands that equal attention be given to minority culture and the boundaries between various people.

(Khan, 1979:83)

Without a framework for incorporating race and ethnicity into models of the family, feminist reformulations cannot be inclusive. Just as feminist theories have reconceptualized the family along a gender axis of power and control, racial–ethnic family scholarship has reconceptualized the family along the axis of race, also a system of power and control that shapes family life in crucial ways. Studying racial–ethnic families enables us to examine race and gender as interacting hierarchies of resources and rewards that condition material and subjective experiences within families (hooks, 1984).

Do interacting race and gender ideologies shape prevailing models of minority groups, appearing in explanations of racial ethnic families as culturally deviant? Do descriptions of cultural diversity explain why families exhibit structural variations by race, although the family nurtures ethnic culture? Families are not the product of ethnic culture alone. We need to acknowledge that beyond universal similarities, there may be vast diffeerences in the experiences of women. Culture remains a powerful force in dictating and signifying the experiences of black and ethnic women.

It is invalid to investigate one group in society and from this to make generalized claims for all races and cultures. There is an urgent and crucial need for a positive thrust in ethnic research, in order to gain a clearer picture of the realities that exist for women of different cultures. Furthermore, much of the literature has a 'malestream' bias. There is a need for white, male middle-class academics to recognize and acknowledge the cultural differences within the society in which we live our daily lives and that these differences are seen to be unique to the individual minority group being studied.

The Influence of Stereotypes

Within feminist analyses and thought and within the social sciences, there exist stereotypical notions of the black woman which are biased. These stem from racist myths that have been incorporated into the literature. For example, there is an image of the submissive, passive, weak Asian woman in her culture with the arranged marriage in which she is brutally oppressed. These images continue to exist within academia, and when Asian women portray an image in opposition to this, they are still often seen in the same light — as being passive and weak. They are unable to challenge the stereotype, and so continue to be treated in these terms. Being an Asian woman lecturer, I was constantly being treated as being weak and in need of being looked after. There was a feeling of not being accepted and not belonging to academia.

Bhachu (1988) has recognized the existence of the stereotype of the passive, weak, submissive Sikh Asian woman. Her research demonstrates, *patrilineality* within the Asian culture, where the seniority of the older male member of the household was much more defined than has previously been recognized. She argues that, as a consequence of Asian women's entry into the labour market and the impact of wage earning on power relations within the family, this is no longer valid. Contrary to popular myth, Sikh Asian women are not powerless.

We live in a society which is inhabited by many different people from various different cultures and societies. There is an indication of difference, whereby each ethnic group will have its own different culture, different rules and norms in which to live their lives. Hence, the definitions imposed upon black women regarding their role in society will be entirely different to those defined by white middle-class women. Ethnicity makes a difference.

Black women are seen as exceptional when they enter higher education, and there are stereotypical notions (such as, they are weak, submissive Asians or Afro-Caribbean single mothers) and unable to cope with academia. We must begin to see an individual's cultural identity in a positive light, instead of simply dismissing it as tradition. hooks (1984) has argued that education is a key area that must be tackled for black women's liberation. Indeed, she argues that the educational needs of all women must be considered by feminist activists if the written word remains the primary medium for the dissemination of ideas. Bourgeois class bias has led many feminist theorists to develop ideas that have little or no relation to the lived experiences of most women. Black women need to develop intellectually and challenge the white feminist movement, where white cultural definition has been used to distinguish the 'abnormal' (black) from the 'normal' (white). Within the study of ethnicity, there is a tendency for over-theorizing and under-researching resulting in vast generalizations being made. Black women are the ones expected to carry out research on their own communities and see this as the focus of attention. White academics do not do so, the reasons given are that the cultures are too different or alien to understand. To examine black women's lives means they be seen as individuals in their cultural complexities rather than seen as problematic and stereotypical.

In order to be inclusive, we need to consider who carries out the research, what the research is on and why it is being done. Black women's work about their lives must be seen to make an active contribution to social research. How can research best help the lives not only of black women, but of all women in society? How do we examine the problems of sameness/difference within academia? What is most important, the things that we have in common as women or our differences as women — colour or culture? As women we share sexist oppression in society and are able to recognize and identity this with other women; at the same time as black women we are different — we may experience racism and we may have fundamental differences in our beliefs and our cultural standards. To what extent can this help us to improve things for black women, by promoting a sense of identity and belonging to a particular group?

Cultural identification, membership and recognition is fundamental, but we must move beyond this to an idea of shared empathy and shared experience to enable us, as women, to understand our commonalities as one group.

Academic Research and Language

The language of academia is white, middle-class and male. There exists a hierarchy within academia, one which has boundaries whose membership are defined by white middle-class academics. As language itself can be seen as a specific form of cultural resistance, the white language of the academic elite serves to exclude black women and does not incorporate black women's realities. Privileged groups, such as white academics, are able to define the boundaries of memberhip, colour is regarded as being deviant and white the norm. The very definitions of intellectual discourse must be challenged. Race becomes the distinguishing feature in which exclusion is reinforced and maintained. Hence, black women and their ideas are silenced and rendered as insignificant. Ideas have been developed that may have little or no relation to the lived experiences of black women. Black women need to examine why there are so few intellectual images of black women. Rediscovering, re-interpreting and re-analysing the works of black women intellectuals will enable us to challenge the definitions of intellectual discourse. This can be achieved by carrying out more research on the black community and incorporating black women's experiences into academic discourse and language. We need to rewrite traditional academic discourse; black feminist research and thought is viewed and continues to be viewed as subjugated knowledge. When we investigate different women's lives and experiences, it is essential that we examine who is doing the investigating, whose views are heard and accepted and what criteria are used to examine the notion of similarity/difference. We need to be able to communicate ideas to an audience of different people, based upon the notion of . cultural diversity.

The terms used to define non-white women are ambiguous and problematic, to be other is to be outside, and this allows racism to construct certain stereotypical categories. Although the use of the term *black* has been appropriated by black people and made powerful through its politicization, certain individuals do not designate themselves as black. Equally the term *women of colour* may be seen as appropriate as it is applied in the context of contemporary politics in the USA, but may not have the same currency in Britain. The term *black* may be problematic, as some individuals may not want to use this as a mode of definition, as an umbrella term to refer to all individuals, as we all have very different cultures. When used in relation to South Asians, the term does not examine specific cultural meanings. There are many differences between South Asian and Afro-Caribbean cultures. Cultures have their own specificity. Asians have felt the term black seems to conceal the cultural needs of groups over those of Afro-Caribbean descent. Ther term *minority* is also unsatisfactory, as it implies Britain is a homogenous society and minorities are outsiders. What terms should we use to define non-white women in Western society and to what extent are the terms important? What do they tell us? The terms tend to confuse colour with culture, and it is important to recognize each black woman is a member of a distinct culture that may separate her from other women, identity is important. White women as well as black women are members of ethnic groups. As academics and as women, we must assert our own identities and define our own terms. Many academics fail to do this, perhaps because they are afraid or are unsure of how to go about this. We must be sensitive to differences; there are many feminisms and there are many differences among women. As academics, we must aim to be 'consciously aware' of such issues. Amos and Parmar (1984) argue, even though there are many differences in the cultures

> between Afro-Caribbean and Asian communities . . . we recognise the autonomy of our separate cultures. By working together we have developed a common understanding of our oppression . . . the black struggle is a political one and it is important that we fight our oppression together.
>
> (Amos and Parmar, 1988:20)

In carrying out research, we have to consider who the researcher is and who the researched are. Who is the best person to conduct research on black communities? Should we encourage white, middle-class males to carry out research on black working-class women within their own cultural environment? Here, issues of objectivity and subjectivity come into play. In such research, playing the role of the objective stranger incorporates a structured balance between distance and nearness. The implication for this is to use the nearness and involvement afforded by shared experience, but at the same time whenever possible to achieve the distance and mystery of the stranger in order to encourage a full account of the participant's experience and to remain objective, because acquaintance with the subject matter will influence the way phenomena are seen. As a result, how researchers report their findings may reflect their own experiences more than the experiences of their participants. Such approaches help us to question the notion of other. Is there a tendency to make these groups appear different, separated out or even marginalized? We may also be falling into adding on the experiences of black women to academic thought. It is possible — respondents may feel some kind of bond, belongingness and identity with the researcher, which may in turn, help to produce data that is highly valuable to social understanding.

Black women within academia may never be accepted completely, but may remain as the other/outsider. As a black woman, and as a lecturer, I am viewed as an 'outsider–inside', I am viewed as one of *them* — part of the academic elite, but never fully accepted into academia. Being in such a position, must we as black women choose between maintaining our own identity and loyalty to our own race on the one hand, and on the other, adapting to the white definition of success? Can we do both? Will we ever be fully accepted into academia? There will continue to be a sense of us and them, I am part of the us *and* I am part of the them. We need to get out of the either/or thinking, but into an *and* state of mind and being.

Black Women and Power

There is a lack of black women in powerful positions within academia; we need them as positive role models. There exists an imbalance of power within academia — black women continue to hold positions in which power is limited and their ideas are rarely heard. Power relations may never be fully overcome and black women are rarely perceived as experts, as those whose contribution is valued. Questions concerning personal experiences, perceptions and interpretations enter into power relationships. Our past experiences inevitably affect the processes of teaching and the processes of learning. When individuals operate from shared realities, there is the idea of shared empathy and shared experience. Such ideas may not have been experienced by students in the academic world. Sharing our different realities as black/white, working/middle-class, hetero/homosexual women can enable our differences to be analysed and understood. This can serve to include experiences of black women and it can serve to obtain and provide insight into the personal experiences of individuals. They may be able to see reality through each others' eyes and share a sense of belonging and empathy. Examining the structures of power and the social practices upon which the power is reproduced will enable us to rediscover, re-interpret and re-analyse the works of black women intellectuals. We need to challenge the very definitions of intellectual discourse itself. Black women within academia must embrace a consciousness that is not only Afrocentric but also Asiocentric. Alternative perspectives exist.

The lack of power for black women is also seen when black women enter academia and higher education. They must change their whole persona in order to be accepted and to have their views heard. The presentation of self within academia is influential and black women have to change what they wear and what they say in order to be accepted. Otherwise, they are again regarded as 'other'. Should they do this? Does this imply a loss of personal identity? This is used to distinguish women on the grounds of race alone. Why are there so few black women in higher positions? Who are the women who manage to achieve acceptable and desirable standards and what makes them different? Why do they achieve, while others do not? Have these black women been socialized into the white, western model of success, where they are accepted into the world of academia, but at the same time regarded as exceptional? We must work to change the direction of the feminist movement in terms of the position of black women academics, so that women of all classes and races can see that their interest in ending sexist and racist oppression is served. A black woman's oppression cannot be understood without reference to her racial and ethnic identity. Rethinking and re-shaping the direction of feminist thought can place emphasis on cultural transformation and eradicating universal ideas of women in society. We need attempts to analyse, understand and work with commonalities as well as heterogeneity of experience. Black women can be sensitive to one another's cultural specificities while constructing common political strategies to confront sexism, racism and class inequality.

Conclusion

In order to create positive images of black women in academia, we need difference without deviance. Difference has been considered to be deviant and is judged alongside white middle-class norms of acceptance and behaviour. Being different is being an inferior other. White stands in a relationship of authority to black. The experience of the dominant group (white, middle-class) is taken as the universal standard. We are no less women because of our difference — we are not deviant. Instead, cultural identity and cultural empathy indicates shared experience and reveals diversity which can then reveal shared experience. The use of experience as a condition of political involvement has also to examine that experience can be as different as different people claim it to be. There may be no end to the divisions and distinctions claimed by an apparently unitary constituency. It is therefore unlikely that all black women will experience racism and sexism in a uniform manner.

Black women's experiences have to be recognized as valid, as women who have something to contribute to academia, rather than women who are just interested in academia. This can be achieved by challenging knowledge and the stereotypical myths about black women, by redefining and re-explaining the importance of cultural diversity and cultural power. This includes understanding and seeing the world from the black woman's perspective in order to perceive a different sense of reality and to define and evaluate of individual meanings of being black. Through self-definition, black women can use their own personal experiences in order to create an understanding of their own reality.

Examining the relationship of the powerful and the powerless within academia enables us to understand who has power and how it is distributed. How can we improve the situation for black women? What can we do to improve and reinforce positive images of black women in higher education? We must move beyond an exploitative relationship between the powerful and the powerless within higher education, rather than seeing this relationship as oppositional. 'Identification with' is important and will serve to maintain the relevance of personal experience and engender a sense of political awareness. Issues of power need to be considered and reconsidered within academia. We can aim to see life from the black woman's own sense of reality. It is important to note that our perceptions as black women, academics and feminists infuse all aspects of the academic process and are fundamentally influential in the processes of inclusion. Being able to hear the many voices of women and understanding who are the 'we' and what the hearing will involve, means using the language of inclusion rather than exclusion. Indeed, by working on learning to listen sensitively to the differences amongst individuals, and hearing and listening to the words that are being expressed, will enable us to explore how maintaining and creating dialogue is crucial; the communication process is a major part of exploring difference.

We need more research on black groups in order to understand the world from the black woman's perspective. This may enable us to gain a different sense of reality which is just as valid as that seen by white middle-class academics. Black women cannot just be added on to the study of gender relations and the study of feminism. Their experiences can be seen as not only experiences of women, but as experiences of women who suffer racism in society and who are exploited and oppressed because of this. Their lives are affected by racism in a fundamental way, through education, employment, housing, etc. The attempt to build a theoretically adequate account of the gendered lives of women may take into account not only the unique experiences of minority women, but also the explanations that they offer about their lives and the communities in which they are situated. As Brah has argued,

> I suggest that black and white feminism should not be seen as essentially fixed oppositional categories, but rather as historically contingent fields of contestation within discursive and material practices in a post-collonial society.
>
> (Brah, 1992:12)

There is a need to recognize, describe and explain the differences that exist between women, this may question the social definition of woman, women's place in society and their political priorities. In their everyday lives in a racist society, the issues that are most immediate for black women are often different from the concerns of white women. The recognition of difference and diversity, that women are a heterogenous group divided by class, race and ethnicity, by nationality and religion, by age and sexual preference, is important. There are very real differences of race, age, sex, etc. But it is not necessarily these differences that separate us. It is rather our refusal to recognize these differences and examine the distortions which result from our misnaming them and their effects upon human behaviour and expectation. We need a greater understanding of the differences and diversities between women's lives in different places and at different times. We may no longer assume the term woman is a unitary category.

Notes

I would like to thank Professor Sylvia Walby (University of Bristol) for encouraging me to present and submit this paper and Martin Myers for reading earlier drafts and providing useful comments. I would also like to thank all those who contributed at the Women in Higher Education Network conference (November 1993), where an earlier version of this paper was presented.
1 I use the term *black* in this paper to refer to individuals of South Asian and/or Afro-Caribbean descent, as a political term. However, black women are an immensely varied social group spanning different histories, classes, sexualities and religions.

References

AMOS, V. and PARMAR, P. (1984) 'Challenging imperial feminism', *Feminist Review*, **17**, pp. 3–20.

BHACHU, P. (1988) 'Apri Marzi Kurdhi, Home and work: Sikh women in Britain in WESTWOOD, S. and BHACHU, P. (Eds) *Enterprising Women*, London: Routledge.

BRAH, A. (1992) 'Difference, diversity, differentiation', in DONALD, J. and RATTANSI, A. *Race, Culture and Difference*, London: Sage.

COLLINS, P. (1991) *Black Feminist Thought: Knowledge, Consciousness and Power*, London: Routledge.

DAVIS, A. (1981) *Women, Race and Class*, London: Women's Press.

FINCH, J. (1983) *Married to the Job*, London: Allen and Unwin.

hooks, b. (1981) *Ain't I a Woman: Black Women and Feminism*, Boston, MA: South End Press.

KHAN, V. (1979) *Minority Families in Britain: Support and Stress*, London: Macmillan.

LAWRENCE, E. (1991) 'Just plain common sense: The roots of racism', in *The Empire Strikes Back*, London: Hutchinson.

LORDE, A. (1992) 'Age, race, class and sex: Women redefining difference', in CROWLEY, H. and HIMMELWEIT, S. (Eds) *Knowing Women: Feminism and Knowledge*.

OAKLEY, A. (1972) *Sex, Gender and Society*, London: Maurice Temple Smith.

PHOENIX, A. (1991) *Young Mothers*, Oxford: Polity Press.

WATSON, J. (1977) *Between Two Cultures: Migrants and Minorities in Britain*, Oxford: Basil Blackwell.

WILSON, A. (1978) *Finding a Voice: Asian Women in Britain*, London: Virago.

Further Reading

ANTHIAS, F. and DAVIS, F. (1992) *Racialised boundaries: race, nation, gender, colour and class and the anti-racist struggle*, London: Routledge.

BARRETT, M. (1980) *Women's Oppression today*, London: Verso.

BHAVNANI, K. and COULSON, M. (1986) 'Transforming socialist-feminism: the challenge of racism', *Feminist Review*, **23**, pp. 81–90.

BRYAN, B. *et al.* (1985) *Heart of the Race*, London: Virago.

BULKIN, E. *et al.* (1984) *Yours in Struggle: Feminist Perspectives on Racism and Anti-semitism*, New York: Itacha.

COHEN, P. and RATTANSI, A. (1991) *Rethinking Racism and Antiracism*, London: runnymeade Trust.

DONALD, J. and RATTANSI, A. (1992) *Race, Culture and Difference*, London: Sage.

FANON, F. (1968) *Black Skins, White Masks*, London: Paladin.

FOSTER-CARTER, O. (1987) 'Ethnicity: The fourth burden of black women – political action' *Critical Social Policy*, **22**, pp. 46–56.

FRANKENBERG, R. (1993) *White Women, Race Matters: The Social Construction of Whiteness*, Minneapolis, MN: University of Minnesota Press.

GEERTZ, C. (1973) *The Interpretation of Cultures*, New York: Basic Books.

GILMAN, S. (1985) *Difference and Pathology: Stereotypes of Sexuality, Race and Madness*,

GILROY, P. (1987) *There Ain't no Black in the Union Jack*, London: Hutchinson. Ithaca, NY: Cornell University Press.

GOLDTHORPE, J. (1987) *Family Life in Western Societies*, Cambridge: cambridge University Press.

KLEIN, G. (1985) *Reading into Racism*, London: RKP.

KOVEL, J. (1988) *White Racism: a Psychohistory*, London: Free Association.

KRAMARAE, C. and TREICHLER, P. (1985) *A Feminist Dictionary*, London: Pandora.

KUPER, L. (1973) *Race, Class and Power*, London: Duckworth.

LORDE, A. (1984) *Sister Outsider*, New York: Crossing Press.

McDOWELL, L. and PRINGLE, R. (1992) *Defining Women: Social Institutions and Gender Divisions*, Oxford: Basil Blackwell.

PHILLIPS, A. (1992) 'Classing the women and gendering the class', in McDOWELL, L. and PRINGLE, R. (Eds) *Defining Women, Social Institutions and Gender Divisions*, Cambridge: Polity Press.

RAMAZANOGLU, C.(1986) 'Ethnoceentrism and socialist-feminist theory', *Feminist Review*, **22**, pp. 83–6.

SEGAL, L. (1987) *Is the Future Female?* London: Virago.

SPELLMAN, E. (1990) *Inessential Woman*, London: Women's Press.

WALBY, S. (1990) *Theorising patriarchy*, Oxford: Basil Blackwell.

WESTWOOD, S. and BHACHU, P. (1988) *Enterprising Women: Ethnicity, Economy and Gender Relations*, London: Routledge.

Chapter 10

Empowering Disabled Women in Higher Education[1]

Julie Mathews

Acknowledging diversity and difference is an integral and important feature of feminism, for the most part, however, disabled women remain invisible from the feminist agenda. Why? Although I myself as a disabled woman have an obvious interest in issues pertaining to disability, this is not the reason why I chose to focus upon it. No one is immune from disability, and disability is less of a minority issue than society would have us believe. For example, according to the Mori/Outset Poll in 1987 questions posed about disability and the extent to which it affected the public were extremely revealing, 'The figures indicate that nearly one in three people have disability in the family, and nearly two in three people have contact with disability (Birkett and Worman, 1988: 4).

In highlighting some of the issues pertaining to disabled women with regard to access, education, and employment, I hope to encourage a new and positive awareness about disability, and to help foster a more enlightened attitude. In attempting to analyse some of the cultural constructions of disability which are predominantly based on perceptions of limitation, I will demonstrate the need for disabled women to be included on the feminist agenda. Before continuing, however, I feel that it is important to recognize that my disability is very much an individual issue, and it is imperative to acknowledge that disabled women are not a unitary category; factors such as types of disability, race, culture, class and sexuality will influence and differentiate individual experiences.

There is a tendency to stereotype and categorize us as a homogeneous group. For example, my disability does not prevent me from speaking to you today. However, if I was a deaf person, or alternatively had a speech difficulty, would this then automatically exclude me? As women we need to look at some alternatives to the disseminating of information. We should be seeking to understand the differing access needs of disabled women, enabling disabled women to be active participants at events such as the Women In Higher

Education Annual Conference. If sign language, for example, was made a compulsory unit at all stages of our education, then not only would we as a society be 'functionally bilingual' (Oliver, 1990) but we would also provide a space, a platform and a voice for women who are, for the most part, denied this right. When we think of access needs, there is much more to consider than wheel-chair provision, although this is of upmost importance — any public building that does not have a ramp is actively discriminating against disabled people. For example, would it not be considered discriminatory practice to exclude women from conferences because they happen to need glasses? In my first year as an undergraduate, the Library, for many reasons, was an unfriendly, disabilist building. We have to be aware of the importance of difference, and this means also the differing access requirements of different disabled people. We need to acknowledge the visibility and invisibility of different kinds of disability.

For some people their disability may be temporary, but the effects that this experience may have on the individual can be for life. Reappraising the processes of discrimination and obstacles faced by disabled women and men, creates an awareness of the polarization and ambivalence inflicted upon us, thereby shifting the focus away from our functional limitations. Therefore, we need to recognize and concentrate on a person's abilities and not disability. I would argue that many of us have been brought up to view disability, dependency, and powerlessness, in a somewhat essentialist way. It is fundamental as women to acknowledge the diversities of women's experience, which includes acknowledging the experiences and work of disabled women. We need to recognize the way in which power between women creates dominant relationships, leading to exclusion and powerlessness for disabled women, who are so often denied the opportunity of attending feminist conferences, due to the lack of appropriate access facilities. As Elspeth Morrison says:

> In the statutory funding world at present, pressure is being exerted on clients to make their venues more accessible. Bits and bobs of money are being made available to start this process. Okay, so a theatre gets a ramp and hearing loop put in, but it's not good enough if that ramp gets cluttered up, or only leads to one part of the venue. And what if none of the staff know how the induction loop works?
>
> (Morrison, 1989: 4)

Within the last decade there has been a growing commitment and movement of disabled people demanding the right to be treated as equal citizens with equal rights. Disabled women, however, claim they experience a multitude of disadvantages. The disability movement has largely been constructed and dominated by disabled men, who fail to identify the extent to which disabled women may in fact be further disadvantaged by virtue of their gender:

Disabled women are concernd to explore questions of sexuality and sexual identity; to challenge stereotypical images and oppressive mors relating to child-bearing and rearing and motherhood; to integrate physical and social aspects of self-presentation with critical analysis of the dependant, non-assertive disabled women which society requires.

(Lloyd, 1992: 213)

Those of us in education should be taking these issues on board in order to change and challenge oppressive representation and its effects. In every discipline disabled people are marginalized, and our experiences as disabled citizens are ignored. Sociology, English, Politics, Women's Studies, Psychology, etc., have failed to give us a voice, unless it is within the medical model, which reinforces the stereotype of disability as dependant, passive and lacking. This is counter-productive, as disability is then seen essentially as a medical problem. As Oliver says:

A major reason for this has been the failure of the medical profession, and indeed all other professions, to involve disabled people in a meaningful way except as passive objects of intervention, treatment and rehabilitation. This has not just trapped professionals within the medical approach but has had oppressive consequences for disabled people.

(Oliver, 1990: 5)

Within education we can counteract the ignorance pertaining to disability, by acknowledging disability is culturally produced and socially structured. People living in former Yugoslavia, for example, will have a higher incident of limb loss compared with people living in Preston. Epilepsy in some countries is seen as evil and bad. How each society deals with disability thus needs to be examined. As Jenny Morris rightly states:

All oppressed groups need allies and by doing research which gives voice to our experience, feminist researchers can help to empower disabled women. However, nondisabled feminists must also ask themselves where are the disabled researchers? students? academics? If they are truly to be allies we need them to recognize the way that discrimination against disabled people operates within their workplace. Why do feminist academics put up with the way that academic institutions fail to comply with the Disabled persons (Employment) Act 1944 which requires them to employ a minimum of 3 per cent registered disabled people.

(Morris, 1993a: 66)

Therefore the next time that we see an advertisement that purports to come from an Equal Opportunities employer, or one who is working 'towards' Equal opportunities, we need to look at how equality is defined.

Many feminists have drawn our attention to the power of language and how it can be an oppressive form of social control. In the same way that a woman is *she* and a man is *he*, feminists have separated out non-disabled women from disabled women by their use of language. 'Gillian Dalley, for example, refers to women and dependant people as if they are two completely separate groups whose interests, what is more, are in conflict' (Morris, 1991: 154).

Furthermore, the lack of positive images represented through language, literature, media, and charity campaigns, foster messages of self-hatred and self-oppression which can be very difficult to overcome. The media promotes disability as bad, evil, sad, ugly and dependant, whereas elsewhere alternative images of female beauty are cultivated and consequently validated: young, slim, blonde and physically active. In the words of E. Boylan:

> The public in industrial countries particularly is bombarded with images of the commercialised ideals of womanhood — young, beautiful active, and physically perfect to the extent that society strips the Disabled Women of her self-respect and sexuality, and regards her not as a person but as an object of charity and pity.
>
> (Boylan, 1991: 13)

The disabled woman who is unable to attain what is perceived to be the desirable bodily image may, therefore, suffer emotional and psychological problems, which are additional to the discrimination incurred by virtue of disability. We are set apart from the non-disabled, and the lack of portrayal and arbitrariness of disability invalidates us as 'other'.

> Similarly if our culture and media promote ideal types giving them status and power then these images and ideas burn very deep in our sub-consciousnsess so that we find ourselves, at least in part, reflecting what society accepts as beautiful.
>
> (Gillespie-Sells and Ruebain, 1992: 7)

These deeply-held fears and prejudices pertaining to disability often prevent us from gaining employment. A woman wearing callipers, for example, could affect an employer's decision to employ her, precisely because either she does not fit the stereotypical image of femininity or the employer is discomforted by her presence. Cultural representation of disability is often based on distorted media images of disability, and is therefore integral to the prejudice and to the economic and social inequalities we experience. Often the hostility and negative attitudes of non-disabled people towards disabled people are more debilitating than the disability itself.

Disabled women, however, are fighting back by creating their own poetry, photography, theatre, and humour. The Disability Arts Forum, and the National Disability Forum, after fighting off interference from the non-disabled community (many of whom wanted to professionalize it and to use it as a kind of therapy), have, for example, encouraged work concerned with the experience of disability — their central aim being to challenge the negative issues surrounding disability. Disabled actresses and actors are paid for their employment; we too have the right to a wage. We need you to acknowledge our differences, and yet respect our privacy and our need for independence. At a conference I attended, and was quite actively invoved in, many people who were concerned for my well-being told me to take a rest and sit down. I pointed out that if I were to do so I would suddenly become invisible — and non-participant. One positive suggestion made was that we should all sit down. Often the solution is quite simple, it just takes a little extra thought.

Breast cancer is on the increase in this country. Those of us who come from a health background, or who are concerned about health issues, could and should be analysing the manner in which different women respond to the diagnosis of breast cancer. The sense of helplessness and hopelessness felt by many women when they are given the diagnosis provokes extreme pessimism, which is often linked to women exhibiting high levels of dysfunction. Despite the terror and silence that shrouds the word *cancer*, and the confrontation with death itself, we also live in a culture where powerful stereotypes predominate. Breasts are linked symbolically to motherhood, femininity and sexuality. Health professionals need to recognize the potential differences in health issues and in the ways that these affect women from different classes, races, or ethnic backgrounds. Perhaps they and we should all read Audre Lorde's *The Cancer Journals*.

At the age of 44 Audre underwent a mastectomy, and through her writing she discusses the possibility of active change, which challenges the masculine model of trauma, at the same time taking control of her own emotions, rather than letting them take control of her.

Just as the female body is fragmented and colonised by various advertisers in the search for new markets for products, and through pornography is fetishised and offered for male consumption so the body is similarly fought over by competitors for its medical care.

(*Spare Rib Reader* 1987: 262)

Audre Lorde successfully manages to bridge the silence of difference, the painful feelings surrounding mastectomy, and the sexism and profiteering involved in silicon implants. Audre's refusal to wear a prosthesis transgresses this fight against the medical professions' influence, where the impaired body is the sight and symbol of all alienation. She forges a positive image, a renewed sense of self. This challenges and threatens the collective, patriarchal and hierarchical values of the *status quo*.

> Black and White, Old and Young, Lesbian, Bisexual and Heterosexual, we all shared a war against the tyrannies of silence. We can learn to work and speak when we are afraid in the same way, we have learned to work and speak when we are tired.
>
> (Lorde, 1980: 15)

When Jo Spence developed breast cancer, through the art of photographic imagery she challenged the oppresion pertaining to disabled women, and succesfully managed to forge her own identity and reality, to create a beautiful, proud and positive imagery of Breast Cancer. While at the Bristol Health Centre, visualization was a technique employed. This encouraged her to use phototherapy, a technique she went on to develop with Rosy Martin, in an attempt to break the silence, fear and invisibility surrounding breast cancer. Her work is about a person-centred, holistic health, which takes into account the whole body — not just the diseased part. Her photographs are a symbol of the profound asymmetry of breast cancer, which gives a wider interpretation of truth and self. However, the status and organization of professionalized medicine has been a major obstacle to a disabled person's identity, often enhancing the stigma associated with disability. Often, in the desire to cure us, we may have undergone unnecessary surgical procedures, where our validity as human beings is overlooked. 'The dominance of medicine has led to the medical condition of people with disabilities being defined as the problem at hand, rather than the social and economic barriers which confront them' (Lonsdale, 1990: 52).

Some feminists have sought to transform the constraints within which science and medicine operate. Women in almost every culture are defined by their reproductive capacity, which has been a cause of concern for feminists for many years. Disabled women, however, are sometimes prevented or actively discouraged form reproducing, often through sterilization. Do we not have the right to reproduce, or more to the point, should I not be standing here now?

Finally I would like to point out that without the support of my family and friends I would be unable to give this talk today. Recently my mother was taken seriously ill. Although some people are recognizing that women need creche facilities, women that have disabled relatives or partners also need some kind of support. I have not yet in any lecture, or at any conference, heard of a support network being offered to people that have other responsibilities, for example, the responsibility of providing support to a disabled person.

We also need to take into account the ethical issues. I was asked to sign a consent form for my mother, who at the time was in a confused state, to have an operation. When my mother changed her mind and said she no longer wished to have the operation, I had already consented. We need to ask whether or not a confused person has any rights, and if the burden of responsibility should fall on the next of kin. This is a crucial issue, just as is the donation of organs. Do any of us have the right, or alternatively, want the responsibility of consenting to the donation of another's organs? None of us at any time know when disability may strike, we need a framework to integrate the experiences and concerns of disability, consenting, and organ donation into our theory, research and politics, with suggestions of ways forward.

Patricia Hill Collins is one of many women, who, when writing about the development of black feminism, has suggested an alternative praxis to represent and understand experiences. As Collins illustrates, although black women may identify with white women and the oppression associated with reproduction, black women often have to defend their right to reproduce. Alternatively, they may receive frightening messags about their sexuality. Disabled women are also challenging oppressive mores pertaining to sexuality and reproduction, yet their experiences remain for the most part invisible in the mainstream of feminist thinking. Discovering the links and common experiences between women should then incorporate the concerns of disabled women.

As feminists we need to acknowledge and construct a new theory which encapsulates the experiences and aspirations of disabled women. It is important and crucial for existing women's groups to make a special effort to extend their memberships to disabled women and to acknowledge that the incidence of disability with the high proportion of elderly people in contemporary society is on the increase. In the not too distant future the proliferation of feminist writers may themselves be writing from the position of a disabled woman. It is not for non-disabled women to assess disabled women's needs and what policies are acceptable, in the same way as white feminists can not assess the needs of black women. We must make the time and space to learn and listen to our disabled sisters. Otherwise all that occurs in reality is that we have fewer choices than existed previously, as policies and decisions are determined by non-disabled people who fail to identify with the oppression incurred by disabled women, or any other oppressed group. In America disabled people have gained support from the Civil Rights movement, in particular from black people and the lesbian and gay community. Therefore, one strategy forward may be to form links with black women and lesbians. There is a connection between knowledge, consciousness and empowerment. Racism, sexism, disablism, heterosexism, and ageism, all incur common areas of oppression. For example, there are links between disabled women, lesbians and black women who are systematically denied the right to reproduce. However, we need to be sensitive to the fact that some disabled women are experiencing multiple disadvantage and oppressions. As Lloyd says, 'I'm a woman, Asian and disabled. Which do I identify with most strongly?' (Lloyd, 1992: 208).

We need to ensure that women from all communities are included and that, for example, lesbians, disabled women, black and minority ethnic women and older women are not marginalized and that their experiences are represented. We must take into account the experiences of all women — including women outside of academia — and accept that all women have an equal voice, effectively rejecting that there is a privileged opinion. There is no way we can be non-political, in the same way there is no neutral position. Only by collective action, and by drawing on each others' experiences can we hope to generate a lasting social and cultural transformation and transcend the oppressive nature of living under patriarchy. As women and feminists we all need to acknowledge and embrace the words of Micheline Mason when she states, 'There is an essential common core to all liberation movements; the right to be both different and equal' (Micheline Mason, quoted in Morris, 1991: 188–9).

Note

1 This chapter was the keynote speech, *The Importance of Difference*, given by Julie Matthews at the Women in Higher Education Network Conference, 20 November 1993.

References

ABEL, E. and ABEL, S. (Eds) *Spare Rib Reader* (1987) London: Pandora Press Ltd.
BIRKETT, K., WORMAN, D. (1988) *Getting On With Disabilities: An Employers Guide*, Institute of Personnel Management.
BOYLAN, E. (1991) *Women And Disability*, London: Zed Books, Ltd.
GILLESPIE-SELLS, K., RUEBAIN, D. (1992) *Disability* Booklet produced by Channel 4 to accompany the OUT series.
LLOYD, M. (1992) *Does She Boil Eggs? Towards A Feminist Model of Disability, Disability, Handicap and Society*, 7.
LONSDALE, S. (1990) *Women And Disability*, Basingstoke: Macmillan Education, Ltd.
LORDE, A. (1980) *The Cancer Journals*, London: Sheba Feminist Publications.
MORRIS, J. (1991) *Pride Against Prejudice*, London: Women's Press.
MORRIS, J. (1993) 'Feminism and Disability', *Feminist Review*, (43).
MORRISON, E. (1989) *Fan Feminist Art News*, 2(10).
OLIVER, M. (1990) *The Politics of Disablement*, Basingstoke: Macmillan.

Part III

Women Challenging the Mainstream Curriculum in Higher Education

Chapter 11

Is a Feminist Pedagogy Possible?

Penny Welch

Feminists engaged in academic work acknowledge that scholarship and teaching are political acts, and that feminist scholarship and teaching can, and should challenge the multiplicity of ways in which women are oppressed. This challenge may occur within the established disciplines.

> Feminists, in stressing the need for a reflexive sociology in which the sociologist takes her own experiences seriously and incorporates them into her work, expose themselves to challenges of lack of objectivity from those of their male colleagues whose sociological insight does not enable them to see that their own work is affected in a similar way by their experience and their views of the world as men
>
> (Roberts, 1981: 16)

Or it may occur in the interdisciplinary area of enquiry that has come to be known as Women's Studies. 'Women's Studies has a most important part to play in ensuring that knowledge, itself a form of social power, is not produced solely in the interests of the powerful and the influential, to the detriment of the powerless and weak' (Evans, 1982: 73).

Feminist scholarship and teaching can be seen as both a development from the Women's Movement that emerged in Britain in the late 1960s and as part of that movement. The need to create and share knowledge about women was recognized from the beginnings of the current wave of feminism. The first National Women's Liberation Conference in Britain in February 1970 was initiated by women dissatisfied with the male-dominated structure and content of the Ruskin College History Workshop. Many feminist writers in the early 1970s demonstrated the way the ideas of theorists, such as Freud and Bowlby, were used to justify the allocation of women to subordinate roles in society (e.g.

Comer, 1974; Figes, 1972). Pamphlets and newsletters were widely circulated within the movement and study groups flourished. *Spare Rib* magazine was set up in 1972, Virago publishing house in 1973. By 1973 seminars and courses on women were running a number of women's centres and adult or higher education establishments, and the term *Women's Studies* was being used to describe them (Dix, 1973). Setting up Women's Studies courses was seen by early practitioners as a form of feminist activism that could make the ideas and debates of the Women's Liberation Movement accessible to a greater number of women (Bird, 1980). Challenging the exclusion of women and their concerns from the curriculum also involved challenging accepted ways of running courses and the prevailing model of teacher–student relationships (Edney, 1974). By 1980, *Spare Rib* could point to the expansion of Women's Studies courses and state that Women's Studies was closely related to consciousness-raising, and was 'similarly at the heart of the Women's Liberation Movement' (*Spare Rib*, (93), April 1980).

Just over three years later, however, practitioners were less positive. 'We are concerned to discuss the political problems thrown up by the contradictions of teaching feminism, and pursuing Women's Studies in the context of a weakened and semi-visible women's movement' (Hurstfield and Phillips, 1983: 94). At the same time Liz Kelly and Ruth Pearson wrote of their decision to set up a Women's Studies collective outside an institutional setting, because of the problems they had experienced with the administrative and financial procedures of their local Adult Education Department (Kelly and Pearson, 1983). The fear of becoming established, incorporated, and de-radicalized had been there for many from the first initiative (Dix, 1973), and the issue of de-radicalization is examined in a number of articles (e.g. Evans, 1982; Currie and Kazi, 1987) and in the collection of papers from the 1990 Women's Studies Network Conference (Aaron and Walby, 1991). The same potential dangers can be perceived in feminist activity within other established institutions. During the 1980s many feminists chose to put their energies into changing policy and practice in political parties, trade unions, the peace movement, local authorities, media organizations and government-funded voluntary organizations. A lot of useful work was done and new contradictions revealed. Feminist challenges, ideas and ways of organizing did reach greater numbers of women during this period, a wide range of groups, activities, and campaigns continued to exist, but no large scale united women's movement emerged in Britain. Elizabeth Wilson and Angela Weir, in an assessment of the British Women's Movement, written for *New Left Review* in 1984, said that they believed

> the ideological impact of feminism has so far been much greater than any changes in women's material position . . . feminism has been more successful in challenging the ideological than the economic contradictions in bourgeois society . . . While women's right to equality is

increasingly (if grudgingly) recognised, the material basis for equality and independence is denied.

(Wilson and Weir, 1986: 131–2)

I believe that this assessment holds true today.

In respect of Women's Studies specifically, it can be argued that whether or not de-radicalization has taken place within the academy, the academic study of women is dominated by the same categories of white, heterosexual, and educated women that predominated in the Women's Liberation Movement. In the absence of a flourishing grass-roots Women's Movement, the majority of feminist theorizing is produced within universities.

The Women's Studies courses which emerged out of argument and struggle have now begun to grow into a little knowledge industry of their own. At the risk of biting the hand that feeds, it is not sufficient to produce for an academic milieu, for this does not engage with the power relations involved in the ranking of certain forms of knowledge and understanding.

(Rowbotham, 1990: xiv)

Similar points have been made about Women's Studies in the USA.

Contemporary feminist movement is sustained in part by the efforts academic women make to constitute the university setting as a central site for the development dissemination of feminist thought. Women's Studies has been the location of this effort. Given the way universities work to reinforce and perpetuate the status quo, the way knowledge is offered as commodity, Women's Studies can easily become a place where revolutionary feminist thought and feminist activism are submerged or made secondary to the goals of academic careerism.

(hooks, 1989: 51)

In the same work, bell hooks offers strategies that counteract these tendencies, drawing on the work of Paulo Freire. Barbara Smith and Patricia Collins also make clear statements about the responsibilities of feminist academics.

Feminism is the political theory and practice that struggles to free *all* women: women of color, working class women, poor women, disabled women, lesbians, old women — as well as white, economically privileged, heterosexual women. Anything less than this vision of total freedom is not feminism, but merely female self aggrandisement.

(Smith, 1982: 49)

151

> To be credible in the eyes of this group (i.e. black women outside
> academia) scholars must be personal advocates for their material, be
> accountable for the consequences of their work, have lived or experi-
> enced their material in some fashion, and be willing to engage in
> dialogue about their findings with ordinary everyday people.
>
> (Collins, 1989: 771)

The key message that I take from the last three quotations is that
feminist academics must look beyond the academy and make a practical
contribution to the fight for the liberation of all women. We all have
knowledge and skills that are or could be useful to local groups. Our teaching
and research would benefit from direct involvement with women's projects
and campaigns. But collective political activity is harder to sustain today than
it was ten years ago. Progressive organizations of all kinds suffer from low
participation and financial difficulties. Women's Refuges and Rape Crisis
centres struggle to keep open. The National Abortion Campaign faced
imminent bankruptcy in November 1993, but just managed to continue
thanks to £9000 in donations. *Spare Rib* magazine has folded. I believe that
the conditions of life for the majority of people inhibit the organized activity
that is needed to change those conditions. Government policies on benefits
and municipal housing have led to a dramatic increase in poverty and
homelessness. Racism, xenophobia, and racist attacks are on the increase,
and fear of interpersonal violence restricts the lives of many people. The push
for higher productivity and lower costs in the economy has led to redundancy
and unemployment for many, job insecurity and low wages for many more,
and greater physical and mental demands on those who remain in paid
employment in all sectors and at all levels. Increased managerial control
through quality control mechanisms, appraisal systems, and performance-
related pay apply, not only in manufacturing industry, but in many areas of
the public services, including Higher Education. Financial cuts and privatiza-
tion have reduced the level of public services, making life materially harder
for most people and high levels of pollution affect our health and quality of
life. There are concrete reasons why so many of us lack the optimism, self-
esteem, time and energy required to challenge government policy and the
social system that it upholds.

In these circumstances, calls to feminist academics to transfer their
restricted leisure time and depleted energies completely to grass-roots
campaigns are unrealistic, but it is worth considering what political work we
can do outside and inside the academy. My recognition that to remain
employed, I had to accept that my job would take up a lot of the effort that I
used to devote to trades union and community activity led me to consider what
more I could do within my job to combat women's oppression. I realized

that I had to stop working on the assumption that a feminist who was a teacher would automatically be a feminist teacher. I began to investigate the possibilities of feminist pedagogy and developed my ideas through reading, through working out strategies and trying them in class, by getting feedback from students and evaluating the methods I have used, and by sharing my ideas with others. I want to acknowledge the value of the contributions made by colleagues at the School of Humanities and Scoial Science Research Seminar and the School of Languages and European Studies Women's Network Seminar (both Wolverhampton), by participants in the workshop at the WHEN Women and the Higher Educsation Curriculum Conference (University of Central Lancashire) and by Diana Holmes, who was there at all three events.

In my deliberations on feminist pedagogy, I rapidly realized that I needed to investigate three more specific questions. First of all, what might be the main elements in a feminist approach to teaching? Second, is such an approach practicable in Higher Education in the 1990s? Third, is feminist pedagogy only feasible in the Women's Studies classroom? I went back to early developments in Women's Studies. When Women's Liberation activists in the 1970s took feminism into an educational setting, they tried to use some of the principles and practices that had been developed in Women's Liberation groups — an informal setting, as little distinction as possible between tutors and students, making space for everyone to speak and be heard, talking about personal experience and collectively reflecting on it, linking study to the needs of feminist campaigns. Many women found such classes individually and collectively empowering, and it seemed that both the content and the approach challenged prevailing educational practices (Bird, 1980). I was involved in establishing undergraduate and postgraduate Women's Studies programmes at Wolverhampton. Our efforts coincided with the demographic changes and the commitment to wider access that made many institutions positive about non-traditional students and the non-traditional courses that might attract them. Aware of the potential for incorporation and de-radicalization mentioned earlier, we were nonetheless confident that teaching Women's Studies in Higher Education was worthwhile. With official backing, Women's Studies attracted more and more students and this felt positive. Informal and egalitarian methods, however, and a concentration on the links between personal experience, academic study, and Women's Movement activism, got harder to sustain as classes got bigger. This contradiction is perceptively addressed in a recent article. 'As Women's Studies becomes something higher education sells as a popular consumption choice, the area itself threatens to move away, practically and politically, from feminism' (Adkins and Leonard, 1992: 33).

Around the same time, developments like the Enterprise Initiative gave official endorsement to student-centred learning of different kinds, and approaches that had a certain amount in common with methods used in Women's Studies were used in other subjects — small group work, group projects, negotiated learning of various kinds. Terms like *learning facilitator* began to be used by institutional management. For quite a while I'd tried to be a facilitator rather than an *expert* in my interactions with students. But when management tell me I've got to be a facilitator, I fear they want to devalue my existing skills, claim that my new role is not very skilled at all, and oblige me to teach even more students in the same number of hours. My personal commitment to Women's Studies and to what I believe it can achieve means that I want Women's Studies classes to be special, both for me and for the students. On the other hand, if I value the methods and approaches I use in Women's Studies, I ought to want to generalize them to the Politics classes I teach, and to encourage colleagues outside Women's Studies to use them too.

In order to try and resolve these contradictions I did some reading. I found two sources particularly inspiring (Culley and Portugues, 1985; and hooks, 1989) and a lot of others thought-provoking (Radner, 1986; Johnson, 1987; Gunew, 1987; Ruggiero, 1990; Cannon, 1990; de Danaan, 1990; Beckman, 1991; Romney, *et al.*, 1992). Most of these writers work in the USA and the others in Australia. All went into detail about what they tried to do in the classroom and the reasons for it. bell hooks led me to Paulo Freire (Freire, 1972). He describes the prevailing system of education in the world as the *banking* model, in which the teacher has the knowledge, the students know nothing, and the teaching deposits the knowledge in the students. The teacher has the power, the students have none, and the whole process reinforces relations of domination and subordination. He advocates instead the *problem-posing* model of education in which oppression and its causes are the object of study, and the teachers and students cooperate to gain a greater understanding of the world and of themselves. In this model, both teachers and students remain human subjects who act. 'This pedagogy makes oppression and its causes objects of reflection by the oppressed, and from that reflection will come their necessary engagement in the struggle for their liberation. And in the struggle this pedagogy will be made and remade' (Freire, 1972: 25). He advocates his model of pedagogy only for educational projects outside the formal system of education, believing that the latter can only be changed once the oppressed take political power. bell hooks nonetheless believes that this approach can be adapted for use in schools and universities. She draws on her positive experience of inspiring teachers in segregated black schools, who 'offered us a legacy of liberatory pedagogy that demanded active resistance and rebellion against sexism and racism' (hooks, 1989: 50), and her negative experience of scorn and humiliation from white male professors in graduate school. Her fears that feminist academics can easily neglect their links with feminist activism were referred to earlier, and she sees a pedagogy that actively challenges domination as a crucial way of linking feminist struggle and Women's Studies. She writes,

> Feminist education — the feminist classroom — is and should be a place where there is a sense of struggle, where there is visible acknowledgement of the union of theory and practice, where we work together as teachers and students to overcome the estrangement and alienation that have become so much the norm in the contemporary university.
>
> (hooks, 1989: 51)

Reading bell hooks, and through her, Paulo Freire, clarified a number of issues for me. I already knew that if my aim was to challenge the oppression of women, I had to address not only gender oppression, but class inequality, racism, imperialism, heterosexism and discrimination on the basis of age and disabillity, because many women also suffer, and resist, these oppressions. My reading, however, convinced me that while it was possible to concentrate on how women experience these oppressions, it was politically and intellectually impossible to concentrate exclusively on women. bell hooks also showed me how ideas like those of Freire were not only applicable to Adult, Community, or Trade Union Education in Britain, but also to formally assessed higher education courses. At the same time, my observations of students (mainly, but not entirely, those from oppressed groups), made me realize that many do not feel entitled to be in higher education. They believe that tutors are powerful experts whose ideas need to be reproduced in order to secure good grades, and have little expectation of finding the subject matter of their studies relevant to their lives. In order to address these perceptions, I felt the need to draw on a source dealing with interpersonal relations, and turned to Carl Rogers. While he does not explicitly deal with social inequalities in general, he does explore power relations between teachers and students. I found his argument that students need to feel recognized as individuals, valued as human beings, unthreatened and free to contribute to the collective endeavour for deeper understanding (Rogers, 1951) filled an important gap in my thinking.

I became optimistic that using a variety of feminist writings as a basis, augmented with ideas from Freire and Rogers, I could construct a viable pedagogy. I have labelled it *feminist pedgagogy*, knowing that some may see this as an inaccurate title, because I have drawn from non-feminist sources in its construction. It could also be argued that the original feminist motivation has been dissolved into a more general, liberal, student-centred approach. On the other hand, I reject a feminism that ignores other sources of oppression, and minimizes the significance of inequality *between* women, and I see the integration of ideas from other traditions as strengthening, rather than diluting, feminist thinking. The pedagogy I advocate is based on three principles:

- to strive for egalitarian relationships in the classroom;
- to try to make all students feel valued as individuals;
- to use the experience of students as a learning resource.

When I use the concept of experience, I am taking account of the major shifts in feminist thinking about the nature and place of subjectivity that have occurred over the last 20 years. In early Women's Liberation Movement consciousness-raising groups, the sharing of experience was used to enable women 'to realize that their problems are not individual, but are part of a collective oppression of the whole sex' (Bruley, 1981: 66), a goal that encouraged those involved to focus on what they had in common as women. When such groups were entirely white, issues of racism were generally not addressed, and when such groups had some black members, the experience of black women were too often treated as a departure from the norm. The tendency for the Women's Liberation Movement in Britain and the USA to generalize on the basis of white, Western women's experiences, and the exclusion, marginalization or distortion of black women's experience within feminsit theorizing, was challenged in a significant number of writings in the early 1980s (e.g. Carby, 1982; Amos and Parmar, 1984; Davis, 1981; hooks, 1981; Hull, Scott and Smith, 1982). The more recent emphasis on difference between women and on the diveristy of women's experiences, has been further encouraged by the engagement of feminism with post-modernism. The editors of a recent collection write 'post-modernism claims that the pursuit of totalizing theory is mistaken, for such theory is inevitably "essentialist" in that it makes invalid generalizations, universalizing what should be seen as local and historically specific' (Crowley and Himmelweit, 1992: 3). In moving away from generalizing about women on the grounds that the identity 'woman' has no universal meaning, there is, however, a risk that what being a woman means in any specific context is de-emphasized, and that the value of testimony by any individual or group of women is discounted. Razia Azis believes that this danger can be avoided. 'If a feminism of difference is to compete with reactionary forces for the spaces caused by political schisms, it needs to incorporate both the deconstruction of subjectivity *and* the political necessity of asserting identity' (Aziz, 1992: 304). In developing a more sophisticated notion of experience and how it can be used, we also need to take account of the insights offered by psychoanalytical theory and recognize that our sense of self has unconscious as well as conscious dimensions. I am convinced that collective reflection on individual experience has value in political organizations, research seminars, and classrooms. It helps us to link theory and practice, to connect with each other to acknowledge those parts of our identity that are not normally explicit in such a setting, to recognize difference and commonality, and to build solidarity across diversity.

At the workshop at the WHEN Conference 1993 I used a small part of this chapter to introduce the issues I wanted the participants to address, and I put the three principles I have identified to the group. I asked them if they agreed with the principles, and if so, what we could practically do to put them into practice. Contributors were by and large positive about the second and third principles. It was pointed out that using experience in the classroom meant that alternative perspectives were heard. Participants stressed that listening to students was an important way of showing that they were valued, as that was encouraging them to recognize their own strengths. The group as a whole were less convinced by my emphasis on egalitarian relationships in the classoom. They stressed the constraints under which teachers operate — regulations, supervision by line management, assessment rules — and advocated instead an open acknowledgment of the power and imbalance between tutor and students, and between students themselves. Practical suggestions for the implementation of our agreed aims covered a wide range. Showing awareness of students' lives outside the classroom — paid work, domestic responsibilities, financial pressures, for example — and negotiating the timing of assessments to meet students' needs, were seen as important. Being positive about students' contributions in class, and involving them in curriculum development where possible, were suggestions that embraced both the valuing of students as individuals and the quest for more egalitarian relationships. All the other suggestions were about assessment. Everyone agreed that clearly communicated criteria for assessment were essential. Marking assignments straight away and getting them back quickly was a way of showing respect for students and their work. Some participants had experience of using an element of self-assessment in group projects and were positive about its value. One contributor made a practice of keeping assignments from previous years and letting the current students grade them and compare their grades with the ones that had been awarded. Many participants agreed that, subject to permission being given by the students who had written the assignments, this was another way of demystifying the process of marking and making assessment criteria very clear.

Reflecting now on the balance of points made by the participants in the workshop, I find it interesting that there was scepticism about attempting egalitarian relationships, and yet most of the practical suggestions referred to assessment, and were directed at making the process of assessment, which is at the heart of the unequal relationship, more open. I wonder if some of the initial resistance to my rather general point about egalitarian relationships was a result of our differing locations in the higher education system. I've got a permanent full-time job and almost twenty years' teaching experience. I'm a Senior Lecturer and my appraiser is generally happy with the teaching methods I use and the evaluations I get from students. Many of the workshop participants were clearly less well established — a number may have been on temporary or part-time contracts although this was not stated. Some may have felt that they did not have a lot of power to share with students, and may have felt squeezed between the demands of students and the demands of line managers. I should have said more clearly that it is important not to disempower yourself to the extent that you cannot fulfil your responsibilities as a teacher. Think about what aspects of your course could be open to negotiation and within what limits. Don't feel obliged to negotiate on issues you really feel are non-negotiable.

There are a number of political and practical objections that can be made to the elements of feminist pedagogy I have put forward. The first is that they require a degree of extra thought and preparation that over-burdened lecturers in higher education in the 1990s shouldn't be expected to undertake. My response is that different methods of teaching and assessment may reduce certain aspects of preparation and marking while increasing others, and, at least for those on continuing contracts, some of the additional thinking may not have to be repeated in subsequent years. The second objection is that the only new methods that are approved of in the current climate are those which enable lecturers to deal with ever-increasing numbers of students at no extra cost. My answer is that we haven't yet managed to collectively resist increased productivity, and experimenting with new methods might at least allow lecturers to regain a little autonomy or even job satisfaction. This would improve our morale, and perhaps even our ability to defend our collective professional interests.

The third and fourth objections relate to women academics specifically. Negotiation with students and other strategies for more egalitarian relationships may be interpreted as a loss of professional authority — something that many women have struggled to claim for themselves and other women. If authority is interpreted as the ability to dominate students or colleagues, I believe we should abdicate it. However, if authority means respect, then communicating our reasons for opening up aspects of our courses to negotiation and encouraging students to voice their anxieties about this more democratic approach may generate a more valuable form of respect. Women who make their classrooms comfortable places to be in, and who show that they value students as individuals, are likely to be in demand for pastoral counselling and project supervision. They may run the risk of overburdening themselves, making it easier for male colleagues to leave the nurturing of students to them. We have to insist that work distribution and resource allocation protect us against overload, and that our skills in relating to students are valued within our departments. A fifth objection is that student-centred learning methods of whatever kind do not challenge the inequalities of the higher education system, and prevent students feeling the need to protest against current conditions. I believe that in a hostile financial climate, disillusioned students are just as likely to drop out as to stay and challenge, and perhaps students who have been encouraged in class have the confidence to speak out and will feel more able to defend the rights of the student body.

I arrive at the position that by reflecting on what we can do to encourage more egalitarian relationships in the classroom, to make all students feel valued as individuals, and to use the experience of students as a learning resource, we start envisaging approaches and methods that challenge the passive and subordinate role still allocated to students. Such a pedagogy has greater legitimacy in Women's Studies, where it complements challenges to curriculum content and prevailing ways of constructing knowledge, than it is likely to have, at present, in other subjects. Teachers who wish to use feminist pedagogy in other disciplines will encounter some resistance from colleagues and students, and may wish to proceed cautiously, changing one aspect of teaching or assessment at a time. Despite being the subject of criticism for 30 years the formal lecture is still the prevailing model of what a lecturer should do. Even with large classes, it is possible to reduce the hierarchical nature of this format, by building in small group work of various kinds, in order to encourage more active involvement by students. The standard academic essay is the most common form of assessment in many subjects and may represent only the reproduction of received wisdom, rather than demand independent thought by students. A wider variety of assessment tasks, both individual and group-based, can allow a greater range of intellectual skills to be tested. It is possible, however, to be immensely innovative in teaching and assessment methods, and yet have no desire to reduce the power inbalance between lecturer and student. In order for non-traditional methods to be part of feminist pedagogy, the teacher must at least explain why she is departing from the expected format, and listen to student responses during and at the end of the module.

There are many simple ways in addition to those mentioned in the workshop of showing that you value students — learning their names; saying hello when you see them on campus; rembering their previous work; making sure criticisms really are directed at the work and not at the student; keeping regular office hours, however short, when your availability is guaranteed. For many teachers these are obvious points, but not everyone consciously adopts them. My recent experience as Course Tutor has made me realize that many students feel anxious about approaching staff when they have personal problems, or when their attendance or performance has been unsatisfactory. They often fear that they will be rebuked or made to feel stupid or inadequate. We need to work out what we can do to make students feel comfortable about approaching us, but at the same time we need to be clear about what, for us, constitutes an unreasonable demand, or unacceptable conduct.

In Women's Studies classes, the issues addressed are bound to make students think of their own experience, and may give rise to strong feelings.

Make it safe to share personal experience if the students wish to, and work out in advance what you will do if students display anger or grief. Remember that there might be disclosures, that you would be comfortable with, but the other students might not be. Decide in advance what information about your own life you are prepared to share with students and in what circumstances. Experience can be used as a learning resource in other classes too. In all subjects there will be some topics that can be discussed in a way that allows students to draw on their existing knowledge, both academic and experiential, and which give scope for individual responses to the issues being addressed. Whatever the discipline, there is one area of experience that should be included — the experience of studying and the feelings students have about it. Students who reflect on their methods of work and who share their experiences with others, tend to grow in confidence, just as, I am arguing, teachers do.

In the present political and institutional climate, there is tremendous pressure on all staff in higher education to work more intensively, and to perform more effectively. Institutions, departments, and individuals are urged to be competitive, whether for students, external funding, or research ratings. Many students suffer financial hardship and the fear of unemployment after graduation. At times it is hard to find any satisfying purpose in what we do. One positive aspect however, is the greater diversity of the student population in some faculties of some institutions. The battle for wider access to higher education has not been won, but many of us will be teaching more women returners, more black and ethnic minority students, more working-class students, and more students with disabilities, than we were in the 1980s. Teaching methods that individually and collectively empower students seem even more relevant and worth generalizing in this situation. What students learn, and how they learn it, impacts on their view of the world, and on their feelings about themselves and other people. If our aim is to help them develop skills for controlling their own lives without oppressing others, then a feminist pedagogy has a positive contribution to make to this process.

References

AARON, J. and WALBY, S. (1991) (Eds) *Out of the Margins: Women's Studies in the Nineties*, London: Falmer Press.

ADKINS, L. and LEONARD, D. (1992) 'From academia to the education marketplace: United Kingom women's studies in the 1990s', *Women's Studies Quarterly*, **3** and **4**, pp. 28–37.

AMOS, V. and PARMAR, P. (1984) 'Challenging imperial feminism', *Feminist Review*, (17), July.

AZIZ, R. (1992) 'Feminism and the challenge of racism: Deviance or difference?' in CROWLEY, H. and HIMMELWEIT, S. (1992) *Knowing Women: Feminism and Knowledge*, Oxford: Polity Press.

BECKMAN, M. (1991) 'Feminist teaching methods and the team based workplace: Do results match intentions?' *Women's Statistics Quarterly*, **1** and **2**, pp. 165–178.

BIRD, L. (1980) 'Setting up women's studies courses', *Spare Rib*, (93), pp. 52–3.

BRULEY, S. (1981) 'Women awake: The experience of consciousness-raising' in Feminist Anthology Collective (1981) *No Turning Back: Writings from the Women's Liberation Movement 1975–80*, London: The Women's Press.

CANNON, L.W. (1990) 'Fostering positive race, class, and gender dynamics in the classroom', *Women's Studies Quarterly*, **1** and **2**, pp. 126–34.

CARBY, H. (1982) 'White women listen! Black feminism and the boundaries of sisterhood' in Centre for Contemorary Cultural Studies (1982) *The Empire Strikes Back: Race and Racism in 70s Britain*, London and New York: Routledge.

COLLINS, P. B. (1989) 'The social construction of black feminist thought', *Signs*, **14**(4), pp. 745–73.

COMER, L. (1974) *Wedlocked Women*, Leeds: Feminist Books Ltd.

CROWLEY, H. and HIMMELWEIT, S. (1992) *Knowing Women: Feminism and Knowledge*, Oxford: Polity Press.

CULLEY, M. and PORTUGUES, C. (1985) (Eds) *Gendered Subjects: The Dynamics of Feminist Teaching*, Boston: Routledge and Kegan Paul.

CURRIE, D. and KAZI, H. (1987) 'Academic feminism and the process of de-radicalization: Re-examining the issues', *Feminist Review*, (25), March.

DAVIS, A. (1981) *Women, Race, and Class*, London: The Women's Press.

DE DANAAN, L. (1990) 'Center to margin: Dynamics in a global classroom', *Women's Studies Quarterly*, **1** and **2**, pp. 135–44.

DIX, C. (1973) 'Where to study women's studies', *Spare Rib*, (18), pp. 35–36.

EDNEY, M. and LANGTON, T. (1974) 'Feminist subversion', *Spare Rib*, (20), pp. 12–14.

EVANS, E. (1982) 'In praise of theory: The case for women's studies', *Feminist Review*, (10), February, pp. 61–74.

FIGES, LE. (1972) *Patriarchal Attitudes: Women in Society*, London: Panther.

FREIRE, P. (1972) *Pedagogy of the Oppressed*, London: Penguin Books.

GUNEW, S. (1987) 'Is academic sisterhood an oxymoron?', *Women's Studies International Forum*, **10**(5), pp. 533–6.

hooks, b. (1982) *Ain't I A Woman: Black Women and Feminism*, London: Pluto Press.

hooks, b. (1989) *Talking Back: Thinking Feminist, Thinking Black*, London: Sheba.

HULL, G. T., SCOTT, P. B. and SMITH, B. (1982) (Eds) *All the Women are White, All the Blacks are Men, But some of Us are Brave*, Old Westbury, NY: Feminist Press.

HURSTFIELD, J. and PHILLIPS, E. (1983) 'Teaching feminism — a contradiction in terms?' *Feminist Review*, (15), November, pp. 94–8.

JOHNSON, L. (1987) 'Is academic feminism an oxymoron?', *Women's Studies International Forum*, **10**(5), pp. 529–32.

KELLY, L. and PEARSON, R. (1983) 'Women's studies: Women studying or studying women?', *Feminist Review*, (15), November, pp. 76–9.

RADNER, S. (1986) 'Operating by consensus: The collective approach to Women's Studies', *Women's Studies International Forum*, **9**(2), pp. 157–61.

ROBERTS, H. (1981) 'Women and their doctors: Power and powerlessness in the research process', in ROBERTS, H. (Ed.) (1981) *Doing Feminist Research*, London: Routledge and Kegan Paul.

ROMNEY, P., TATUM, B., JONES, J. (1992) 'Feminist strategies for teaching about oppression: The importance of process', *Women's Studies Quarterly*, **1** and **2**, pp. 95–110.

ROGERS, C. (1951) 'Student-centred teaching' in ROGERS, C. (1951) *Client Centred Therapy*, London: Constable.

ROWBOTHAM, S. (1989) *The Past is Before Us: Feminism in Action Since The 1960s*, Rickmansworth: Penguin Books.

RUGGIERO, C. (1990) 'Teaching women's studies: The repersonalization of our politics', *Women's Studies International Forum*, **13**(5), pp. 469–75.

SMITH, B. (1982) 'Racism and women's studies' in HULL, G. T., SCOTT, P. B and SMITH, B. (Eds) (1982) *All the Women are White, All the Blacks are Men, But Some of Us are Brave*, Old Westbury, NY: Feminist Press.

Spare Rib (1980) (93).

WILSON, E. and WEIR, A. (1986) 'The British women's movement' in WILSON, E. (1986) *Hidden Agendas: Theory, Politics and Experience in the Women's Movement*, London and New York: Tavistock.

Chapter 12

Transforming the Household: Mature Women Students and Access to Higher Education

Madeleine Leonard

Introduction

During the past two decades, universities have attempted to widen access by encouraging the participation of previously under-represented groups such as women, members of the working-class and minority ethnic groups. Part of this strategy involves offering a second chance to mature members of these groups by establishing non-traditional access routes to institutions of higher education. Aptly named *Access* courses have been designed and developed to facilitate entry into higher education for mature students without conventional qualifications (Pearson, 1990).

The 1987 White Paper 'Meeting the Challenge' identified access courses as one of three popular routes into higher education along with traditional 'A' level and vocational qualifications. In 1984 when the first national survey of Access courses was undertaken (Lucas and Ward, 1985), there were 130 courses in England. In 1987 (Wisker and Millins, 1988) there were 334, while a survey undertaken in 1989 (Jones and Millins, 1990) revealed no fewer than 529. In Northern Ireland, Access courses are a relatively new phenomenon. Compared to the 529 access courses available in England, Northern Ireland provides only 24 Access courses. This is due mainly to the small size of the geographical area concerned, and the fact that Northern Ireland has only two universities, the University of Ulster and Queen's University. Nonetheless, access courses are expanding rapidly as a significant avenue for entry to university for mature students, particularly women (Edwards, 1990; Lyon, 1988).

Widening access to Higher Education is a laudable concept, but concern has emerged over whether current attempts to widen participation incorporate rather than challenge the structural characteristics of traditional education. For example, Pearson *et al.* (1989) found that there tends to be a heavier concentration of mature women students in Arts and Humanities and a lower concentration in the Sciences. Access co-ordinators I spoke to in Belfast state that they have considerable problems in recruiting female students to science subjects. Hence, Access courses seem to perpetuate rather than transform the traditional gendered nature of subject choice. On the other hand, a recurring theme in feminist writing about education has been that education turns girls towards domesticity (Deem, 1978; Delamont, 1980; Finch, 1984). However, research on mature women students carried out by Pascall and Cox (1993) reveal that their respondents saw education as the route away from domesticity. Although 41 of the 43 respondents interviewed were following Arts and Humanities degrees, the majority of the women saw education as a way of escaping from traditional family structures and in particular, the housewife role. The family circumstances of mature students is given scant coverage in studies concerned with their participation in higher education. Rather, the focus tends to be on educational policy such as widening access in general terms, the implication being that education exists in a vacuum separate from the rest of society. One of the key concerns of my research is to pursue the relationship between mature women's family circumstances and educational reform aimed at widening access. While the aim of the women interviewed by Pascall and Cox (1993) was to escape domesticity the women in this study were prevented from such action by the patriarchial attitudes of their partners, who gave conditional support of the women's decisions to return to education on the understanding that traditional domestic roles were not threatened.

Background to the Research

The research draws on the experiences of 23 women involved in a Sociology degree course at Queen's University in Belfast. Fifteen of the sample entered Queen's through a Humanities and Social Science Access course. The remainder studied A-levels at part-time evening classes before entering Queen's. The respondents were aged between 23 and 51, with the majority falling betwewen 30 and 49. Twelve of the sample were married, five were divorced or separated, two were single parents and the remaining four respondents were single. Fifteen of the 17 respondents who were married or divorced/separated had children. Three-quarters of this group had between one and three children while the remaining quarter had four or five children. One third of married respondents had husbands who were long-term unemployed.

All of the women classified themselves as working-class, although in three cases the women claimed they had achieved middle-class status through their husbands' occupations. Seventeen of the sample left school between the age of 15 and 16 with no academic qualifications, although two of this group had shorthand and typing skills. Four of the sample left school between the age of 17 and 18 with O level qualifications, while the remaining two respondents left school at age 18 with A level qualifications. This meant that the majority of the sample worked in traditional low-paid gender specific occupations. Half the sample had worked for a period in shops, factories or in hairdressing salons. Two had worked as nurses while the remainder had worked in mainly low grade clerical occupations.

All the respondents were interviewed by the author. The interviews were tape-recorded and later transcribed, the analysis is based on these transcripts. The interview was semi-structured and sought to elicit information on the women's motivations for returning to study; their evaluation of Access courses as a preparation for university; their experiences of university life and the effects returning to education has had on their personal relationships and domestic commitments. While the author recognizes that there is no one method that can be termed the feminist methodology, nonetheless the author utilized a range of techniques that can be loosely described as sympathetic to the concerns of feminist methodology.

Doing Feminist Research

Much of the most widely quoted research on mature students has relied on quantitative techniques, in particular self-completion questionnaires (Smithers and Griffin, 1986, Woodley *et al.*, 1987). While such procedures are extremely useful for providing background details concerning the structural characteristics of mature students, they are less useful for exploring women's lived-in experiences of being mature students and the effects returning to education has on their personal relationships. As a result, much of this research has maginalized women's experiences and silenced their voices (Smith, 1993). While qualitative research, including in-depth interviewing, is a common method for collecting data in mainstream sociology, nonetheless feminists approach in-depth interviewing in ways that Graham (1983) refers to as 'a female style of knowing'.

Classic sociology textbooks on interviewing techniques suggest that the interviewer 'while friendly and interested [should] not get too emotionally involved with the respondent and [the] problem' (Moser, 1958: 186–7). Social researchers are encouraged to interact with research participants in a 'neutral', 'value-free' way, always remembering that the interviewee is the object of study.

However, Mies (1983) argues that feminist researchers must not do research from their ivory towers, but must become involved with the people they study. Feminist methodology places great value on women-to-woman research, based on personal identification with the subjects' experiences, as a mechanism to produce more meaningful and insightful research. Part of this strategy involves self-disclosure (Edwards, 1993) on the part of the researcher, to promote reciprocity, empathy, trust and mutual interaction.

All of the interviews I conducted with the mature female students utilized the in-depth interviewing technique. All of the interviews were tape-recorded, as I felt that taking notes during the interview would reduce the intimacy I was attempting to create. I tried where possible to structure the interviews around natural conversation and adapt the interviewing style to the individual concerned. Thus, while all respondents were gently probed to focus on specific areas, I tried to interrupt as little as possible in order to allow the women's own experiences and perceptions to emerge. Throughout the interviews, I shared with the respondents my own experiences of being a mature student, and felt that this was essential in order to reduce the exploitative power balance between researcher and subject (Graham, 1984). Oakley (1981) argues that a non-hierarchical relationship and personal involvement on the part of the researcher is required in order to reach the goal of being admitted to interviewees' lives.

Such an empathy with one's respondents is difficult to achieve in practice. It is not enough to rely on the status of being a woman interviewing a woman to overcome the potential power balance between researcher and researched. Edwards (1990), for example, found that being a white woman was not enough to overcome the apprehension of the black women she was interviewing. Structural disadvantages in terms of race and class may affect the power imbalance between researcher and researched. While I was partly able to overcome these difficulties, sharing a working-class background with the women I interviewed, nonetheless, I remained their lecturer and tutor, responsible for setting and, more importantly, marking their exams. On the whole though, I felt that the technique was successful, although at times emotionally draining. By using the above approach, I feel I was able to learn more about the aspects of the women's lives which crucially affecct their chances of success.

Motivations for Returning to Study

All of the respondents were asked what motivated them to return to education. Their responses fell into two broad categories, instrumental motivation and personal motivation. Those who returned to education for instrumental reasons included those who were motivated by a desire to change their careers or enhance their career prospects in general terms. Interestingly, the responses of the four single respondents all fell into this category. For the majority of the remaining respondents, motivations were more personal, including the desire to enhance self-confidence or fulfil a private challenge. The following quotes typify the responses received:

I just wanted a new challenge. I felt I had missed out on something.

I always had a complex about having no exams. It always bothered me as I felt I was capable.

I always felt I could do better. My life was like clockwork. I did the same thing day-in and day-out and people around me, particularly the people I worked with, thought I was stupid.

For some of the married women, the desire to return to education was motivated by the decision to have children, or to fill the vacuum created by children becoming more independent when they became older. The following responses illustrate this aspect of the data:

I never thought about education until my son was born in 1989. He was definitely the jolt that made me sit up and think about what I was going to do with my life. I had someone to provide for. I had a responsibility to look after another person until he was at least eighteeen. I could work at dead-end jobs to support myself but not to support another human being as well. I decided I was going to give him the background he deserves. I was going to have a solid job for him.

When my kids grew up, I was left with the empty nest syndrome. I had devoted my whole life to them but they were becoming independent and as they became independent, it created a vacuum in my life and I had to replace it with something.

I waited until my husband and children were independent and didn't really need me. My husband has his own career. He isn't really around very much. My daughter doesn't really need me either so I thought what am I going to do with the rest of my life, just sit here and vegetate?

To a large extent, these quotes reflect the enormous impact the wider structural characteristics of the household have on women's personal so-called 'decisions' to return to education.

Evaluation of Access Courses

The main purpose of Access courses is to prepare students for university. Therefore, one of my key concerns in asking students about their impressions of Access courses was to evaluate the extent to which they felt Access courses had prepared them for university life. According to Green and Percey

> By adopting a highly flexible understanding and supportive posture to students, access tutors may do a disservice to women in two respects: first, a flexible pedagogy may also be a non-demanding pedadogy . . . second, an understanding, kindly, hand-holding pedagogy fosters dependency. It suggests that students cannot cope and makes the transition to the tough world of higher education much more difficult
>
> (Green and Percey, 1991:155–6)

The whole ethos of Access courses is to specifically prepare disadvantaged students for higher education. The intake consists of students who for one reason or another failed to take the opportunity to go to university at age eighteen. Their recruitment policies specifically focus on students who were generally labelled as failures by the education system first time round. Consequently, Access tutors are given enormous responsibility in tackling the hurdles which prevent certain groups from achieving their full potential. To overcome the disadvantages of non-traditional students, Access tutors are accused of pampering students in their counselling and support duties without paying enough attention to notions of academic standards (Green and Percey, 1991). According to this argument, the end result is that Access students may be ill-equipped to deal with the academic demands of university life. I put these observations to the 15 respondents who had undertaken Access courses before entering Queen's university. Only two of the respondents agreed with the views expressed above. The majority of respondents felt that Access courses provided a useful bridge between returning to education and entering university. Most respondents felt that without the support of Access tutors, they would not have had the confidence to apply for a university place.

University Experiences

According to Pantziarka,

> The transition from further education to higher education is probably the most difficult that the access student has to make . . . and

is certainly more traumatic than the initial return to education after a long period of absence (1987: 33)

All 23 respondents were asked to recall their first impressions on coming to university and whether they considered the transition as traumatic. Most students stated that they felt nervous and apprehensive, but this was tinged with elation that they had actually made it. One respondent expressed her feelings in the following way:

> I kept thinking you're here but you're not really here. It's a mistake. You shouldn't really be here. . . It was like a big juicy apple that you were afraid to take a bite of in case somebody took it away from you.

I asked all respondents how they handled the university lecturing and tutorial system. First year Sociology courses generally attract around 400 students at Queen's. Most of the respondents felt initially very intimidated by the huge lecture theatres, and were very conscious of being older than the majority of their fellow students. Queen's tends to draw its intake from Northern Ireland. Most traditional students tend to transfer *en masse* from school to the university. Hence, most first-year students enter university with a ready made set of friends from their school days. This tended to increase the isolation of mature students who were unable to plug into these pre-existing social circles. Many students stated that they felt inadequate regarding their ability to take lecture notes. Access course tutors had dictated notes at extremely slow speeds, whereas lecture notes had to be taken down at the speed of normal conversation. All the mature students came from working-class backgrounds and felt intimidated by the sophisticated language that seemed to come from academic staff.

Most respondents found the tutorials manageable and enjoyed the opportunity to discuss aspects of the course in a tutorial setting. However, they tended to feel that they dominated tutorial discussions, and this often resulted in mature and younger students feeling ill at ease with each other. The mature students were aware that their participation in group discussions was seen by younger students as a sign of self-confidence, yet many mature students felt their participation was motivated by their desire to escape the uncomfortable, prolonged silences which seemed to occur when they did not participate.

Effects on Family Relationships

Often mature students face hostility and a lack of support from partners. Disapproval can be particularly acute if participation is seen to threaten gender roles. Married men, in particular, fear that their partners' educational endeavours will affect the relationship and that household obligations will be traded off against university obligations. Smith (1993) identifies three main aspects of support which husbands could give their wives when they return to education. These are: practical support — the extent to which husband share domestic duties and childcare responsibilities with their wives in order to allow them time for study; financial support — the extent to which husbands assist their wives in economic terms; and emotional support — the extent to which husbands were generally supportive and encouraging. In no case were the married respondents receiving all three of the above types of support. Financial support was dependent on the financial circumstances of the household, in particular on whether or not the husband was employed. When the hushand was unemployed, or in a low paid occupation, spending money on books and other study materials was seen as a luxury the family could ill afford. In two out of the four households where the male was unemployed, the wife engaged in part-time work as well as attending university, and part of the earnings from part-time employment was utilized to subsidize university expenses. One woman stated that she felt less guilty about attending university because of her ability to contribute to the household budget through her part-time employment. As she says:

> I work two afternoons a week and at the weekends I work at cleaning in the local hospital. I get £56 a week and that salvages my conscience. I can put my £56 on the table and say — there you are, that's for the house. I'm doing my bit. . .

Some husbands in well paid jobs gave financial support to their partners, but this was seen as temporary and justified because of the possibility of a future lucrative career for the wife which would benefit the whole household economically. This view is typified by the following quote:

> I think I realized that he only encouraged me when he thought there was a chance of a job on the horizon which would be beneficial for everybody, but if there hadn't have been any benefit at the end of it and he had to sacrifice things, I don't think he would have been too enhusiastic. If it had been just for me, I don't think he would have been too supportive. . .

Other husbands were less generous in helping alleviate the expenses their wives incurred on returning to education. This aspect of the data verified the proposition that money is the source of power that upholds male dominance in the family (Pahl, 1989). These males felt that because they were bringing in a wage to the household, they were entitled to domestic and childcare services from their wives. Wives were given money to be spent on the household and not on their personal needs. University expenses were seen as personal needs. Often these men would use 'domestic sabotage' ((Lovell, 1980) to prevent their wives from achieving their objectives, by making wives feel guilty for not fulfilling their domestic roles. The following quotes illustrate this aspect of the data:

> When I was working during the summer and bringing in a wage, he often made the dinner but not when I am at Queen's. I think he looks on this as a pastime and feels it shouldn't interfere with my housekeeping duties.

> He tells me how good he is to me. I get away on holiday every year and I have a dishwasher and all. Anything I want for the house I can get it, but he is not very good about financing me here. Only for the student loan, I don't know what I would do. My housekeeping wouldn't stretch to buying books and he won't give me money for books, only for housekeeping.

> I'm not bringing in any money and that's part of it. He says I'm just on an ego trip and don't deserve to be encouraged. That really hurt me. I though how could I put myself through all this just for an ego trip.

Practical and emotional support were linked together and often interdependent. Husbands' emotional support was often dependent on not having their lives disrupted by their wives returning to study. While there were some instances where husbands were generally encouraging, in other cases, emotional support was limited to passive acceptance or a mere lack of opposition. The following quotes represent the diversity of responses received:

> My partner has been very supportive. He knows that deep down I have always wanted to do this and it is him who encourages me to fulfil my ambitions. He helps me build up my confidence.

> Well he doesn't mind me coming here. He accepts that this is what I want to do but he doesn't really understand why I want to do it. When I first started the Access course, he asked me would I not be better doing a course in flower arranging or a cookery course as I would find that more enjoyable. He can't understand how I can get pleasure out of what I am doing but he's happy enough to go along with what I want to do.

However, this emotional support rarely translated into practical help. In most instances, wives were still overwhelmingly responsible for housework and childcare. At best, husbands helped out. At worst, husbands' assistance was practically negligible. The following comments were typical:

> I still try to be the housewife he wants. I still do everything at home. I make all the meals and do all the housework. He has a business and doesn't have time for any of that . . . he feels housework is my responsibility and if I can't handle my household duties, then I shouldn't be here

> He's very Victorian. He feels a woman's job is to look after her kids and home and nothing should stand in the way of that. He has very high housekeeping standards and feels that my coming here should not interfere with the house.

In a third of cases, women met with considerable resistance from their husbands over their decision to return to education. The following quotes exemplify this:

> He would say — Oh there's educating Rita, thinks she is above everybody else . . . I couldn't study at home. I always had to wait until he went out. I used to keep my books on top of the ironing board to look at them when I was ironing and when he came into the kitchen I used to quickly hide them under the ironing.

> Do you know we never, ever discuss me being here. Never, ever. He has never ever asked me about how I'm doing. He's never asked me if I passed my exams. When I passed my exams and told him, he said, 'You know I don't want to discuss any aspect of your life at university. That's your business. You decided to do it. I'm not stopping you but I don't want you going on about it.'

> As I became more interested in what I was doing, he became less willing to discuss it. He keeps saying, 'Don't give me any of your Queen's talk here.' If I speak at all about it, he refuses to listen. He walks around the house as if I am not there. He ignores me to punish me. I don't know what the hell he thinks I'm doing at Queen's. He thinks I'm meeting all these men, whoring about while I'm here. I can't talk to anyone about him. They would think I was pathetic. I'm always running everywhere. He keeps a note of my timetable and I have to come straight home after the lectures or tutorials. If I'm late, I start to panic. I don't want him to start when I go home.

In 1991, Christine Jarvis, an Access co-ordinator at Huddersfield Technical College, and her colleagues carried out a survey of 64 of their Access students and found that one in three of the women had experienced domestic violence during their year on the course. Among the 12 married women interviewed at Queen's, one-quarter had been the victims of domestic violence.

Several respondents felt that their husbands' lack of general support, non-cooperation and sometimes violent action was due to feelings of insecurity at their wives returning to education. The following quotes illustrate this view:

> My husband feels a little threatened at times. 'You're more independent. You steal the ground more. There is a chance that you might walk away,' although I never would.

> He's very insecure because in my first year all he said was, when he got a couple of whiskeys, 'you're going to get educated and leave me. You're going to get a brilliant job and one day I am going to come home into the house and you will be gone' . . . I know that deep down he is very insecure. He sees my horizons widening and his standing still.

> I think he is starting to feel very insecure. I keep telling him all that goes on here about how so and so has split up from their husbands. Three out of our wee group of nine have split up already. I just don't think when I tell him. To me it's just idle chit-chat but I think he is reacting to these tales. I think he is starting to think that this might happen to me.

These responses indicate the extent to which women's university careers may impinge on their family life. They also illustrate the conflict between widening women's access to the public world of higher education, while leaving domestic patriarchal ideologies, which promote the confinement of women to the private sphere, unchallenged.

Several of the women did experienced a sense of empowerment through returning to education. This is exemplified by the following quote:

> I dress differently at home. At home I am a wife and mother. When I am here I am a student and I think that I have to dress appropriately. At home you always belong to someone else. You can't do your own thing. You always have to perform the role that is expected of you. I still fit in with the mainstream role that is expected of me. But at home I'm still me inside, only with different clothes on on the outside . . . I'm more independent in my head now even if I go through the same motions.

Institutional Responses

Access courses have met with some resistance from higher education institutions. Some institutions take pride in adopting a gate-keeper role and despite all evidence to the contrary (Walker, 1975; Woodley, 1984; Bourner and Hamed, 1987; Smithers and Robinson, 1989), continue to associate non-standard entry with the lowering of standards. This is clearly seen in the tendency for some institutions to rate their status in terms of the number of applicants that they have to turn away, rather than those they are able to admit (Woodrow, 1988). Woodrow goes on to suggest that reliance on 'A' levels point scores absolve admissions, personnel, and academic staff from the need to make difficult decisions about their student intake. This in turn transforms itself into an unwillingness on the part of higher education institutions to adopt flexible facilities to enhance the access of non-traditional students. Gray (1993) argues that often academics hide behind rules and these rules save the rule followers from making difficult decisions. Harrison (1990) suggests that a true commitment to accessibility demands that universities adopt a more diverse and pluralistic approach to pedagogy. Access students require a different form of interaction with the tutor and socio-psychological support on a scale not associated with traditional intakes. The presence of Access students in large numbers do inevitably distort the curriculum and necessitate changes to the curriculum.

My research findings were first presented at the WHEN conference 1993, University of Central Lancashire, which focused on women and the curriculum in higher education. In her keynote address to the conference, Marilyn Schuster argued that the content of the curriculum and the educational climate needs to reflect the needs of women. Creating an equitable learning climate necessitates bringing about positive change for women as learners. Schuster suggested that achieving meaningful curriculum change requires tackling the invisible as well as the visible structures of disadvantage. The workshop discussion on this chapter focused on mature women students in higher education. One of the participants pointed out that the climate mature students enter is an individiual one, a competitive one, and yet access courses encourage students to operate as a group. Schuster (1993) argued that women more than any other group challenge this deap-seated faith in individualism. The general conclusions from the workshop discussion were that genuine commitment to equality means that we move beyond more equality of access. Equally important is the need to promote equality of outcome. There is no point in expanding access to under-represented groups, if these groups are going to flounder within the university system. We need to follow policies and practices to ensure that certain groups do not under-achieve. This may mean establishing mature student support services and creche facilities to fulfil the specific needs of mature women students.

Universities should also implement policies to ensure that specific groups are not discriminated against in the higher education system. Queen's University, in response to this, holds equal opportunities workshops throughout the year. It is compulsory for all staff, academic and non-academic to attend these workshops. The sessions deal with the law concerning religious and sex discrimination and inform participants of what procedures to follow if they suspect discrimination has been practiced. The Sociology department at Queen's University has recently appointed a member of the academic staff to deal with equal opportunities issues within the department, and all Sociology students are given a handbook giving information about how to contact this person if a complaint arises. While these responses are commendable attempts to deal with the issue of discrimination in legislative terms, they are less successful in tackling the everyday subtle forms of discrimination that permeate many large scale public institutions. Even in legislative terms, statistics from Queen's equal opportunities monitoring unit reveal a strong gender imbalance among academic staff. In October 1990, only 12 per cent of academic staff at Queen's were female. Patriarchal structures and attitudes are not confined to the private lives of mature women students, but also persist in the public sphere to which they have gained access.

Acknowledging the presence of non-traditional groups in teaching materials is one way of transforming the curriculum to their skills, experiences and aspirations should be treated as valid. The curriculum should, where possible, include issues of relevance to women students, and course materials which enhance stereotypical images of under-represented groups should be avoided. To some extent, sociology courses may find such transformations unproblematic since the subject material focuses heavily on issues of gender, race and class. Other subject areas such as science with their reliance on male illustrations and examples have a long way to go to promote the needs of non-traditional groups such as women (Kelly, 1981).

With varying degree of enthusiasm, institutions of higher education are seeking ways of making their provision more accessible and relevant to adult students. Queen's university, for example, has set up a student support services group. Under the direction of one of the pro-vice chancellors, the group meets regularly to discuss the needs and problems of specific types of students. Mature students have been singled out for special attention and Queen's holds an induction day specifically for them. During the induction day, the problems that mature students might face are addressed. For example, students are informed about where in the university they can undertake study skills courses, as many Access students feel greatly inhibited when the study skills component of their Access courses is no longer available. Students are also informed about the financial problems they are likely to specifically encounter as mature students, and are put in touch with a university appointed financial adviser. Queen's has also recently appointed a mature students' officer with special duties of looking after the needs of mature students. All mature students receive an opportunity to meet on a one-to-one basis with the mature students' officer to discuss any problems they might be experiencing. Within the department of Sociology and Social Policy, a mature students' society has also been set up this year. Social evenings and functions have been planned and partners and children of mature students are encouraged to attend. Smithers and Griffin's (1986) study of mature students found that most felt it invaluable to have such an organization within the university.

In many ways, Queen's, as an institution, can be commended for adopting policies to effectively respond to the needs of non-traditional entry students. However, as my research indicates, the greatest drawback mature students may face is the patriarchal attitude of their marital partner and their continued adherence to ideologies of gender stereotyping, which results in women having to engage in a endless juggling act of trying to balance home, family and university committments.

References

BOURNER, T. and HAMED, M. (1987) *Entry Qualifications and Degree Performance*, CNAA Development Services Publication.

DEEM, R. (1978) *Women and Schooling*, London: Routledge and Kegan Paul.

DELAMONT, S. (1980) *Sex Roles and the School*, London: Meuthen.

EDWARDS, R. (1990) 'Connecting method and epistemology: A white woman interviewing black women', *Women's Studies International Forum*, **13**, 477–90.

EDWARDS, R. (1993) 'An education in interviewing: Placing the researcher and the research', in LEE, R. and RENZETTI, C. (Eds) *Researching Sensitive Topics*, CA: Sage.

FINCH, J. (1984) *Education as Social Policy*, London: Longman.

GRAHAM, H. (12983) 'Do her answers fit his questions? Women and the survey method', in GAMARNIKOW, E. MORGAN, D. PURVIS, J. and TAYLORSON, D. (Eds) *The Public and the Private*, London: Heinemann.

GRAHAM, H. (1984) 'Surveying through stories', in BELL, C. and ROBERTS, H. (Eds), *Social Researching*, London: Routledge and Kegan Paul.

GRAY, B. (1993) 'Women in higher education: Expanding definitions of "academic"' Paper given at Women and the Higher Education Curriculum Conference, University of Central Lancashire, November.

GREEN, M. and PERCEY, P. (1991) 'Gender and access' in CHITTY, C. (Ed), *Post-16 Education: Studies in Access and Achievement*, London: Kogan Page.

HARRISON, M. J. (1990) 'Access — the problem and potential', *Higher Education Quarterly*, **44** (3).

JARVIS, C. (1992) 'Keeping them down: Women and access provision', *Access News*, **3**, June.

JONES, P. and MILLINS, K. (1990) *A Survey of Access Courses to higher Education*, CNAA Briefing Paper (22).

KELLY, A. (1981) *The Missing Half: Girls and Science*, Manchester: Manchester University Press.

LOVELL, A. (1980) 'Fresh horizons: The aspirations and problems of intending mature students', *Feminist Review*, (6).

LUCAS, S. and WARD, P. (1985) *A Survey of Access Courses in England*, Lancaster University.

LYON, E. (1988) 'Unequal opportunities: Black minorities and access to higher education', *Journal of Further and Higher Education*, (12).

MIES, M. (1983) 'Toward a methodology for feminist research' in BOWLES, G. and DUELLI KLEIN, R. (Eds), *Theories of Women's Studies*, London: Routledge and Kegan Paul.

MOSER, C. A. (1958) 'Interviewing women: A contradiction in terms', in ROBERTS, H. (Ed), *Doing Feminist Research*, London: Routledge and Kegan Paul.

PAHL, J. (1989) *Money and Marriage*, London: Macmillan.

PANTZIARKA, P. (1987) 'The step from further to higher education', *Journal of Access Studies*, (2), London: Fast.

PARKER, S., EMMETT, T. and SMITH, P. (1990) Managing Equality in Access, *Higher Education Quarterly*, **44** (4).

PASCALL, G. and COX, R. (1993) *Women Returning to Higher Education*, Buckingham: SRHE and Open University Press.

PEARSON, R., PIKE, G., GORDON, A. and WEGMAN, C. (1989) *How Many Graduates in the 21st Century? — The Choice is Yours*, Brighton Institute of Manpower Studies.

PEARSON, R. (1990) 'Doubling student numbers — What are the Prospects?' *Higher Education Quarterly*, **44**, (3).

SCHUSTER, M. (1993) *'Transforming the curriculum'*, paper given at the Women and the Higher Education Curriculum Conference, University of Central Lancashire, November 1993.

SMITH, S. (1993) 'Uncovering key aspects of experience — The use of in-depth interviews in a study of women returners to eduction', paper preseented at the British Sociological Association Annual Conference at University of Essex.

SMITHERS, A. and GRIFFIN, A. (1986) *The Progress of Mature Students*, Manchester: Joint Matriculation Board.

SMITHERS, A. and ROBINSON, P. (1989) *Increasing Participation in Higher Education*, University of Manchester: BP Educational Services.

WALKER, P. (1975) The University Performance of Mature Students, *Research in Education*, (14).

WISKER, A. and MILLINS, K. (1988) *Access Courses to Higher Education:* Development of a Database, CNAA.

WOODLEY, A., (1984) The Older the Better? A Study of Mature Student Performance in British Universities, *Research in Education*, (32).

WOODLEY, A., WAGNER, L., SLOWERY, M., HAMILTON, M. and FULTON, O. (1987) *Choosing to Learn: Adults in Education*, London: Society for Research in Higher Education and Open University Press.

WOODROW, M. (1988) The Access Course Route to Higher Education, *Higher Education Quarterly*, **42**.

Chapter 13

Health and Caring in a Feminist Context

Doreen MacWhannell

Introduction

Higher education in the UK is currently experiencing some of the greatest academic and economic challenges that it has ever had to face. Decreasing funding levels and increasing student numbers are two of the most crucial features of this ever changing and fluid environment. New contractual arrangements and organizational restructuring are now commonplace. Academic staff who work within these institutions are now involved in decision-making and problem solving that goes well beyond the boundaries of academic issues. Consumerism and value for money, in addition to education for the masses, is the new language of academic life, but cynicism prevails as the majority view such language as mere rhetoric. Staff at the chalkface literally observe the reality: mass education indeed, but with a feeling that lowering standards are a fact of life, despite the student now being the consumer. Most of this change has been implemented in a top-down manner by senior managers. It is driven by government policy, which in Britain is driven by a market ideology.

At this point little has been said of the students and their experiences, yet a major reorganization of the curriculum is currently taking place. Colleges and universities up and down the country are now moving to modular systems of curricular provision. This is certainly a challenge to all who work and study in HE, but has unfortunately come about at such a time of massive change that it has not been exactly welcomed and wholeheartedly embraced by academics. Yet, modularization has facilitated a process of being able to deliver new and exciting academic subjects into the mainstream curriculum. The purpose of this chapter is to explore this positive aspect of modularization. In managerial terms, modularization could be a classic bottom-up approach enabling staff to change, update and enrich the curriculum — the fast and flat, flexible system of the 90s in organizational terms. As Jarvis (1992) remarked that the modular structure seems ideal for contemporary society. He claims that it is the educational structure for a late-capitalist society. The modular curriculum might also be defined as postmodern, utilizing features of decentralization, fluidity and flexibility (Thompson, 1993).

The focus of this chapter will be a module entitled Feminism, Health and Caring. This will be used to demonstrate how the mainstream curriculum within health programmes can be challenged — using modularity as the structure to enable the inclusion of 'stand alone' modules, such as this. The chapter will demonstrate ways in which feminist perspectives can be developed within health care courses by the use of distinct modules, enabling such perspectives to be channelled into modular programmes. It will consider the institutional approach whereby health students are now able to gain access to feminist theory as part of their programme, specifically discuss a module entitled Feminism, Health and Caring which gives students access to feminist theory and feminist concepts of women's health, review the literature concerning the teaching of women's health within a feminist context and suggest that Women's Studies modules can be easily accessed by health students within traditional programmes for professional education. Action such as this would mean engaging with and informing current practice. This would enable a more holistic approach to patient care to be offered. This would affect healthcare provision, not only for women, but also for men. It will be suggested that the provision of even one module can be successful in redressing some of the imbalances that exist within the current health curriculum of many institutions. It will also be demonstrated that the process of modularization has enabled the inclusion of feminist perspectives into discrete subject areas of the curriculum where previously they had not been taught. The area to be considered will be the teaching of women's health.

An Institutional Approach to Modularization

The module, Feminism, Health and Caring, was offered as one of four options within a BSc (Hons) Health Sciences and a BSc (Hons) Nursing Studies degree at a Midlands University, which was previously a Polytechnic. These degrees are offered within a School of Health and Social Sciences. The modular structure allows a defined number of core modules to be offered, in conjunction with a number of optional modules. The latter may or may not be academically related to core subjects. This allows the students to package a chosen route of study and gives far greater flexibility and choice within that route. Many health professionals in the UK are now undertaking education at undergraduate level to supplement their original diploma-level professional qualification. These groups are comprised of nurses, midwives, health visitors, district nurses plus the whole range of health professions, which in the United Kingdom are referred to as the 'professions allied to medicine'. This includes such groups as dieticians, physiotherapists, occupational therapists, radiographers, and chiropodists.[1]

There are many reasons why individuals want to upgrade a professional qualification, and institutions on their part have responded to and exploited this situation by providing a variety of programmes to enable a whole range of health professionals to gain degrees. The need to gain knowledge and skills in research is of paramount importance to health professionals. In some instances this lack of research in diploma-level education has been the only significant difference between a degree and diploma-level course. For the professions allied to medicine, diploma-level education is a thing of the past. There has also been a knock-on effect here as pressure is felt by those students who are themselves now involved in the delivery of teaching at degree level to health professionals. There is a perceived need by those who both deliver and teach health care, to update *their* qualifications to, at a minimum, keep u with their own students!

The two degrees previously mentioned, Health Sciences and Nursing Studies, are offered on a part-time basis. Similar programmes are being offered up and down the country providing flexible modes of education. These degrees lend themselves to being provided in a modular pattern as core subjects which usually include research methodology and are combined with optional subjects. This allows the student to put together a comprehensive package of study. This is welcomed by mature students who are busy practitioners needing the flexible arrangement of modular part-time study. Feminism, Health and Caring was offered as an optional subject. It proved to be popular, with 25 per cent of the student cohort choosing to take this module from a choice of four options, but the validation, adoption and development of this module raised many issues that will be familiar to those who teach Women's Studies in the UK. Ignorance of the subject area and initial hostility by a minority of academic staff were encountered in relation to the module proposal in its progress towards validation.

The fact that this module was optional and not core could be a discussion point in itself. One has to be realistic however. The fact that it *was* included within a traditional health programme can be seen as a positive and potentially exciting move. What is core or optional in a modular degree is always an area of great debate. This particular module was offered alongside more traditional modules seen in health programmes, such as Health Psychology. It is important, however, to recognize the wider effects and implications. This module was included in the Women's Studies degree being planned at that time as an already validated module and a core subject within that degree. The potential is obvious.

The planning of a modular degree is facilitated by stand-alone modules of this type being initially validated as individual modules. Selected modules can then be utilized in the planning of degree programmes around that subject. This incremental approach can be a useful way forward and an enabling process for subject areas such as Women's Studies which are still met with hostility in some institutions.

The Student Cohort

Questionnaires were used to survey two cohorts of students over a two-year period (1991–93). One questionnaire was distributed prior to commencement of the module and a second was utilized on completion. The students who chose the module were all women. Some had more than 30 years' experience of working in healthcare settings, others had been qualified and practicing for only three years. The majority held professional diplomas in an area of health or nursing. However, four students were final year undergraduates taking an Honours degree in Occupational Therapy. Responses showed that the practising students had had little or no opportunity to study women's health from feminist perspectives. Even those who were only recently qualified, with perhaps three or four years' experience, had had no opportunity to study women and their health needs from such perspectives. Some of these practitioners were actually working with women's groups, for example, with women who had been referred for psychotheraphy or who had an eating disorder. A situation of even greater concern to the author was the fact that those students still in training in 1993, and not yet practising, had had no opportunity to address health issues from either a gendered or feminist perspectives. When the practitioner students had been taught about women and their health behaviour, this had followed a traditional pattern. Motherhood and childbearing were the only areas which had been addressed. Traditional, patriarchal medical values and traditions had been adhered to and a biological model was commonly adopted.

Feminist Perspectives Within a Traditional Health Curriculum

Providing students with feminist approaches to concepts of caring and healthcare provision through the module Feminism, Health and Caring resulted in a powerful combination. The students' enthusiasm and excitement was palpable. They had chosen to take this module, therefore motivation was high, but being at last able to academically access what they knew existed, but had not been able to procure, was overwhelming. They could access both theory and research which other lecturers had been unable or unwilling to provide. Being able to teach a subject area such as this was also an enriching experience for the author. For the students, however, it seemed to have a far more powerful effect. As one student said, 'This module has changed my life.' This response needs to be stated as it must raise questions for those who teach and work in the area of health.

Women make up 79 per cent of the National Health Service workforce (Langridge, 1993), and women are the main users of healthcare systems (Abbott and Wallace, 1990). Yet it would appear that some students are being denied access to a wealth of literature and research which would enrich their practice and, in turn, their care of patients and clients. In relation to this absence of feminist thinking Miles succinctly supports the author's view stating, 'This state of affairs is deplorable,' adding that 'ignoring the feminist contribution distorts and misleads' (1991:141). Miles raises the issue that healthcare professionals are mainly women and that they regularly work with women. She discusses the supposed balance and objectivity of curriculum material that institutions are required to provide. A crucial and fundamental point is raised here. The majority of training and education of health professionals emanates from a scientific and medical model of health. It has been, and often still is, an ongoing challenge to the curricular of some health professionals to adopt a more psychosocial approach to care. However, not long ago there was a complete absence of the Social Sciences within the education of some health students. The subject matter can still be viewed as soft, lacking in rigorous scientific and rational reasoning. Again such debates are well known among feminists, especially feminist sociologists. If the Social Sciences can still be seen in themselves as a challenge to the curriculum content, then it is a simple matter to understand the delay in health students being able to study Women's Studies. As we are reminded, Women's Studies take us even further along a challenging path to the 'malestream' curriculum (Richardson and Robinson, 1993).

Planning and Content of the Module

The content of the module Feminism, Health and Caring was challenging to both lecturer and student. From the lecturer's point of view, and in the context of planning, these students were taking a third-level module at Honours degree level, having no understanding of feminist theory. It was crucial therefore to plan a course of study that would raise awareness of feminist thought, yet would also provide a rigorous and analytical course, providing students with knowledge and information. To do this within one module is a challenge indeed, yet, in the students' view, objectives were successfully achieved. Application of this theory, in the context of women's health, was the ultimate aim of the module. As with all successful teaching, enthusiasm, good planning and a sound theoretical grounding in the subject to be taught were essential elements. Preparation included meeting the students and requesting the completion of questionnaire to determine their professional backgrounds, aspirations, needs, wants and outcomes (both professionally and personally) from such a course of study. This knowledge would subsequently inform the content of the module. One aspect of this personal meeting was fascinating. In discussion with the students at this first meeting, it appeared that the most important aspect of this event was *not* finding out about the module but finding out about the lecturer! Some students wanted to know 'how feminist' I was, did they have to be feminists to take the module and whether I came over as being too 'strong'. When as a group we discussed this later some interesting issues arose (mainly to do with the admission that they had all wanted to see what I looked like, what I was wearing and whether I was radical). One student wanted to know if there were any other married students taking the module. These comments (anxieties) were all discussed when the group had formed and the environment felt safer for them, and they expressed embarrassment when they were able to recognize their own ignorance and negative views of feminism. To pose such questions, however, highlights the crucial need to provide feminist perspectives in order to be able to dispel fears and challenge prejudices.

In recognition that the majority of students had never read any academic Women's Studies material, a pre-reading pack was supplied. This was comprised of a selection of articles taken from journals and texts from a variety of sources — none concerned with women's health. Articles on feminist film critiques, politics, literature, sexuality, Women's Studies and feminist theory were included. These proved to be very successful. The readings highlighted both the variety and range of academic research and writings to which the students had not been exposed. A comprehensive booklist was also supplied and details of teaching methods were discussed.

Teaching and Learning Strategies

The nature of teaching and learning approaches were addressed in recognition that students might not have been previously exposed to feminist teaching practices. They had not. As has been noted (Shrewsbury, 1987), respect for difference, democratic and participative approaches are some of the components of feminist pedagogy. The use of discussion and validation of the students' own experiences was also recognized. That this needed to be stated to students is supported by Shrewsbury, who argues that critical thinking cannot be an abstracted analysis but is a 'reflective process firmly grounded in the experiences of the everyday'. This tied in well with preliminary discussions as to the nature of feminism, subjectivity and difference which formed core discussions early in the module.

In the first session an ice-breaker was used to define *feminism* — an invigorating, challenging and educational experience, never to be forgotten by all! The first two sessions dealt solely with feminist theory. Concepts such as patriarchy, oppression, sexism and women as 'other' were discussed, supported by the research and current literature in these areas. Interesting debates ensued and each group responded — as would be expected — in different ways. The pace was regulated to allow all students to engage with the subject areas being discussed. The responsibility of putting theory into practice was ever-present for both teacher and student. Students need to be reminded that sessions such as these will raise personal issues and this is expected and validated. It never ceases to amaze me how bright and articulate students are. Yet they remind me that they have never been able to discuss, debate and learn in this way about women's health needs. The mainstream curriculum could indeed learn much from feminist pedagogy.

Students felt a gap in their education, a void that was never filled in any sense of the word by their professional education. *Sadness* seems an inappropriate phrase to use, but it was the emotional response expressed by many students, *anger* being another, plus *joy* and *delight* at being able to tackle such a stimulating and challenging subject. There was always a wonderful urgency as if these women were desperate to be heard to tell their stories. This is familiar territory for those who teach Women's Studies. These students did not necessarily define themselves as feminists at the beginning of the module, but, interestingly, most were happy to give themselves that label on completion of the module. They somehow felt they could now justify their political and personal position if required to do so. One student told us that she knew all this was going on but could never articulate it. She felt happier now that she could understand and coherently debate. But she suggested, as did her peers, that it was a pity that she had to defend all the time. She also felt even more concerned for the practices she saw going on around her in the clinical environment.

Module Content

The content of subsequent sessions was well planned in relation to the students' knowledge base and professional background (See Table 1). A flexible approach was required, however, as the wide variety of professional backgrounds

Table 1: Module Content

Sociobiology and social construction
Biological reductionism
Medical metaphors of women's bodies
Biological sex differences
Sex stereotyping
Historial debates with reference to women's health
Witches, healers and wise, wise women
Sexuality
Women and ageing
Women and mental health: A touch of the vapours!
The AIDS and HIV debate — Where are the women?
Black women's health issues
Medicalization and the medical control of women
Feminist critiques of IVF
Health issues for lesbian women
Hormone additive therapy — a feminist perspective on HRT
Women as workers in the National Health Service
Caring. The nature/culture debate
Researching women.

necessitated alterations to the programme at times, in keeping with the specialist areas of work in which the students were involved.

A book box was brought to every session in order to create an awareness of the wealth of feminist literature, particularly that related to women's health. The students' thirst for knowledge and their level of debate dispelled any fear by the author that providing one module of undergraduate study would be tokenism — another fear being it might also create frustration and discontent, instead of providing a stimulating course of study. The survey of the last two cohorts of students demonstrates that the provision of a module such as this can make some impact in addressing issues that have never been included in undergraduate programmes for education and training of health professionals.

Current Developments in the Healthcare Curriculum

This is an interesting time in the development and undergraduate education of health professionals in the UK, especially in nursing. Many schools and departments have become amalgamated into HE colleges and universities. This has been a major cultural change. It is now becoming common practice that students will learn alongside other health students, and will often be taught by someone who does not possess their professional background and training. Modularization has both explored and exploited, but also challenged this situation. The curriculum, by virtue of this process, becomes overt and visible, and traditional core and non-core subject matter is challenged, while validation processes seek out and test traditional values, attitudes and beliefs. The curriculum looks very different today from even five or six years ago. The inclusion of the Social Sciences in the health curriculum has already been alluded to, yet this is just one of the many changes. Interestingly, and in the context of this paper, a major shift has taken place in relation to moves away from a biomedical model. As Ruzek (1993) states in her discussion regarding 'the strains and tensions between a narrow biomedical model and a more inclusive social model of health', the latter would put 'women's core needs at the centre of analysis' (1993: 6). She also reminds us that women are not a homogenous group and that diversities among women must be addressed. This brings us back to the earlier point that courses in women's health can fail to address *all* women if feminist perspectives are not given. All women do not have the same health problems, and all do not choose, or are able to choose, similar lifestyles.

Within a modular system, scrutiny of the health curriculum by non-health professionals is now common. This has brought about major changes and has had the effect of greatly expanding the curricular content, for example, management, information technology, law and ethics are subject areas now included. The impact on content of both health and educational policies such as Project 2000 cannot be negated. However when the debate centres on the inclusion of feminist perspectives, we can see that in the majority of institutions change has also been in response to the changes brought about by second wave feminism in the late sixties.

Where are the Feminists in Women's Health Professions?

The literature that addresses this issue is mainly North American and related to the nursing profession. We are reminded (Hagell, 1990) of a growing awareness with the health concerns of women and the subsequent development of educational programmes interestingly mostly offered through Women's Studies programmes. One view (Thomas, 1992) is that nursing itself 'has been conspicuously absent from the Women's Movement'. This is contradicted by Fogel and Woods, who in 1981 were raising the issue that nursing was likely to emerge as the most responsive profession with regard to women's health. However, even in professions, where women hold the majority of posts, women's needs can be, as demonstrated, ignored, marginalized or negated. The healthcare system may not be good for women (McBride, 1993). Why do women who work in health not recognize this? Why do they collude with the existing system? Why do they not seek to change it? It is suggested that they do not because of the power differences that exist within patriarchal institutions, such as those involved in the provision of health (Turner, 1987).

The literature overwhelmingly demonstrates that nurse education has been slow to develop courses that address women's health issues from a feminist perspective. Andrist (1988) agrees that when women's issues have been taught it is in a traditional, patriarchal model, both supporting and reinforcing medical dominance. She cites obstetrics and gynecology as being typical areas to be taught under a heading of women's health, in addition to menstruation and the menopause. Other authors support her findings, giving voice to this very narrow definition of women's health. (Saunders and Taylor, 1985; Oakley, 1993)

Boughn (1987) raises the fundamental question as to why nursing education neglects to include feminist theory into their curricula even though the profession is populated primarily by women. The response to this, recognizing patriarchy as a crucial element, is that all nurses are not feminists, although one can empathize with Boughn's view. She also notes that feminist perspectives 'provides a solid theoretical base upon which nurse education can be restructured'. But she agrees that nursing education has resisted the inclusion of such a perspective (Boughn, 1991).

A Relationship Between Nursing Theory and Feminist Theory?

Recognizing that professionalization is in itself a patriarchal process (Hearn, 1982), it is important to move the debate on. Nursing, as a profession, has made a great impact upon notions of health, illness and care and has developed a theoretical framework. Major changes have been taking place in the development of theory and practice of nursing. Chinn and Wheeler support this, yet provide a counter argument to the notion that there can be little connection between feminist theory and nursing theory stating, 'Nursing practice typically occurs in the oppressive, reductionistic milieu of the patriarchal order, the hospital, which does not foster, tolerate, endorse, nor approve nursing practice based on nursing's own theories and values' (1985: 76).

The concept of patriarchy is raised time and time again by authors writing with regard to the subject of teaching women's health within nursing, but women work within many other health professions, it is unfair to lay blame at the nursing profession alone. But *who* else *is* challenging the health curriculum?

Andrist (1988) discusses how crucial it is for those who teach women's health to understand patriarchy. She cites the paternalistic system, the 'perpetuation of women as sexual objects', and medicalization and control as key issues necessary to both enable understanding and to develop a feminist consciousness in nursing theory. Developing this argument further, she talks of the early days of second-wave feminism, reminding us that nurses, like most women . . . 'were unaware of their oppression'. More crucially she describes the current system where when doctors 'have traditionally been in control, nursing . . . internalised the values of medicine, consequently identifying with medicine'. She helpfully provides an explanation to this notion of male identification by quoting (Barry, 1984) who herself explains such identification as 'the path of least resistance for women in patriarchy'.

The Contribution of Feminist Theory to the Health Debate

The curriculum of health care students has been shown to have altered in many aspects in relation to the subject matter that students are now expected to learn as part of their professional education. Modularization has been shown to be both a vehicle and a route into this expanded curriculum. An example has been given as to the process in which one module can provide a new, innovative, and, it is suggested here, essential contribution to the education of a wide variety of health students. One focus here has been the development and delivery of a module and the students taking this module. The students' views were extremely positive. One aspect of particular importance to them was that they now felt able to challenge the content of their previous educational experience and the modules within their current programme. The latter related to an absence of gender and feminist perspectives in other subject areas. It also related to sexism within the curriculum. They felt confident and able to challenge practices they observed or were expected to participate in, in their clinical work. They recognized that they could act as agents for change, yet they realized the enormity of such a role. These students had been teased by their peers (and other lecturers) for their choice of module. Some had to fight with their employers for the opportunity to take this module. It was deemed by line managers to be unsuitable, inappropriate, not academic and (frighteningly, yet unsurprisingly!) not relevant to the workplace. Raising awareness of women's issues is just one component of introducing subject matter such as this into the curriculum.

It is important to recognize, however, the extra stress and strain it puts on students, whether mature or otherwise. These health students will provide many differing treatments and care models, but the majority of them will be women providing support and healthcare to many other women. Women are 'an oppressed minority despite being a statistical majority' in relation to their healthcare needs and provision by the healthcare system within the United Kingdom (Oakley, 1993).

Neither *The Health of the Nation* (Department of Health, 1991) nor *Scotland's Health: A Challenge to us All* (The Scottish Office, 1992) really radically challenge or redress gender inequalities in healthcare. Priorities and targets remain predominantly male, coronary heart disease and suicide being two examples. The Royal College of Nursing (1991) has attempted to increase the debate regarding women's health. It has also attempted to move the debate on from one which merely discusses women in relation to their reproductive health and their role as mothers. Nursing has been used throughout this chapter as an example of a profession where the majority of workers are women but which has done little to address women's health from feminist perspectives. Yet it, and the other women-dominated professions, hold prime positions to be able to do this, both in practice and in theory, through the education of its workforce.

An attempt has been made to demonstrate ways in which feminist perspectives enrich the health curriculum. As Chinn and Wheeler remind us 'feminism provides a personal, philosophic and political means for analysing the realities of women's lives . . . It is not a single line of thought' (1985: 77). Any enrichment of the curriculum will inform practice and improve the care provided to both women and men.

Conclusion

A student commented after attending a women's health course similar to that described by the author that she had learned not to be afraid of issues that would slap her in the face when she graduated (Boughn, 1987). Those who teach health students would surely wish to ensure that our students are best equipped to cope with the fundamental changes taking place in providing healthcare. Removing inequalities in health is the responsibility of all who teach and practice. Feminist theory, according to Thomas (1992), suggests that women's experiences have never been adequately articulated, because men rather than women have described and explained women's experiences. Feminism has questioned and challenged how we form and validate knowledge. It would be expected that the place for debate regarding this would be in the academy, but it would appear that this is not so.[2]

Chinn and Wheeler, in relation to nursing in the USA, argue that feminist perspectives require 'uncompromising questioning of the forces that divide us from one another, the ethics of our actions, and our co-optation into the unhealthy environment of the healthcare system' (1985: 77). Those who are involved in the education of health students have a responsibility to provide a rigorous and challenging educational experience for them. This may encompass areas of the academy which some would wish did not exist. Securing the health of the nation means just that — securing health for all. Feminist perspectives, offered through just one module, by the process of modularization, can facilitate this and more.

Notes

1 It is important to note, within the context of this paper, that these occupational groups are defined as semi-professions. For a detailed discussion see Witz, A. (1992) *Professions and Patriarchy*, Routledge: London.
2 For a debate regarding feminist knowledge and thought see Gunew, S. (1990) 'Feminist knowledge: Critique and construct', in Gunew, S. (Ed.) *Feminist Knowledge: Critique and Construct*, Routledge: London.

References

ABBOT, P., WALLACE, C. (1990 'Women, health and caring', in *An Introduction to Sociology: Feminist Perspectives*, London: Routledge, pp. 94–120.
ANDRIST, L. C. (1988) 'A feminist framework for graduate education in women's health', *Journal of Nursing Education*, 327(2) February, pp. 66–70.
BARRY, K. (1984) *Female Sexual Slavery*, New York, NY: NYU Press, cited in ANDRIST, L. C. (1988) *op cit.*
BOUGHN, S. (1987) 'A strategy for increasing student autonomy: Women's health course', *Nurse Educator*, 12(6) Nov/Dec. pp. 31–3.
BOUGHN, S. (1991) 'A women's health course with a feminist perspective: Learning to care for and empower ourselves', *Nursing and Health Care*, 12(2), pp. 76–80.
CHINN, P. L. and WHEELER, C. E. (1985) 'Feminism and nursing: Can nursing afford to remain aloof from the women's movement?' *Nursing Outlook*, 33(2), pp. 74–7.
DEPARTMENT OF EDUCATION (1992) 'Aspects of women's studies courses in higher education', A Report by HMI, April 1991–March 1992, Ref. 371/92/NS.
DEPARTMENT OF HEALTH (1991) 'The health of the nation', London: Her Majesty's Stationary Office.
FOGEL, C. and WOODS, N. (1981) 'Health care of women: A nursing perspective', St. Lo uis, MO: Mosby, cited in THOMAS, B. (1992) *op cit.*
HAGELL, E. I. (1990) 'Time for change: Women's health education in Canadian University Schools of Nursing', *Health Care for Women International* 11: pp. 121–31.
HEARN, J. (1982) 'Notes on patriarchy, professionalization and the semi-professions', *Sociology*, 16, pp. 184–202.
JARVIS, P. (1992) 'Certification and the bureaucratic statre' in PLARJANEN, M. (Ed.)

Legitimation in Adult Education, Julkaisusarja, A2/92 Publications, Institute of Extension Studies, Finland: University of Tampere, pp. 13–29.

LANGRIDGE, C. (1993) 'Women on the edge of a workforce breakthrough', *Health Service Journal*, 7 October, pp. 28–30.

MCBRIDE, A. B. (1993) 'From gynecology to gyn-ecology: Developing a practice-research agenda for women's health', *Health Care for Women International*, **14**, pp. 315–25.

MILES, A. (1991) 'Women in medicine', in *Women, Health and Medicine*, Buckingham: Open University Press, pp. 124–52.

OAKLEY, A. (1993) *Essays on Women, Medicine and Health*, Edinburgh: Edinburgh University Press, Introduction, p. ix.

RICHARDSON, D. ROBINSON, V. (1993) 'Introducing women's studies', in *Introducing Women's Studies*, London: The Macmillan Press Ltd, pp. 1–26.

ROYAL COLLEGE OF NURSING (1992) 'Health of half the nation', London: Royal College of Nursing.

RUZEK, S. B. (1987) 'Towards a more inclusive model of women's health', *American Journal of Public Health*, January 1993, **83**(1), pp. 6–8.

SAUNDERS, R.B. and TAYLOR, R. H. (1985) 'Women's health: Developing a course for open enrollment', *Nurse Educator*, Mar/April, pp. 25–30.

SHREWSBURY, C. M. (1987) 'What is feminist pedagogy?' *Women's Studies Quarterly*, **XV**(3)(4), pp. 6–14.

THE SCOTTISH OFFICE (1992) 'Scotland's health: A challenge to us all', London: Her Majesty's Stationary Office.

THOMAS, B. (1992) 'Challenges for teachers of women's health', *Nurse Educator*, **17**(5), pp. 10–14.

THOMPSON, P. (1993) 'Postmodernism: Fatal distraction', in HASSARD, J. and MARTIN, P. (Eds) *Postmodernism and Organizations*, London: Sage, pp. 183–203.

TURNER, B. (1987) 'Women's complaints: Patriarchy and illness' in TURNER, B. (1987) *Medical Power and Social Knowledge*, London: Sage, pp. 82–110.

Chapter 14

Transforming the Curriculum

Marilyn R. Schuster

A landmark of feminist scholarship and teaching has been attention to cultural context; curriculum transformation work, in particular, needs to be shaped by local needs, strengths, and values. I will count on you to help make the translation from our work in the US to yours in the UK; I'm quite certain that the tasks and motives and obstacles we face bear much resemblance. I can only speak, however, from what I know and what I have learned from colleagues throughout the United States, hoping that it will prove helpful to you.[1]

I will address issues of curriculum transformation in three ways. First, I will propose working definitions of Women's Studies and curriculum transformation and consider the relation between Women's Studies, coeducation and the curriculum in general. Second, with the help of a chart, I will outline the stages of curricular change that Susan Van Dyne and I have identified to track the process of change, the motivation of faculty members to participate in the process and the connections between curricular content and pedagogical practice. Finally, using several images from the American press, I'll present a cautionary tale about forms of resistance to Women's Studies and curriculum transformation.

Women's Studies and Curriculum Transformation

What is Women's Studies?

Women's Studies is an interdisciplinary, multicultural field that has grown over the last 20 years. In the US there are now formal programs on over 600 campuses and women's courses are taught at 75 per cent of all colleges and universities. As a field, Women's Studies includes research in all the disciplines of the humanities and social sciences and increasingly in mathematics, and the natural sciences, especially biology.

Women's Studies programs thrive on campuses where there is also a commitment to ethnic studies. Often courses in both programs are cross-listed, recognizing that Women's Studies must include attention too all women and ethnic studies must pay attention to the experience and cultural production of women as well as men.

Historically, Women's Studies as a field accomplishes three tasks — it corrects errors of fact, adds new information, and provides new analytical frameworks. As all of us engaged in this work know well, Women's Studies not only increases what we know about women, it enriches our understanding of men, and allows us to understand gender relations — how the roles assigned to men and to women structure our societies and shape our personal intractions and public policies.

We need to define *higher education* and *curriculum* broadly. Students learn not only in seminars, lectures, study groups and tutorials but in all their experiences in and outside of the university. Equity for women in our universities leads us to think about all aspects of the university. In the classroom we need to think about creating equal access to the teacher's attention and equal representation in the curriculum (seeing the experience of women and people of color represented in the curriculum). Equity also requires the creation of a university community in which women's activities outside of the classroom are valued as highly as men's and it means assuring that all women and men of color see models for their own success mirrored throughout the university — on the faculty and at all levels of the administration and staff.

The curriculum includes all the ways and places a student learns: choice of extra-curricular activities, advising as well as teaching, interaction with staff, patterns of friendship groups, social interaction in the coffee lounges, values reinforced by celebrations, prizes, recognition throughout the university as well as courses and the classroom experience *per se*.

Women's Studies and Coeducation

As a faculty member in a women's college, I'm often asked what place Women's Studies has in a coeducational university. A comprehensive definition of coeducation would include the composition of the student body, the profile of the teaching faculty and administration, the content of the curriculum and classroom climate.

Having roughly equal numbers of women and men students in the student body is not enough to assure that both women and men have equal access to the educational opportunities on a campus or equal chances of realizing their intellectual potential. Studies have shown that the academic and career achievement of women is positively correlated to increased numbers of women on the faculty and in positions of authority in the administration.[2]

The content of the curriculum and classroom climate must also figure in a comprehensive view of coeducation. Male students as well as women need to understand the historical contributions of women and the condition of women today throughout the world. As students begin to take Women's Studies courses they recognize the need for curriculum transformation. As one student put it to me, 'Once I had discovered what was possible to learn about women from a course that focused on women, I felt cheated in the courses in my major because they didn't pay any attention to women.'

The most powerful message we sent to students about the world and what we value in it is the curriculum. A second powerful message, of course, and one which equally influences feelings of self-worth, possibility and responsibility for both women and men students, are the teachers we hire and retain to teach them. Men as well as women students are inadequately educated if women are missing from the curriculum and under-represented in the faculty.

Women's Studies and Curriculum Transformation

Curriculum transformation involves the incorporation of Women's Studies and ethnic studies scholarship throughout the curriculum. Curriculum transformation programs encourage all members of the educational community to create an equitable learning climate. Curriculum transformation projects incorporate faculty development as a means to curricular change. Faculty members in all fields need to have an opportunity to read together current feminist scholarship in order to rethink what they are teaching and to identify new materials to include in their courses. Curriculum transformation is even more difficult to accomplish than Women's Studies because it makes us bring new paradigms created in feminist scholarship into courses shaped by disciplines that are still defined by conventional paradigms.

Stages of Curricular Change

I'd like to turn now to a discussion of curricular change as we have watched it over the last ten years in North American universities. The chart outlining stages

Table 14.1 Stages of Curriculum Change

Stages	Questions	Incentives	Means	Outcome
1 Invisibility	Who are the truly great thinkers/actors in history?	Maintaining 'standards of excellence'	Back to basics	Pre-1960s exclusionary core curriculum Fixed products Student as 'vessels'
2 Search for missing women, men of color	Who are the great women, female Shakespeares? Who are the Black Darwins?	Affirmative action/compensatory	Add data within existing paradigms	'Exceptional' women added to syllabus; 'Contribution history' Role models for students of color and for women
3 Minorities as oppressed, women as subordinate group	Why has African-American experience been devalued? distorted? Why is women's work marginal?	Anger/Social Justice	Protest existing paradigms but within perspective of dominant group	'Images of women' courses Black Studies begins; 'US Minorities' courses
4 Women studied on own terms, cultures studied from insiders' perspective	What was/is women's experience? What are differences among peoples of color? among women? (attention to race, class, cultural differences, different meanings of gender)	Intellectual	Outside existing paradigms; develop insiders' perspective	Asian-Americans Latino writers Links ethnic, cross-cultural studies and women's studies Interdisciplinary courses Student values own experience
5 New scholarship challenges disciplines	How valid are current definitions of historical periods, greatness, norms for behavior? How must questions change to account for gender, ethnicity, class in context?	Epistemology	Testing the paradigms. Gender, race, class as categories of analysis	Beginnings of transformation Theory courses; Teacher as coach Student as collaborator
6 Visibility; Transformed curriculum	How do class and race intersect with gender? How can we account more fully for the diversity of human experience?	Inclusive vision of human experience based on differences and diversity, not sameness and generalization	Transform the paradigms	Reconceptualized, inclusive core Dynamic process Transformed introductory courses Empowering of student

Prepared by Susan Van Dyne and Marilyn Schuster, Smith College, Northampton, MA.

of curricular change presents an overview of where we're going, but the landmarks are more recognizable once we've been there. The stages present a process that academic disciplines, individual teachers, and even institutions are going through, but at different rates. Even an individual teacher may find herself at different stages in different courses.[3]

This chart, like all feminist scholarship, grows out of collaborative conversations. The first effort to chart stages of disciplinary change was Gerda Lerner's characterization of history in *The Majority Finds its Past: Placing Women in History* published in 1979.[4] Peggy McIntosh outlined five interactive phases of teaching and learning in history.[5] Susan Van Dyne and I first developed our chart in 1983 and have modified it several times since, in an effort to capture the ways that research on women and marginalized cultures continue to change what we know and how we know it.

The stages chart hopes to illustrate the process of curricular change as teachers have experienced it — identifying incentives, obstacles, and connections between questions raised in scholarship and course design and between course content and the classroom.

Stage one: Invisibility

The first stage we identified corresponds to the curriculum that dominated North American universities in the 1950s and 1960s. The absence of women and people of color was simply not noticed. Questions related to gender, race, ethnicity and sexuality were not raised and so the *generic* man (white, male, Eastern European, publicly heterosexual, primarily Christian) could seem to stand for a common human experience. The question underlying curricular choices at this stage tended to focus on singular individuals and public events: who are the great thinkers/actors; what public events have changed the course of history?

This stage could have remained a historical marker, but in the 1980s as educators sought to define coherence in curricula that had seemed to grow without direction in the 1960s and 1970s, they looked back instead of forward for models. *Back to basics* has become a rallying cry that responds to a real need for direction but looks to a solution that is expedient and retrograde. The assumption is that we all agree on what the basics are, that standards of excellence are fixed and not subject to debate. Often the new requirements that would establish coherence replicate the curricula with which educators now over 50 grew up. The focus is on fixed products (Great Books, for example) and eternal principles rather than on the educational process itself. The most dangerous effect of this curricular nostalgia is that scholarship about women and historically marginalized cultures is excluded from the Basics, and appears in footnotes or as enrichment rather than at the center of what we consider essential for educated people to know. In the classroom at this stage of the curriculum the teacher lectures students who are passive vessels.

Stage Two: Search for the Missing Women and Marginalized Men

As the percentage of women students and students of color in higher education increases, committed teachers were moved to look for role models in history, literature and the sciences that these students could emulate. The search for missing women and absent, marginalized men may be well-meaning, but it risks being short-lived because the criteria for inclusion in the curriculum have not changed. The models for what is worthy of study lead to such questions as: Who are the great women, the female Shakespeares? Who are the Black Darwins? The figures and events that have been missing from the curriculum are assumed to resemble the men and public events that are already subjects of study. The problem of exclusion is understood as oversight.

Even using these (unexamined) criteria to search for new material, signficiant numbers of 'women worthies' and influential men of color are uncovered at this stage and find their way into courses. They tend, though, to be exceptions to their gender or race. The larger topic remains ungendered and seemingly racially neutral. For example, a history course might include some attention to Susan B. Anthony or Frederick Douglass, but the dominant narrative line remains unchanged. This stage, however, does make important new data available.

Stage Three: Minorities as Oppressed, Women as a Subordinate Group

The new data of stage two begins to unsettle the underlying criteria in stage three. Disciplinary paradigms that had privileged individuals begin to shift as we look to social structures that shape individual experience and opportunity. Instead of searching for the exceptional woman, we might begin to ask why women's work has been marginalized or why African American experience, for example, has been devalued in accounts of US history. New material has begun to make the invisible paradigms shaping the curriculum visible, but no new paradigms have been developed to replace them. As a result, the classroom climate may heat up. To focus on oppression or subordination may provoke resistance among students who long for enfranchisement. For middle-class, white male students, this focus may feel like an accusation of guilt or *political incorrectness*, to borrow the term that is being used to trivialize efforts at fundamental change in the last few years.

This is the stage where Women's Studies and ethnic studies begin to emerge. But this is only the beginning; both fields have moved far beyond a focus on oppression or victimization, even though this characterization had been used to discount both fields in recent years. Oppression and victimization are the most noticeable aspects of the experience of women and marginalized cultures only if one considers them from the dominant point of view.

Stage Four: Women Studied on our own Terms, Cultures Studied from Insiders' Perspective

The anger, struggle, and resistance that may characterize the classroom at stage three subside at stage four as we begin to consider women and marginalized cultures in their own terms rather than from the perspective of the dominant group. There is an epistemological shift as we move outside the prevailing paradigms and try to develop new ones shaped by the experience and cultural production of women and marginalized men. In the US, black studies led the way to understanding the signficance of developing an insider's perspective. For example, from a white, propertied, male point of view, the oustanding characteristic of African American experience is slavery, the condition of being owned as property. Looked at from an insider's perspective, a much broader range and diversity of black experience, both within and outside of the North American context becomes visible. Rather than focusing exclusively on social and political subordination, black studies demonstrated the multicultural realities of black experience — African, African-American, African-Caribbean, for example — highlighting cultural continuities and political resistance rather than cultural suppression and political subjugation.

Similarly, Women's Studies courses, growing out of feminist scholarship, have sought to uncover and define the character of women's experiences as women themselves have understood their lives. This stage takes as its premise the eye-opening declaration of Gerda Lerner that 'to document the experience of women would mean documenting all of history: they have always been of it, in it, and making it . . . half, at least, of the world's experience has been theirs, half of the world's work and much of its products.'[6]

The most compelling motivation described by teachers at this stage is a voracious intellectual appetite: What was and is women's experience, known as a subject rather than object? What are the differences among women? How do race, sexuality, ethnicity, religion and age change our understanding of gender? This stage produces the cross-cultural comparisons that complicate the questions we ask and enable us to avoid inaccurate generalizations about women that derive from a limited sample. Even as we discover more about women, the definition of *woman* is destabilized.

When we develop courses that focus on the experiences of *ordinary* women, we often find illuminating patterns that allow us to understand the politics of domestic life, the artistic values of noncanonical forms (such as letters and diaries) or of collective or folk forms (quilts, for example). Just as a female student may be inspired by the extraordinary women in stage two, she learns to reflect more self-consciously on her own daily behavior and choices for self-expression by studying the 'nontraditional' materials made available in stage four.

Stage Five: New Scholarship Challenges the Disciplines

At stage four, separate paradigms are developed to organize and account for the new material being studied and the shift in perspective being used to orient study. The accumulation of data from stage four research and the newly emerging paradigm(s) cause us to question the paradigms that continue to organize our traditional disciplines and courses. We begin to question the validity of our definitions of historical periods, of norms for behavior, of standards of greatness. We begin to focus more on context and process. Teachers who have developed women-focused courses focusing on black experience (or the experiences of Latinos or Asian-Americans or Native Americans, for example) and who are familiar with feminist and ethnic studies scholarship are the best equipped to undertake curriculum transformation. Stage five is where this sort of deep transformation of the curriculum can begin, a transformation that brings new paradigms to bear on conventional ones.

In institutional terms, the movement from Women's Studies and ethnic studies to curriculum transformation is rarely seen as a welcome development. When faculty members who have enjoyed a stage one curriculum for most of their professional lives are asked the question typical of stage five, they often feel that their credentials are challenged. In questioning the paradigms we use to perceive, analyze and organize experience, we are pointedly asking not only what we know, but how we came to know it; the intellectual investment on both sides of the debate may be higher here than at earlier points in the process of change.

Carefully designed faculty development is necessary to engage teachers whose own research will never focus on women or marginalized cultures to understand that the new scholarship not only challenges their courses but can enrich them significantly. Using gender, race, class, ethnicity and sexuality as categories of analysis can transform our perspective on familiar materials as well as account more responsibly for new material. Although the conventional syllabus is purported to be gender-neutral and color-blind, the new scholarship helps us understand that it has always been pervasively gendered and racially marked. Recognizing the relevance of gender and race to all materials allows us to understand conventional syllabi in a new light. This stage means the loss of old certainties, but the gains are the recovery of meaningful historical and social context, the discovery of previously invisible dimensions of old subjects and the development of analytical tools (gender, race, class, sexuality as significant variables) that expose strata of formerly suppressed material.

Stage Six: The Transformed Curriculum

What are the paradigms that would make it possible to understand women's and men's experiences together, without privileging one over the other? What would a curriculum that offers an inclusive vision of human experience, that attends as carefully to differences as to commonality look like? Although we possess the tools of analysis that allow us to imagine such an education, we cannot, as yet, point to any institution that has entered the millennium. What we can imagine, from the lessons we've learned in the earlier stages, is that this stage will attend to process and focus on the student's learning experience in contrast to the stage one curriculum where passive students absorb lessons about immutable products. In a world in which knowledge changes rapidly, the ways a student learns, the tools she acquires to continue teaching herself, become every bit as important as the content of any particular course.

The goals of a stage six curriculum — to equip students for lifelong learning, to impart an inclusive vision of human experience — are often readily adopted, but the means may seem costly or cumbersome to administrators and faculty members. They want to believe that the promised land can be attained without passing through the difficult terrain of Women's Studies and ethnic studies. The vital work of stage four — studying women on our own terms, understanding historically marginalized cultures from an insider's perspective — generates the data and the transformative questions that enable the change process. Only well supported faculty development can provide the means for responsible curriculum transformation. Not all faculty members will shift their research, and only specialists with research experience in women's studies and ethnic studies will teach courses in those fields, but all faculty members engaged in curriculum transformation need to be given the opportunity (and appropriate institutional recognition and rewards) to read feminist and ethnic studies scholarship and to work through the ways in which this scholarship might reshape the courses they teach.

A Cautionary Tale in Three Images

Transforming the curriculum means moving through these stages of change and resistance, challenging deep and often invisible structures in our fields and our institutions. As women have gained more visibility in positions of authority on our campuses and as subjects of study in our curricula, resistance has taken interesting and revealing forms. I'd like to consider three images from three very different US publications that tell us something about women, men, power and fear. I'll end with a visualization exercise suggested by a Women's Studies major at Smith College.

The first image is a two-part cartoon printed on the front page of *Heterodoxy* a tabloid published by a well-financed right wing group in Southern California. The name implies variety of opinion, but the tabloid was established to provide a forum for resisting change in the academy; like most of the attacks in *Heterodoxy*, the attack on Women's Studies depends on caricature, sarcasm and misrepresentation rather than argument.

The article accompanying the cartoon specifically attacks recent growth in Women's Studies; they attribute this growth to funding from private, philan-thropic foundations, a most precious, scarce resource in American higher education.

A look at the two sides of the cartoon can teach us a lot about the kinds of resistance curriculum transformation encounters. This first half, on the left, represents the first decade of Women's Studies. We see a dowdy, unfashionable white woman with an unflattering haircut, buck teeth, sensible shoes and a baggy skirt and jacket; her hand is thrust gracelessly into her pocket. She appears to suffer from acne, and her big nose could be read as anti-Semitism.

The second half of the caricature represents Women's Studies in the eighties. We see a grotesquely outsized body-builder. Very few signs indicate that she's female, except for an unnecessary bikini top. The image displays an emphatic rejection of conventional femininity (unshaven legs, aggressively displayed hair in armpits, spiky short hair, oddly dark lipstick). The big lips encode racism just as the nose in the first image encodes anti-Semitism; the figure on this side is emerging from darkness like a monster. Unlike her anemic sister, this woman is aggressive, even violent; her upraised left arm recalls the 1970s symbol for black power, her right arm is drawn back as if to strike. If the first image figures an odd duck, frumpy and easily dismissed, the second represents rage, Women's Studies on steroids, out of control as she bursts out of the frame.

Both images represent women who are easy to read as 'unfeminine'; Women's Studies is presented as deviant from cultural norms of what's attractive in women; these 'Women's Studies' women lack the comforting signs of femininity: a smile, good hair, the shapely legs and breasts that signify conventional female heterosexuality. The two halves taken together suggest that the growth of Women's Studies has spawned women who are progressively more frightening in their resemblance to men; female rage is now endowed with a body to enact it (but if the first image looks like absent-minded professor, the second is clearly out of place in academy — the incredible hulk invades the halls of ivy).

The caricature acknowledges in spite of itself a fundamental insight of Women's Studies: that *gender is culturally constructed*. We are made uneasy by these images because we've learned to read what is rewarded as feminine (and mocked as unfeminine) in our culture. Women's Studies has taught us that gender is not fixed, not a natural or a biological given. Rather, cultures define what is feminine and masculine.

The *Heterodoxy* cartoon demonstrates the power of *dominant cultural scripts* for women; we can easily read, through these distortions, what the good, or nice, or desirable woman looks like, we participate in the discomfort provoked by these images that show us as deviant, we feel these images as somehow punishing us (even — especially — if we *like* to wear sensible shoes or to work out). Women's Studies explores how Woman is 'constructed' through images and stories that are constantly reproduced by the media. The *Heterodoxy* caricature reminds us that departures from the norm are policed, punished, ridiculed or dismissed.

One goal of Women's Studies is to write new narratives of gender, to appreciate the ways that gender, race, sexuality are not only individual attributes but organizing features of social and political relations, narratives about our place in the larger world. The *Heterodoxy* caricature unwittingly demonstrates the urgency of this task. The *Heterodoxy* caricature also reveals an inability to imagine women's strength as positive, attractive. The bursting body of the second image also expresses homophobia.

The next image is the September 1993 cover of *Mother Jones* which, unlike *Heterodoxy*, considers itself a progressive magazine, a gadfly to powerful institutions, unafraid to take on corporate America. It is named for a heroic union organizer who worked with mine workers in the early twentieth century in the western United States. The article purports to investigate Women's Studies today by looking at four programs: Berkeley, Iowa, Dartmouth and our own at Smith. The journalist accuses Women's Studies of being unacademic, confessional, ideological and — at the same time — too immersed in what she characterizes as current theoretical fads such as poststructuralism and postmodernism.

A photo of Dartmouth sophomore, Gina Vetere, dominates the cover: She could be the daughter of the average reader of *Mother Jones*, white, middle-class, enrolled in an elite school. The title, 'Our minds, ourselves' echoes the Boston Women's Health Collective whose very popular publication *Our Bodies, Our Selves* posited self-help for women to fight institutionalized medicine; this early feminist critique probably pleased *Mother Jones* readers in the 1970s. One of the contentions of the article is that Women's Studies has betrayed this earlier feminist message of self-help.

The journalist trivializes Women's Studies content by alleging that women together only talk *girl talk* — they endlessly swap stories of menstruation, orgasm. This trivialization assumes that talk about the body or sexuality has no place in the academy and that the personal should be left outside of the classroom. If the *content* of Women's Studies is ridiculed as inappropriate discussion of what's most taboo, private, least connected to our minds, Women's Studies *pedagogy* is ridiculted as uncensored 'sharing' of personal experience — rapping as opposed to intellectual rigor. Twenty-five years of scholarship in Women's Studies and ethnic studies is simply left out of the journalist's consideration. At the same time, her attacks on both the content and pedagogy of the field as she represents it, betray anxiety about violating limits that delineate what's appropriate to study or what's expected in the classroom.

Like the *Heterodoxy* cartoon, the *Mother Jones* article parodies, in part, what we would describe as a strength: Women's Studies does value the voices of individual women who seek to understand their experience; Women's Studies seeks to transcend arbitrary divisions between bodily experience and the mind, feelings and reason that have cut the academy off from the world and that have isolated the life of the mind from daily life and common concerns. In *Heterodoxy* and *Mother Jones* we can detect deeply seated fears: fear of the body, fear of sexuality, fear of what women will do with power.

Many of the attacks against Women's Studies charge the field with demagoguery, thought control, the tyranny of the politically correct (one popular radio talk show host has coined the term *femi-Nazis* to refer to feminists today). The fear that underlies these charges is a guilty one that the previously disenfranchised will use power as they have experienced it to exclude, punish or silence.

The accusation that Women's Studies is too political is linked to the charge that Women's Studies is not an intellectual discipline with objective criteria for argument and proof, rational discourse, or internal debate, that it is instead an *ideological* program, a political agenda being imposed on vulnerable young minds. This attack conceals the politics of the traditional curriculum and it inadvertently recognizes something important about Women's Studies — our conviction that *knowledge and power are inevitably joined.* Curriculum transformation projects recognize that to change shape of knowledge is to change the exercise of power. And yet, the most insidious lie about Women's Studies told by media, and exemplified in the contradictions of the *Mother Jones* article, is that it's a story of victimization. *Mother Jones* accuses us of producing victims but fears that we're creating confident women who will work for change.

The *Mother Jones* photo of a lone, white woman contrasts with the four different women on the September 1993 cover of *Ms.* magazine who debate feminism from insiders' perspectives. *Ms.* shows feminists announcing their willingness to disagree in contrast to the totalitarian mind-control that threatens the Dartmouth sophomore on *Mother Jones.* The group debating on the cover of *Ms.* suggests a cross-section of people whose work a student might read in a Women's Studies class. The four women are Gloria Steinem, now in her sixties, a founder of *Ms.* magazine and a spokeswoman for feminism since the earliest days; bell hooks, a literature professor in her forties, who identifies the importance of her links to African-American communities *outside* the academy; Urvashi Vaid a former director of the National Gay and Lesbian Task force, a community organizer, attorney, worker for civil rights and legislative solutions as well as for self-directed grassroots organizing; and, Naomi Wolf, in her early thirties, the author of *The Beauty Myth* and *Fire with Fire*, the youngest of this group of four. This group portrait forefronts diversity of age, ethnicity, work, and sexuality and explicitly values debate.

The article itself focuses on the question of why women are reluctant to call themselves feminists, even though they support feminist goals: reproductive rights, equal pay for equal work, an end to domestic violence, an end to discrimination for other groups. Steinem identifies fear of feminism with resistance to seeing beyond the individual to the real revolutionary impact of feminism. The 'me first' media representation of feminism in the 1980s stated, 'I'm for equal *rights* for *me*' — this constitutes at best a reform. Steinem says that to say, 'I'm a feminist' is to say 'I'm for equal *power* for *all women*.' This is a revolution. Bell hooks emphasizes that unmasking the harm of patriarchy heals more than women, it can enfranchise marginalized men — 'feminism as a critique of masculinity can be life-affirming for black men' too. 'If you care about black men as an endangered species, then feminism has something to offer black men in the struggle for their lives.'

Urvashi Vaid understands from long experience that resistance to feminism is often barely disguised *homophobia*. Even though some progress has been made in changing attitudes toward homosexuality (seeing that the problem is homophobia, not homosexuality) the media still accuse strong women of being lesbians with the explicit understanding that to be a lesbian is deviant, undesirable. This puts all of us into contradictory positions. Straight women often feel they have to deny being lesbians while insisting that there's nothing wrong with it anyway. Lesbians and bisexual women are put into the position of challenging the unspoken homophobia, justifying their own legitimacy and defending feminism while simultaneously maintaining that there is not an inevitable link between feminism and lesbianism. Given the limits of television news in the US these arguments have to be made in ten-second sound bites.

Some people have suggested that homophobia is just another form of misogyny — fear of power in women and of the conventionally feminine in men. Because Women's Studies tries to help women gain more power and at the same time contests conventional understandings of gender it is particularly vulnerable to homophobic attack.

As Women's Studies faces the millennium we can see in the fears expressed by the backlash from the new right and the old left that female power is still seen as a threat in our society. But I would like to echo the real Mother Jones (the labor organizer) who upon the death of her colleague said to their people, 'Don't mourn, organize.'

With that in mind I offer you the following *visualization*, one student's dream of what an ordinary school day might be.[7]

Imagine Jennifer Reed. She is your typical 17-year-old high school student. In the morning she wakes up, throws on a pair of jeans and a sweatshirt, and runs out the door. At school she meets up with her friends and they stroll down the hallways to their classes with heads held high, checking out the other students who pass them by. She begins the day with her favorite class, physics. Her teacher, Ms. Smith, calls on her often and whatever Jennifer's answer may be she is never laughed at or ridiculed — Ms. Smith helps her discover the right answer or praises her for having discovered it on her own. At lunch she and her friends eat a good meal, not worrying about the calories in each bite, and they talk about their accomplishments.

In her afternoon history class they discuss the contribution of women inventors in the late nineteenth century, and in English they analyze Virginia Woolf's *A Room of One's Own*. At no time during the day is Jennifer ogled by one of her teachers — she is never made to feel guilty or stupid for rejecting such an advance. After school Jennifer rushes home to change for the big rugby game that night. As she and her teammates run out onto the field at the start of the game there are loud cheers from the stands filled with parents, teachers and classmates. Jennifer goes to bed that night feeling confident and excited about what the next day will offer her.

This student's dream graphically illustrates that students instinctively understand the term *curriculum* in its broadest sense and that equity leads to an empowering appreciation of women rather than an angry denunciation of men. Our hope is that curriculum transformation can make her dream a reality.

Notes

1 This chapter incorporates work that I have done in collaboration with Susan Van Dyne, Professor of Women's Studies and Director of the Women's Studies Program, Smith College.
2 Tidball, E. M. (1986) 'Baccalaureate origins of recent natural science doctorates', in *Journal of Higher Education*, 3(6), November/December, pp. 606–20.
3 Part II is based on an article I wrote with Susan Van Dyne called 'Placing women in the liberal arts: Stages of curriculum transformation,' in *Harvard Educational Review*, **54**(4), November 1984, pp. 413–28. It was revised for inclusion in a sourcebook on teaching and learning published by the National Center on Postsecondary Teaching, Learning, & Assessment, the Pennsylvania State Unviersity, University Park, PA 16801-5252, in 1994.
4 Lerner, G. (1979) *The Majority Finds its Past: Placing Women in History*, New York: Oxford University Press.
5 'Interactive phases of curricular re-vision', in Spanier, B., Bloom, A. and Borovniak, D. (Eds) (1984) *Toward a Balanced Curriculum: A Sourcebook for Initiating Gender Integration Projects*, Cambridge, MA: Schenkman Publishing Company, Inc., pp. 25–34.
6 Lerner, G. (1977) *The Female Experience: An American Documentary*, Indianapolis, IN: Bobbs-Merrill, p. xxi.
7 Created by Deveny Dawson, a Smith College Women's Studies major from the class of 1994.

References

LERNER, G. (1977) The Female Experience: An American Documentary, Indianapolis, IN: Bobbs-Merrill, p. xxi.
LERNER, G. (1979) The Majority Finds Its Past: Placing Women in History, New York: Oxford University Press.
SCHUSTER, M. and VAN DYNE, S. (1984) 'Placing women in the liberal arts: Stages of curriculum transformation', in *Harvard Educational Review*, **54**(4), November, pp. 413–28.

SPANIER, B., BLOOM, A. and BOROVNIAK, D. (Eds) (1984) Toward a Balanced Curriculum: A Sourcebook for Initiating Gender Integration Projects, Cambridge, MA: Schenkman Publishing Company, Inc., pp. 25–34.

TIDBALL, E. M. (1986) Baccalaureate origins of recent natural science doctorates', in *Journal of Higher Education*, 3(6), November/December, pp. 606–20.

Contributors

Barbara Bagilhole is a Lecturer in Social Policy and the Director of MA in Women's Studies in the Department of Social Sciences, University of Loughborough. Prior to this she worked in a local authority in the field of equal opportunities and race relations.

Kalwant Bhopal is a full-time PhD research student at the University of Bristol and part-time lecturer. Her research focuses on the position of Asian women within the family, with specific reference to patriarchy and is being funded by the ESRC. Her interests include feminism, ethnicity and gender.

Trev Broughton is a lecturer as the Centre for Women's Studies, University of York. She teaches and (sometimes) writes on the subject of women's auto-biography, and is working on a book on Victorian masculinities for Routledge.

Chris Corrin teaches Politics and Women's Studies at Glasgow University. Her research work has been concerned with women's situation in Hungary. Her current work focuses on issues of violence against women internationally and women's human rights. She is currently co-chair of the Women's Studies Network (UK) Association, convenor of Glasgow University Women's Studies Centre and a member of the International Lesbian and Gay Association (ILGA) which is active on lesbian and gay human rights.

Sue Davies Job Shares the post of Equal Opportunities Development Officer at the University of Central Lancashire. As a committed feminist she has spent much of her career promoting the interests of women in her private and professional life. She has previously held posts at the National Council for Voluntary Organizations and Oxford City Council where she worked both as

Women's Officer and in the initiation of the council's work on anti-poverty issues. She has two children.

Breda Gray is doing postgraduate research at the Department of Sociology and Centre for Women's Studies at Lancaster University and lectures part-time in Sociology at the University of Central Lancashire.

Millsom Henry is presently working at Stirling University as the Deputy Director of a Research, Training and Consultancy Centre for Sociology and the New Technologies. Her research interests are gender, ethnicity, culture and new technologies. Millsom is currently working on research into the 'Images of black women in popular culture' and the 'Impact of new technologies in higher education'.

Madeleine Leonard is a Lecturer in the Department of Sociology and Social Policy at Queen's University, Belfast. Her research interests include women and informal economic activity and mature students in Higher Education.

Pauline Leonard is a lecturer in the Department of Sociology and Social Policy at the University of Southampton. Her research interest are in poststructuralist theory and gender, and she is currently looking at the intersections of these with organizational literature. She has recently had her third child, Edward, who together with William and Frances, are the greatest joys for herself and her partner Guy.

Cathy Lubelska is Principal Lecturer in Social History and Women's Studies, and course Leader for Women's Studies at the University of Central Lancashire. Her current research interests include the exploration of experiential approaches within feminist methodology and women's history and the history of women and professionalization. She has published studies and chapters on feminism within the curriculum and is co-editor (with Mary Kennedy and Val Walsh) of *Making Connections: Women's Studies, Women's Movements, Women's Lives* (Taylor & Francis, 1993).

Doreen MacWhannell is a Senior Lecturer in the Department of Management and Social Sciences at Queen Margaret College in Edinburgh. She previously worked as a manager in both the Health Service and Higher Education. Her teaching and research interests include Women's Studies, feminist theory, women's health and organization studies.

Danusia Malina lectures in Employee Relations and Gender in Organizations in the Faculty of Management and Business at Manchester Metropolitan

University. She is currently working on research addressing the manoeuvres of sexuality, power and desire in organizational contexts. At the same time, she is loving Fred, George, Jack, Tom and Harriet as they grow up, beautifully. Unpredictably, she is 31 and still sane.

Julie Matthews a graduate in Single Honours Women's Studies from the University of Central Lancashire. She is about to embark on a PhD into women as users, providers and mediators of health care, 1948–1979. She also hopes to examine and develop new research on disabled women.

Mairead Owen lectures in Women's Studies at the Liverpool John Moores University. Her research interests are eclectic, anything to do with the lives of women, but centre at the moment on media studies, especially popular fiction (which was the subject of her relatively recent PhD on women's reading of romantic fiction), equal opportunities and the theories and practice surrounding the teaching of Women's Studies.

Jocey Quinn Job Shares the post of Equal Opportunities Development Officer at the University of Central Lancashire, and also teaches Women's Studies. She has a background in Women's education, and has also worked as a Women's Officer in the public sector for some time. Her current research interests include the experience of women students in mainstream degree courses. She has one child and is expecting her second.

Deryn Rees-Jones is researching anxiety in contemporary women's poetry. **Rebecca D'Monté** is working on the construction of female identity in seventeenth century drama. **Joanne Winning** is researching Dorothy Richardson's textual practice. **Sally Kilmister** is examining ideas about music within literary and cultural modernism. All four are doctoral students at Birkbeck College, University of London.

Marilyn R. Schuster is professor of French and Women's Studies at Smith College. She completed her BA at Mills College and her PhD in French literature at Yale University. She has published articles on curriculum transformation and co-edited *Women's Place in the Academy: Transforming the Liberal Arts Curriculum* (Totowa, NJ: Rowman & Allanheld, 1985) with Susan R. Van Dyne. She has also published articles on nineteenth- and twentieth-century French and North American literature, especially fiction written by women. *Marguerite Duras Revisited* was published by Twayne in 1993; she is currently writing a book about the Canadian lesbian novelist, Jane Rule, for New York University Press.

Penny Welch teaches Politics and Women's Studies at the University of Wolverhampton. She has been active in NATFHE and the wider trades union movement since the late 1970s. She lives in Wolverhampton with her partner and their son.

Index